THE SOVIET COLLECTIVE FARM, 1929–1930

THE SOVIET COLLECTIVE FARM, 1929–1930

R. W. DAVIES

Professor of Soviet Economic Studies
University of Birmingham

Harvard University Press
Cambridge, Massachusetts
1980

Library of Congress Cataloging in Publication Data

Davies, Robert William.
  The Soviet collective farm, 1929–1930.

  (His The industrialisation of Soviet Russia; v. 2)
  Bibliography: p.
  Includes index.
  1. Collective farms—Russia—History.   2. Russia—
Economic policy—1928–1932.   3. Russia—Industries—
History.   I. Title. II. Series.
HD1492.R9D35   338.7′63′0947   79–15273
ISBN 0–674–82600–0

CONTENTS

v

LIST OF TABLES

PREFACE

During 1929–30 the collective farms (kolkhozy) achieved a commanding position in the Soviet countryside, although they still included only a minority of households. The present volume discusses in some detail the emergence of the kolkhoz as an economic unit. During the heady months of the first collectivisation drive in the winter of 1929–30, the kolkhozy were planned as giant, fully socialised enterprises modelled on the state-owned factories, and employing wage labour. Such schemes soon proved both impracticable and too costly, and aroused much peasant hostility. By the summer of 1930, a compromise system had been introduced. The kolkhoz henceforth roughly coincided with the boundaries of the settlement or village, or of a natural part of the village. Within this smaller kolkhoz, collective farmers were permitted to retain a personal household plot and their own animals, while arable land was collectivised, and was cultivated in common. A free market was reintroduced side by side with state planning. The collective farmers were remunerated for their work on the collective lands—in principle, though not yet in practice—in 'labour days'; these were proportionate to the quantity and quality of work, though they were paid only after the harvest, by sharing out what remained after state and collective needs were satisfied. In this compromise between state and peasant interests, the state predominated, by its power and its material advantages. The collective product was firmly controlled by state collection agencies, and, after a lengthy controversy, available tractors and other modern machinery were transferred to state-owned Machine-Tractor Stations, each of which served and controlled a number of kolkhozy.

The main features of the kolkhoz, as they emerged in the summer of 1930, continued throughout rapid industrialisation; the kolkhoz became an integral and major unit of Stalinist economic organisation, and many of the arrangements made in 1930 continue in the Soviet Union today. The emergence of the kolkhoz in 1929–30 was thus a crucial stage in the formation of the Soviet system.

The present volume, like the others in this series on *The Industrialisation of Soviet Russia*, has been written so that it can be read independently, and it has its own bibliography and index. Thanks for advice and assistance from many colleagues and organisations were expressed in the Preface to volume 1, and need not be repeated here. The reader's attention is also drawn to the 'Technical Note' in that volume, which briefly describes the organisation of Soviet central and local government, and sets out various conventions used throughout the series.

July 1979   R. W. DAVIES

CHAPTER ONE

THE STATE AND THE KOLKHOZ

(A) THE BACKGROUND

In 1929–30, much closer central control was established over agricultural production; and in the main grain-surplus regions most agricultural land and a large minority of peasant households were collectivised. Simultaneously several hundred thousand 'kulak' households were expropriated. The Soviet leaders carried out this 'revolution from above' with such violence and haste because they were convinced that it would provide the solution to the crisis in agricultural marketings which had developed since 1927, and was becoming more acute as they pressed forward and enlarged their industrialisation programme. They were confident that the consolidation of the planned state collections, and the replacement of individual peasant farms by kolkhozy, would immediately increase food supplies for the urban population, agricultural raw materials for industry, and agricultural exports generally.

The collectivisation of agriculture, and its planned control, were thus seen as conditions for industrialisation. But they were not undertaken with narrowly economic objectives. This was proclaimed to be a 'socialist offensive', a decisive stage in the construction of the first socialist society in the world. And, on the Soviet—or rather Stalinist—analysis, it was bound to be resisted, for both economic and political reasons, by the petty-capitalist peasant class, the kulaks who, together with their 'henchmen', had to be treated as irreconcilable enemies. According to Soviet theory, always stubbornly maintained in public, this battle of the regime against the petty-capitalist peasants was supported by the poor and middle peasants, who voluntarily participated in the collectivisation drive; but there is no doubt that the Soviet leaders were privately well aware that many ordinary peasants behaved like their image of petty capitalists when faced with low state collection prices for their products, and when invited to relinquish the family farming they knew for the unknown and alien kolkhoz. Moreover, the grain collections of the autumn of 1929 already amply demonstrated—and this was officially and publicly recognised at the time—that even the kolkhozy, themselves influenced, in the party view, by the kulaks, could not be relied upon automatically to submit themselves to commands and requisitions from the socialist state. For all these reasons, the Soviet authorities were determined to establish firm state political and administrative controls over the whole of agriculture, including its socialist sector, so that 'market spontaneity' would be replaced by central planning, and the peasant community would be subordinated to the state.

The socialist transformation of agriculture was, however, never seen by the Soviet authorities merely as an instrument for the exploitation of the peasantry. While an increased flow of agricultural products to the state was confidently expected, efforts were also made to provide definite quantities of industrial goods in return for agricultural products; 'market spontaneity' was to give way not simply to planned collections but also to 'product-exchange'. Even more important, in the Soviet view of future state – kolkhoz economic relations, was the supply by the state of tractors and agricultural machines in large numbers. The Soviet authorities cherished great hopes that mechanisation would bring about a rapid technical revolution in agriculture, and they believed that the replacement of the petty economies of the individual peasants by large-scale socialist agricultural economies was essential if this revolution was to succeed. The 'metal link' between the state and the kolkhoz would thus come to predominate over the 'textile link' between the state and the individual peasant. The political and administrative controls over the kolkhoz must therefore incorporate agencies and methods not only for exacting grain and other products from the peasants but also for coping with the reverse flow of products and assistance from the state and with the inculcation of mechanised agriculture.

Within this framework of state controls, an appropriate internal structure for the kolkhoz needed to be established. This was a new environment and a new system of agriculture; and the past experience of small market-oriented kolkhozy was of limited relevance. The type of kolkhoz now being established must simultaneously respond to the new and daunting requirements of state planning, and replace the deep-rooted family economy of the individual peasantry. If it were to work effectively, its size and structure should be such as to enable the efficient organisation of agricultural production, and its system of income distribution should promote adequate investment in the collective economy while providing economic incentives to collective farmers more powerful than the market incentives which stimulated the individual peasants.

In the summer of 1929, the Soviet political leaders had no clear idea either of the future pattern of controls over the kolkhoz, or of the shape and functioning of its economy. But they were strongly biased towards industry in their ideology and organisation, and, in an atmosphere of mounting enthusiasm for industrialisation, industrial experience and factory methods came to be seen as fully applicable in agriculture, and capable of greatly improving its efficiency. In September 1929, an editorial in *Pravda*, insisting that the example of the United States had 'compelled bourgeois economists to admit that in 10–15 years agriculture will have reached the level of an extractive industry', roundly asserted:

> All the most recent developments in agriculture, especially in technically more developed capitalist countries, have revealed that attempts to find methods and laws of development of agriculture different from the methods and laws of industry are completely groundless and stupid.[1]

Markevich, head of Traktorotsentr, declared in the same month that 'there is no difference in principle between agriculture and urban industry'.[2] The November 1929 plenum of the central committee argued that large kolkhozy and comprehensive collectivisation 'require the establishment of unity in the management of agricultural production on the basis of the utilisation of the experience of the management of Soviet industry'.[3] At the plenum, Molotov succinctly summed up the approach of the leadership to agricultural organisation with the slogan:

> Kolkhozy, in organising social production, model yourselves on the sovkhozy![4]

[1] P, September 5, 1929.
[2] EZh, September 10, 1929.
[3] *KPSS v rez.*, ii (1954), 654.
[4] B, 22, November 30, 1929, 20.

The sovkhozy, in their turn, were closely copying the experience of large industrial plants; it was not accidental that the new large grain sovkhozy were always described as 'grain factories'.

Uncritical enthusiasm for the application of industrial methods in kolkhoz affairs did not survive the winter of 1929–30. It soon became clear to the party leaders that the industrial model was too costly to apply immediately to peasant agriculture as a whole, and that the peasants were not ready for it. In July 1930, a resolution of the XVI party congress implicitly refuted Molotov's dictum of November 1929:

> All attempts to transfer the organisational system of management of the sovkhozy to the kolkhozy are anti-Leninist, because *unlike the sovkhoz*, which is a *state* enterprise, created by state resources, the kolkhoz is a voluntary social association of peasants, *created by the resources of the peasants themselves*, with all the ensuing consequences.[5]

This tactical retreat did not, however, change the fundamental assumption that the kolkhoz would eventually become an enterprise controlled and organised on factory lines. The resolution of the XVI congress also envisaged that the kolkhozy would create a 'new social discipline' in the peasants, who would, under party guidance, abandon their 'petty-bourgeois psychology and thirst for private accumulation'; to this end a large-scale mechanised economy would be provided for the kolkhozy, skilled collective farmers would be trained and the cultural level of the mass of collective farmers would be fundamentally improved. But it was now much more strongly emphasised that all this would require 'years of stubborn effort' by the party.[6]

(B) STATE CONTROL OF THE KOLKHOZ

On the eve of collectivisation, Soviet power in the villages was weak and ineffective (see vol. 1, pp. 51–5). Party membership was small, party members often unreliable; the village soviet commanded less respect, and had less influence on the peasants, than the mir and the

---

[5] *KPSS v rez.*, iii (1954), 53.
[6] *Ibid.* 61.

skhod, the traditional agencies of peasant self-government. The vast majority of the peasants were unsympathetic to the new policies of the party leadership. The extension of state control over agriculture in 1929–30 therefore required the invasion of the countryside by large numbers of temporary plenipotentiaries and brigades from the towns, supported as required by the militia, the army and the OGPU. The major instruments of state control in the villages were not the party cell, which did not exist in most villages, or the village soviet, but the plenipotentiaries; and agriculture was not controlled primarily by ordered and regular plans but by successive grain, livestock and sowing campaigns, above all by the drive for collectivisation and dekulakisation.

For more than a quarter of a century, campaigns by urban plenipotentiaries, backed by the power of the state, would remain a crucial element in state control of the countryside. But already in 1929–30 the outlines began to emerge, at the centre and in the localities, of a regular system of administration and control, which in part took over management of the campaigns, in part coexisted uneasily beside them.

At the centre, the most important development was the establishment at the end of 1929 of a Narkomzem and a Kolkhoztsentr for the whole USSR (see vol. 1, p. 169). The Narkomzem of the RSFSR had been dominated, until the end of 1927, by 'bourgeois specialists' strongly committed to the preservation of small-scale peasant agriculture; even after the expulsion of Kondratiev and his colleagues from its staff early in 1928 it continued to be a centre of resistance to the new agricultural policies. In contrast, the new Narkomzem of the USSR was dominated by party members whose loyalty to the Politburo was not in doubt. Yakovlev, the People's Commissar for Agriculture of the USSR, was the former deputy head of the People's Commissariat for Workers' and Peasants' Inspection, Rabkrin, which, as well as watching over government institutions and their bourgeois specialists on behalf of the party, was by this time the principal agency advising the Politburo about both policy and administration. A number of senior officials of Rabkrin were also transferred to the staff of both Narkomzem of the USSR and Kolkhoztsentr of the USSR at the end of 1929. A few weeks later, the rural department of the party central committee was abolished, one of the main arguments for this being that the establishment of a USSR Narkomzem made it redundant (see vol. 1, p. 216). All this seemed to indicate that strong and loyal governmental institutions were emerging in agriculture, responsible for transmitting party policy to the kolkhozy and the individual peasants, and in charge of the new kolkhoz system throughout the USSR; their control over agriculture was intended to correspond to the control of Vesenkha over industry.

From the beginning of 1930 Narkomzem and Kolkhoztsentr immediately plunged into the work of administering the kolkhozy, supplementing and continuing the work of their republican equivalents. But the changes in agriculture were so novel, so vast and so important to the regime that the Politburo and the party apparatus intervened more frequently and extensively than in industry; in practice Narkomzem and Kolkhoztsentr were of relatively minor importance in comparison with Vesenkha. Moreover, the executive responsibility for the grain, livestock and vegetable collections rested not with Yakovlev and Narkomzem but with Mikoyan and Narkomtorg. Appropriately, perhaps, Yakovlev was a second-rank political figure, and, unlike Mikoyan or Kuibyshev, the chairman of Vesenkha, he was not a member or even a candidate member of the Politburo.

Narkomzem and Kolkhoztsentr were also weaker than Vesenkha in another important respect. In industry, the major factories throughout the country were directly subordinate to powerful departments of Vesenkha located in Moscow. This imposed strict limits on the influence on industrial affairs of local party and soviet organisations, and of the local industrial committees, the sovnarkhozy, and strengthened the position of Vesenkha, which the Politburo and the central party apparatus found it difficult to by-pass. In agriculture, however, the kolkhozy formed part of the local 'kolkhoz unions', the kolkhozsoyuzy, at district, okrug, regional and republican level. While the kolkhozsoyuzy were formally subordinate to their republican Kolkhoztsentr (which was identical with the USSR Kolkhoztsentr in the case of the RSFSR), they were much weaker organisations than the departments of Vesenkha. Designed for a small voluntary kolkhoz movement, they were suddenly confronted with the immense tasks imposed by mass collectivisation. They did not, even formally, acquire executive authority in relation to their kolkhozy until June 1929 (see vol. 1, p. 120). Soon after, they were plunged into a confusing series of reforms which continued throughout 1929 and 1930, and were intended to rationalise the control of the kolkhozy and the agricultural cooperatives. An attempt was first made to coordinate the work of the kolkhozsoyuzy and the koopsoyuzy (the local agencies of the various agricultural cooperatives), and then to fuse them; subsequently, in the summer of 1930, their functions were again divided (see vol. 1, pp. 301–2, 351–2). These reforms failed to strengthen the kolkhozsoyuzy. In October 1930, Yurkin, after touring nine districts in the Central Black-Earth region and the Ukraine, complained that 'most districts, it seems, only "plan" and are not directly leading the production work of the kolkhozy'; the kolkhozsoyuzy even lacked detailed information about kolkhoz activities:

It is surprising how the kolkhozy, left to their own devices, and deprived of live leadership by the system, manage to cope with tremendous production tasks.[7]

A month later, a deputy chairman of Kolkhoztsentr reported that in the Lower Volga region the district kolkhozsoyuzy 'in essence are doing nothing'.[8] A district kolkhozsoyuz was supposed to have a full-time staff of ten, but a Narkomzem investigation at the end of 1930 reported that 'the extent of understaffing presents a threatening picture'; in many districts with a low percentage of collectivisation kolkhozsoyuzy separate from the koopsoyuzy had not even been established.[9]

The enforcement of the major agricultural campaigns, which required the recruitment of large numbers of townsmen for temporary work in the countryside, and often also involved a show of force, clearly lay far beyond the capacities of the local kolkhozsoyuzy, or of the well-established but conservative local departments of Narkomzem (the *zemotdely*). During 1929 and 1930, the secretaries of the local party organisations, supported by the chairman of the soviets, together with their respective committees and 'bureaux', became the effective local controllers of agriculture and the kolkhozy, intermediaries between the kolkhozy and the central party apparatus. The party leadership, attaching supreme importance to the subordination of agriculture to the will of the state, and to the transformation of its structure, bombarded its local organisations with instructions and appeals, and agricultural and

---

[7] SZe, October 14, 1930 (report to board of Kolkhoztsentr); *Kollektivist*, 20, October 31, 1930, 3; see also I, September 4, 1930; Yurkin see pp. 135–6 below.
[8] SZe, November 11, 1930 (Tataev's report to board of Kolkhoztsentr).
[9] NFK, 24, [December?] 1930, 52, 54–5, 57.

kolkhoz affairs soon came to predominate in the activities of the local party and soviet authorities, particularly in view of the relative insignificance of their role in relation to industry.

During the collectivisation drive of the winter of 1929–30 the party and soviet apparatus at the level of the administrative district (raion) gradually emerged as the main focus of administration in the countryside. With the abolition of the okrugs in the summer of 1930, the 3,000 districts, each including an average of 8,000 households, became the sole administrative level between the large administrative regions (oblasti or krai), each with a million households or more, and the 70,000 village soviets. The district, already the main executive agency of Soviet power for the collection of grain and other foodstuffs, became the main planning and reporting unit for the second phase of comprehensive collectivisation which began in the autumn of 1930. The gap between region and district soon proved to be too large. It was closed in the course of the 1930s not by increasing the average size of the district, which remained more or less constant, but by greatly increasing the number of regions.[10] From 1930 onwards, then, the district was a stable unit of control in the countryside.

Much remained uncertain at the village level in 1930. Collectivisation and dekulakisation greatly weakened the mir and the skhod throughout the USSR, particularly in villages where the kolkhozy included a high proportion of the population. Comprehensive collectivisation also, for a time, threatened the village soviet; many officials argued that the kolkhoz could itself act as the primary unit of Soviet power, now that it was planned to correspond in size with the village (see vol. 1, p. 226n.). At one moment, comprehensive collectivisation even threatened the district soviet, when influential officials and publicists proposed that a single giant kolkhoz should be formed in each district (see pp. 41–7 below). But the principle that Soviet power in the village should be separate from the kolkhoz, even when their boundaries coincided, was strongly reaffirmed by the Soviet government as early as January 1930 (see vol. 1, pp. 225–6). By the end of 1930, there were already 113,000 kolkhozy,[11] as compared with 70,000 village soviets; henceforth, particularly in villages containing more than one settlement, a single village soviet frequently contained several kolkhozy. The village soviet emerged from the first collectivisation

[10] See *Nar. kh. 1958* (1959), 37.
[11] *Ezhegodnik po sel. kh. 1931* (1933), 442.

drive with strengthened authority: it was now the unchallengeable primary unit of Soviet government, responsible for taxation and policing, and for various minor public services, with its own separate sources of finance. But the functions of village soviet and kolkhoz board remained in many respects confused and overlapping.

Within this structure of authority, the arrangements for the collection of grain and other foodstuffs from the kolkhozy and the individual peasantry were relatively clear-cut by the summer of 1930. The collections, while carried out by campaign methods in which party organisations and plenipotentiaries were decisive, were planned and organised by Narkomtorg, using the grain cooperatives as its agents. Agricultural cooperation, in its traditional meaning of a voluntary organisation to assist peasant agriculture, was in a state of collapse; the agricultural cooperatives, instead of marketing peasant products, now acted as agents of the state in the collection of grain, livestock and vegetables from kolkhozy and individual peasants. For this purpose the district koopsoyuzy were both simplified and strengthened; significantly, in the autumn of 1930 the permanent establishment of staff was 50 per cent higher for the average district koopsoyuz than for the kolkhozsoyuz.[12]

The contracts signed by kolkhozy and groups of individual peasants with the agricultural cooperatives provided both for the supply of grain and other products by the peasants to the state and, in return, for the supply of industrial consumer goods, agrotechnical assistance and machinery by the state to the peasants. But the arrangements for the supply of industrial consumer goods, unlike the arrangements for the collections, were weak and ineffective. This was not entirely due to the shortage of industrial goods. Arrangements to cope with the shortage by earmarking supplies of goods to the value of 20–40 per cent of the value of the collections were tried out in the autumn of 1929, and revived in the autumn of 1930, and seem to have been viable in principle. But they rarely worked in practice (see vol. 1, pp. 80, 253). This failure was mainly due to the priorities imposed by the authorities, who concentrated their manpower, their decrees and their punishments on the drive for the collections, and failed to provide adequate support for the systematic distribution of industrial goods. Social policy also came into it; the authorities hesitated about enforcing

[12] NFK, 24, [December?] 1930, 54–5.

the exchange of industrial goods for grain because they feared that too many of them would go to the well-to-do middle peasants who supplied much of the grain. But even here devices were available to correct this danger (see vol. 1, p. 80). Significantly, the authorities overcame social scruples and supply difficulties only in the case of industrial crops, particularly cotton, where they were convinced from experience that 'special-purpose supplies' in return for crops were essential to the urgently needed expansion of production. But here, ironically, the main product supplied efficiently by the state was not an industrial good, but grain, which had been collected from peasants in the grain-surplus areas without an adequate return.

With tractors and agricultural machinery, the authorities soon resolved that only the socialised sector should receive supplies, and henceforth they were not available to stimulate individual peasants to meet the grain quotas. Another element thus disappeared from the 'product-exchange' equation. Even in the case of the kolkhozy, while supplies of tractors were often used as a spur to further collectivisation (see vol. 1, pp. 383–4), they were rarely offered as an incentive to deliver grain.

Substantial resources, including foreign currency, were, however, devoted to increasing the present and future supplies of machinery in 1929 and 1930; mechanisation was genuinely regarded as the key to future success. Much effort was devoted to finding the best way of organising the tractor economy, culminating in the decision in September 1930 to concentrate all tractors used by the kolkhozy in state-owned Machine-Tractor Stations (MTS). The MTS thus became the principal embodiment of the main economic benefits provided by the state to the kolkhozy, and, in those districts in which they operated, a parallel centre of control to the kolkhozsoyuz. Chapter 2 deals with the story of their rise to a monopoly position. It should be borne in mind that the decisions about the tractor economy and internal kolkhoz organisation were inter-related. If the kolkhozy were to be giants incorporating many villages, they could manage and repair their own tractors; if the kolkhoz-village and the kolkhoz-settlement were the norm, then, particularly when few tractors were available, the tractor economy must be separately organised, whether by agricultural cooperatives, by the kolkhozsoyuzy or by the state. *Per contra*, if the state decided to establish its own multi-village MTS—whether to enhance its own control over the kolkhozy or to take advantage of economies of scale—then the main argument in favour of multi-village kolkhozy would collapse. The discussion of the rise of the MTS in chapter 2 is thus closely related to the discussion of the size of the kolkhoz in chapter 3.

(c) THE STATE AND KOLKHOZ INTERNAL ORGANISATION

In the months preceding the collectivisation drive, it was a platitude in official circles that almost nothing was known about how to organise the kolkhoz, and that the attention devoted to this crucial subject was woefully inadequate. At the XVI party conference in April, Kubyak, People's Commissar for Agriculture of the RSFSR, complained that 'we have been discussing collectivisation and the kolkhozy for two days and no-one has so far mentioned that it is necessary to organise farming properly in the kolkhozy'.[13] At the conference of large kolkhozy in July, one of the rapporteurs in the organisation section declared that 'questions of the organisation of labour in kolkhozy are little studied, and have been still less studied in large kolkhozy'.[14] At the November plenum, Vladimirsky, chairman of the Union of Unions of agricultural cooperatives, strongly emphasised the lack of information:

I have read all the publications about the kolkhoz movement. They can almost be put in one pocket, and there is almost nothing there about the organisation of labour in kolkhozy.[15]

These criticisms were somewhat exaggerated. Vladimirsky would have needed a capacious pocket; the relevant items in the bibliography of the present volume contain over 1,000 pages, and are a small selection from a large literature. Much of the information about the organisation of small kolkhozy which was assembled and published in the early and mid-1920s was evidently not known to the party leaders. Some of it was known, but curtly discarded in the ambitious attempt to introduce industrial methods into kolkhoz management in the winter of 1929–30, only to be taken up again in the spring of 1930. Much of the experience of the small

---

[13] *XVI konf.* (1962), 421.
[14] ZKK (1929), 145.
[15] Chigrinov (1970), 50.

kolkhoz of the 1920s was, however, irrelevant to the typical kolkhoz of 1930, containing dozens of households.

During the collectivisation drive, the Soviet leaders refrained from prescribing the structure and *modus operandi* of the kolkhoz except in a rough outline; on the face of it, this was a sound approach, given their ignorance and lack of experience. When the November plenum insisted on 'unity in the management of agricultural production', this was a unity in which much was deliberately left to local initiative. Even Molotov, while reproaching the central kolkhoz administration for an insufficiently serious approach to kolkhoz organisation, left the door open for independent action:

> Kolkhozy can learn much from the well-organised Soviet factory, but the variety of conditions and the differences in the stages of development reached by the kolkhoz movement in particular [geographical] areas makes necessary an exceptional degree of flexibility in the forms and methods of kolkhoz construction.[16]

Symptomatic of the unwillingness of the party leaders to undertake the resolution of these questions at the centre, or of their indifference to them, was the failure to include a subcommission on kolkhoz organisation among the eight subcommissions of the Politburo commission on the kolkhoz movement of December 1929. The subcommission on organisational questions under M. Katsenelenbogen, who was on the staff of the central committee rural department, appears to have dealt only with the relations between kolkhozy and higher authorities.[17] At the conference of marxist agrarians in the same month, an agronomist from a Ural RSK reproached the central authorities with having no theory which could provide guidance about 'what to do, how to do it, and where to do it' with the result that 'there is complete chaos in the planned organisation of the land area, in the socialist organisation of the masses and of genuinely large-scale production'. 'Why don't you provide anything from the localities?,' called out someone in the audience. 'We do a bit,' the speaker replied, 'but we are practical officials.'[18] At a

---

[16] B, 22, November 30, 1929, 14–15.
[17] IISO, [i] (1964), 265–7. For Katsenelenbogen see *Trudy . . . agrarnikov-marksistov* (1930), i, 430.
[18] *Trudy . . . agrarnikov-marksistov* (1930), i, 146–7.

kolkhoz conference, also held in December, representatives of local organisations were said to be 'swimming on the waves of an unknown sea, improvising, talking in general terms rather than on the real theme'.[19] The central authorities continued, however, to abstain from any detailed prescriptions, and on February 20, 1930, Syrtsov complained of the 'organisational muddle and lack of commonsense' which had left the peasant without leadership.[20] Even at the XVI party congress in July 1930, after all the upheavals of the previous six months, Yakovlev told critics that, apart from its ruling on the proportion of the crop which should go to the state, the central committee did not propose to make specific provisions about the way in which the harvest should be divided up between the kolkhoz and its members:

> *Such bureaucratic castles in the air should not be permitted; in future instead of issuing new instructions one should be making sure that questions about the distribution of the harvest are decided not behind the backs of the collective farmers in some office but, as is laid down by the directives of the party central committee, by the collective farmers themselves, by the general meeting of collective farmers, with the approval of the general meeting of collective farmers.* That will be the best guarantee against mistakes.[21]

In October, in the course of his critical speech about the organisation of the economy, Syrtsov called for the 'standardisation of organisational forms and production methods' in the kolkhozy, but was condemned for his bureaucratic approach; 'this proposal', said one of his critics, 'would get first prize at a competition of Soviet bureaucrats'.[22]

The complicated questions of kolkhoz organisation were not, however, decided by a kind of Benthamite self-acting democracy. In each kolkhoz, in each district, okrug and region, decisions were reached within a definite framework of national policy; and local decisions on matters of organisation were pushed in different directions by the changes in policy at the centre. This was a learning process on a vast scale, and in an extremely brief period of time, in

---

[19] EZh, December 27, 1929; this conference is discussed further on pp. 44–5 below.

[20] B, 5, March 15, 1930, 48; for Syrtsov see vol. 1, p. 375, n. 10.

[21] *XVI s"ezd* (1931), 643–4.

[22] NAF, 11–12, 1930, p. xiii (Tal'); for this speech see vol. 1, pp. 375–6.

which party leaders and their advisers, local party officials, the peasants and economic regularities all contributed to the outcome. Out of the chaos and the brutality of the winter and spring of 1929–30, important features of the kolkhoz system gradually emerged, in the course of the failure of impossible solutions and the rejection of solutions unacceptable to the central authorities, or intolerable to the peasants. Major features of the kolkhoz system established in 1929–30 endured until Stalin's death, and for some time after it.

CHAPTER TWO

THE MACHINE-TRACTOR STATIONS

In the spring of 1929, new forms of organisation of the tractor economy were distinguished more by their potential than by their achievement. A couple of state-owned Machine-Tractor Stations attached to sovkhozy, with about a hundred tractors,[1] and some fifty 'tractor columns' of the grain cooperatives with over 1,000 tractors ploughed between them a mere 90,000 hectares or so of the 4 million hectares sown by the kolkhozy in the spring of 1929 (see Table 2(b)). In addition, several thousand tractors belonging to agricultural cooperatives were available for loan to kolkhozy through hiring points. A further 800 tractors were owned by 147 large kolkhozy (see vol. 1, p. 122, n. 60). But the vast majority of the 20,000 tractors serving the kolkhozy in the spring of 1929 were scattered among 57,000 small kolkhozy. Almost all tractors had been removed from individual owners; according to official statistics, none remained in their possession by October 1, 1929 (see Table 1).

In the rancorous and protracted discussions about the organisational forms through which tractors should be made available to kolkhozy, no objection was raised to the proposition that the small kolkhozy of 10–15 households were not capable of using a tractor efficiently. Their land area was insufficient—the sown area of the average kolkhoz in June 1929 was 73 hectares, but a 10 h.p. tractor, if fully used, would plough at least 200 hectares a season. In a substantial minority of kolkhozy, in which the land was not consolidated, conditions for using tractors were particularly difficult. Facilities for maintenance and repair were also usually lacking. While large kolkhozy, covering a whole village or several villages, were able to make full use of their tractors, maintenance

[1] Carr and Davies (1969), 213, list three such MTS as in existence in the spring of 1929, but other accounts state that only one or two state MTS existed throughout 1929 (see Table 2(b), and SZe, February 11, 1930, which reports that only two state MTS existed on February 1, 1930).

was difficult except in the few kolkhozy large enough to use several tractors. The cooperative columns, with an average of 25–30 tractors each (see Table 2), were in principle sufficiently large to make reasonable maintenance feasible. But the state-owned Machine-Tractor Station, modelled on the successful experience of the Shevchenko sovkhoz in the Ukraine, seemed to offer considerable additional advantages. Markevich, the founder of the Shevchenko MTS, in his widely distributed booklet (the second edition alone was printed in 10,000 copies), claimed that in Soviet conditions by far the most efficient arrangement was to concentrate some 200 tractors, serving an arable area of 40,000–50,000 hectares, in a single station. Owing to the scarcity and expensiveness of capital, tractors must be used for longer periods in each year, and for a longer period altogether, than in the United States. Adequate maintenance was therefore essential and would carry with it higher productivity and fuel economies.[2] But this required a well-equipped repair shop, including for preference a casting shop, so that work need not be put out. Such a shop would not be economical for a small number of tractors. With a large number of tractors, it would also be possible to keep some spare tractors for emergencies. Markevich presented calculations of capital and current costs for different sizes of MTS, and claimed that total tractor costs per hectare fell steadily with the growth of the area served by the MTS.[3] Costs continued to fall for areas larger than 50,000 hectares, but Markevich argued that until technology improved and experience accumulated, a larger MTS was not justified in view of 'the complexity and difficulties of organisation'.[4]

Markevich's conclusions suffered from the important weakness that a few minor adjustments to the data made it possible to show that an MTS of 10,000 hectares was as efficient as one of 50,000 hectares.[5] But the viability of his general concept did not depend on

[2] Markevich (1929), 92–3.

[3] *Ibid.* 163–7. Total costs per hectare fell from 30 rubles 46 kopeks for 500 hectares to 15r 36k for 5,000 hectares, 13r 20k for 10,000 and 11r 10k for 50,000. These figures include (a) capital outlay, depreciation charge and interest at 6 per cent, on workshops, housing, staff, tractors and vehicles, (b) wages for the central staff of the MTS and its repair shop, and (c) running costs (materials, spare parts and fuel but *not* the wages of the drivers, which were to come from the village itself).

[4] *Ibid.* 169.

[5] A critic argued, on the assumption that the MTS acted as a grain collection point, that Markevich ignored the rising cost of transporting the marketed harvest

such calculations. He tried to combine in the MTS what he saw as two essential requirements for the advance of Soviet agriculture. The first was that agricultural technology should be managed by a *'unified organisational centre'* for the whole USSR. The unified centre would select the priority districts and okrugs for development, survey world technology to find the best systems and types of machinery for Soviet conditions, and then impose its requirements on Soviet industry; huge economies of scale could be obtained from standardisation and centralised supply.[6] Markevich regarded it as highly desirable, though not absolutely essential, that the MTS should be owned by this unified centre rather than by the group of villages served by the MTS; ownership by a group of villages would 'inevitably involve an artisan approach'. He rejected, on rather flimsy grounds, proposals resuscitated by Khrushchev 30 years later that each kolkhoz-village should possess its own tractors, but be served by the MTS as a repair base; this scheme would have been at least as profitable in terms of Markevich's own calculations.[7] But he did not insist that the unified centre should be a state enterprise; it could equally well be owned by the cooperatives or by a mixed joint-stock company.[8]

According to Markevich, the second requirement, if advanced technology were to be successfully introduced, was that it should be palatable to the peasants, while simultaneously leading them towards collectivisation. Markevich took it for granted that the existing village, or part of a village, must be the basic unit with which the MTS dealt; he made the obvious point that it would be much too expensive to rearrange the villages so that each had the same area.[9] According to Markevich, the minimum condition for economical use of the tractor was that all boundaries between strips within each village should be removed, and that all work should be carried out under the guidance of an agronomist and a mechanic from the MTS; the village would supply and pay all the labour, including tractor drivers trained by the MTS. The harvest would, at first, be distributed among the peasants according to the land

---

to the MTS; if this were taken into account the optimum size was 50,000 hectares *total* area (SZo, ix, October–November 1930, 21–3; see also SZo, vi, July 1930, 51–66).

[6] Markevich (1929), 274–7, 288.
[7] *Ibid.* 288–92.
[8] *Ibid.* 280.
[9] *Ibid.* 67.

each household contributed.[10] The peasants need not join formally into a kolkhoz, and, if they did, the best form in the first instance would be the simplest type of kolkhoz, the TOZ, in which each household kept its own animals, and only arable farming was undertaken in common.[11] Finally, whether the village became a kolkhoz or not, its payments to the MTS must be such as to provide a *'clear gain obvious to the peasantry'*. In Shevchenko the village handed over to the MTS a quarter or a third of its harvest, an arrangement which provided an incentive for both the MTS and the peasant to produce more; the alternative of a fixed charge per hectare would provide no incentive for the MTS and would cause the peasant insupportable losses in a bad year.[12]

In the spring of 1929, Markevich's call for centralised state control and his intention of separating the tractors physically and organisationally from the kolkhoz were strongly criticised. In the opinion of the agricultural cooperatives, state-managed MTS would inevitably be isolated from the kolkhozy and would not be able to take advantage of the contacts established over the years by the cooperatives.[13] At the XVI party conference in April 1929, considerable enthusiasm was shown for the Shevchenko experiment, but the conference resolution, adhering to the course strongly advocated by Kaminsky in the debate (see vol. 1, p. 115), impartially recommended the development of 'state and cooperative' MTS and tractor columns, and of large kolkhozy at the level of modern technology.[14]

After the XVI conference, events moved fast. On May 8, STO decided to establish an 'all-Union centre' to manage the Machine-Tractor Stations, and during the next few weeks inter-departmental meetings convened by Rabkrin, and a special commission of STO, prepared the appropriate legislation. The rival merits of kolkhoz and state ownership were much debated; the majority of the commission agreed that the development of the MTS should be concentrated in the hands of the state. Some members of the majority wanted the 'all-Union centre' to be a state trust; others proposed that it should be a 'joint-stock' enterprise. The draft

[10] *Ibid.* 298–301.
[11] *Ibid.* 18–19.
[12] *Ibid.* 182–5.
[13] For an account of the arguments advanced by the cooperatives see Lewin (1968), 365–7; Miller (1970), 72–8.
[14] *XVI konf.* (1962), 393–4; *KPSS v rez.*, ii (1954), 580, 587.

decree by Rabkrin supported the 'joint-stock' form, with state capital predominating; this would ensure that the kolkhoz and cooperative organisations were fully involved, and make it possible to collect peasant funds for the construction of MTS.[15] This proposal was accepted by STO in a decree of June 5, 1929, which established 'VTsMTS', the All-Union Centre of Machine-Tractor Stations, as a state joint-stock company in which the main government and cooperative organisations concerned with agriculture participated. VTsMTS, which soon became known as Traktorotsentr, was allocated 5,000 tractors 'as a minimum' for the year 1929/30, to begin the establishment of a network of MTS, the structure of which, as outlined in the decree, closely resembled that proposed by Markevich. A provision that sovkhoz MTS which were mainly cultivating peasant land should be transferred to the new centre enabled Shevchenko to be incorporated as the first unit in the new system.[16] The legal constitution of Traktorotsentr was thus a concession to fears of too much central control; it was later described as 'a special semi-state, semi-cooperative organisation'.[17] But, as with the other state joint-stock companies which existed at this time, this was almost entirely a legal fiction. All the property of Traktorotsentr and its MTS remained firmly in state ownership, even though peasant contributions were solicited for their establishment; and the whole operation was directed in detail by the central authorities.

The promised allocation of 5,000 tractors was substantial: in 1928/29 the total stock of tractors in the kolkhozy and the agricultural cooperatives increased by only 8,000 (see Table 1). At the conference of large kolkhozy in July 1929 one delegate complained that it was likely that as a result of the allocation to the new MTS no tractors would be left for the large kolkhozy.[18] But most existing tractors belonged to agricultural cooperatives, or to the kolkhozy themselves, and no hint was given in the decree of June 5 that Traktorotsentr would have any control over these tractors, or over the cooperative MTS and tractor columns; the establishment of MTS was described merely as 'one of the basic paths' to collectivisation.

The relation between the tractor and the kolkhoz was further

[15] IS, 2, 1978, 68 (Vyltsan); this account is based on the archives.
[16] *Kollektivizatsiya . . . 1927–1935* (1957), 179–80; SZ, 1929, art. 353.
[17] NAF, 11–12, 1929, 142.
[18] ZKK (1929), 302.

discussed at the conference of large kolkhozy, and the course of the discussion made it abundantly clear that the decree of June 5 had not settled the problem. Kaminsky, departing from his earlier impartial support for different forms of tractorisation, urged that the tractor columns of the agricultural cooperatives, at this time quantitatively much more important than the MTS, should be transformed into group holdings (kusty) of the kolkhozy, and that collective farmers should acquire resources to buy up the state-owned MTS.[19] Another official spokesman of Kolkhoztsentr, however, wanted Kolkhoztsentr itself to take over those tractor columns which served the kolkhozy.[20] In the debate at the conference, the common thread was the resistance by the kolkhozy to MTS or tractor columns which were independent of the kolkhoz system. Many delegates criticised Kaminsky for his conciliatory attitude to the cooperative tractor columns, and urged that they should be brought under the direct control of the kolkhoz system or preferably of the kolkhozy themselves. 'The instruments of production', one speaker declared, 'cannot be in someone else's hands', and a Kolkhoztsentr official complained that the main allocation of tractors had been made to tractor columns rather than to the kolkhozy themselves until Kolkhoztsentr got the decision reversed.[21] The resolution of the conference called for the eventual 'transfer by sale' of the tractor columns to the 'population of the kolkhoz'.[22]

During the summer, Traktorotsentr approved the locations of 100 MTS, each with 50 tractors in the first instance, which were to be set up in the spring of 1930; most of them were to be situated in RSKs.[23] In the meantime the agricultural cooperatives greatly expanded their tractor columns, which were now also frequently and confusingly described as 'MTS'; they contained 2,000 tractors by September 1929 (see Table 2(b)). This expansion was achieved not by acquiring new tractors but by removing existing ones from hiring points, small kolkhozy and producers' associations within the cooperative system.[24]

[19] ZKK (1929), 284–5.
[20] ZKK (1929), 292–3.
[21] ZKK (1929), 295, 298–301, 314–15.
[22] ZKK (1929), 318–20.
[23] P, September 12, 1929; *Krasnyi Khoper*, September 5, 1929 (referring to a Traktorotsentr plan dated August 28).
[24] There were 6,673 tractors in the agricultural cooperatives on October 1, 1928,

In August 1929 Rabkrin issued a highly critical report about the cooperative MTS and columns, criticising the absence of careful planning, the lack of preliminary preparation of the population, by either propaganda or technical training, the use of old tractors, the absence of repair shops, the frequent stoppages (amounting to 40 per cent of the working time) and the failure to involve the peasants in the provision of finance. The report castigated the whole operation of setting up the columns for 'hastiness', and for aiming at 'looking good from outside'.[25] In its report to the party central committee of September 7, 1929, Kolkhoztsentr, following up a further point in the Rabkrin report, criticised 'tractor columns outside the kolkhoz' because they failed to stimulate socialisation except in arable farming, and resulted in peasants transferring their activities to the development of other branches of farming on an individual basis. It also reproved both the tractor columns and Shevchenko for failing to attract peasant resources to their construction.[26] The inability of state MTS and cooperative columns to persuade the peasants to contribute to the cost of the tractors was frequently stressed by those who argued that the kolkhozy themselves should own the tractors; this must have been an important consideration for the authorities.

The November plenum of the central committee showed no disposition to favour any particular form of organisation for the tractor economy. At the plenum Molotov reproved Traktorotsentr for planning 102 MTS for the next spring and failing to notice that about 100 already existed; some were known as tractor columns, but this was a purely organisational distinction:

> In the last resort this is one and the same thing. Who has found in reality, or can find, a difference in principle between tractor stations and tractor columns?[27]

---

but only 3,769 in the cooperatives and 2,387 in 'MTS' (at this stage this must refer to cooperative columns), 6,156 in all, on October 1, 1929 (see Table 1). On the removal of tractors from kolkhozy by the cooperatives, see *XVI konf.* (1962), 422 (Kubyak).

25 P, August 2, 1929; the similar criticisms cited by Lewin (1968), 422–4, also all refer to the cooperative columns—Tsil'ko's article in NAF, 11–12, 1929, was presumably a version of the report cited above (Tsil'ko was at this time an official of Rabkrin).

26 *Materialy*, vii (1959), 228, 267.

27 B, 22, November 30, 1929, p. 12.

The resolution of the plenum again commended both MTS, as future 'centres of comprehensive collectivisation of whole districts', and the 'large mechanised kolkhozy'.[28] But it also made clear its anxiety to obtain finance from agriculture itself for the production of agricultural machinery: it recommended that kolkhozy ordering new tractors and other machinery should pay a deposit amounting to 20 per cent of their value, to be used to finance the construction of new tractor factories.[29]

With the reorganisation of the kolkhoz and cooperative system announced at this time (see vol. 1, pp. 301–2), which aimed at bringing together agricultural cooperatives and kolkhozsoyuzy into a common organisation at the regional, okrug and district level, the cooperative MTS and columns appeared to fall naturally into place as the tractor agency of the single district organisation. At the height of the collectivisation drive, the agricultural cooperatives supported attempts to establish giant kolkhozy each embracing a whole district, or a substantial part of a whole district, and running their own tractors and other machinery. On January 18, 1930, in a telegram to the Central Black-Earth region, Khlebotsentr ruled that every column or MTS which owned more than 20 tractors should set up a giant kolkhoz.[30] In the following month Belenky, a senior official of Khlebotsentr, announced that it had already organised 185 MTS and columns with over 5,000 tractors, and planned to set up a total of 490 with 18,000 tractors by the end of 1930 (see Table 2(b)).

Schemes to obtain payments for tractors from the kolkhozy were promoted during the collectivisation drive as part of the general campaign to obtain more money from the peasants (see pp. 120–4 below). The Politburo commission of December 1929 recommended in its draft resolution on collectivisation that deposits should be increased during 1930 to 60 per cent of the value of the tractors and 40 per cent of the value of agricultural machines; in addition tractor 'obligations' covering 120,000 tractors should be issued to the kolkhozy and paid in three instalments.[31] On December 30, a Sovnarkom decree ruled that in the case of MTS and tractor columns the peasants served by them must pay at least 25 per cent of

[28] *KPSS v rez.*, ii (1954), 646.

[29] *KPSS v rez.*, ii (1954), 645–6; Nemakov (1966), 80.

[30] IS, 4, 1969, 33; according to IZ, lxxiv (1963), 21, a decree of January 21, 1930, ordered the transfer of all grain cooperative MTS and tractor columns to giant kolkhozy before the spring sowing, or at the latest by the end of 1930.

[31] VIK, 1, 1964, 38.

their cost before construction began; payments were to be made via kolkhozy at the rate of 3–5 rubles per hectare of arable land.[32] In January and February 1930, the agricultural cooperatives collected substantial advance payments of 60 million rubles from the kolkhozy for the purchase of 25,000 tractors,[33] and in the course of 1930 the state-owned MTS collected 24 million rubles as compared with a capital investment in 1930 of 110–113 million rubles.[34]

Meanwhile, a cloud loomed over Traktorotsentr. At the beginning of December 1929, after the formation of Narkomzem and Kolkhoztsentr of the USSR, a Kolkhoztsentr conference proposed that as well as Traktorotsentr becoming an 'autonomous centre' within Kolkhoztsentr, as already proposed by the November plenum, the local agencies of Traktorotsentr should be placed under the leadership of the regional or okrug kolkhozsoyuz.[35] This recommendation was not immediately accepted, and both Kolkhoztsentr and Traktorotsentr continued to be autonomous organisations not formally subordinate to the new Narkomzem of the USSR (see vol. 1, p. 169, n. 95). But, significantly, Markevich, in spite of his status and popularity, was made neither a deputy People's Commissar nor a member of the collegium of Narkomzem of the USSR, unlike, for example, the chairman of the sovkhoz grain trust Zernotrest or the chairman of Kolkhoztsentr.[36] In December 1929, the ideas of Markevich, which had seemed very advanced six months before (see pp. 18–20 above), were sharply criticised for their moderation. At the conference of marxist agrarians a report on the MTS rebuked him for allegedly believing that 'motive power' as such would automatically lead to socialism; in the discussion, a speaker from the Lower Volga region, while conceding that the 'energy theory' or 'energy approach' of Markevich and Krzhizhanovsky had played a positive role, suggested that the failure to link it in practice with social problems

---

[32] SZ, 1930, arts. 16, 130; see also Danilov (1957), 380–1.

[33] P, May 22, 1930, disk. listok 1; SO, 3–4, 1930, 109, reported that 61·2 million rubles were collected for tractors by March 10, 1930.

[34] Danilov (1957), 381; IS, 2, 1978, 69, states that peasant contributions in 1930 amounted to 55 million rubles and capital investment in MTS to 99·3 million rubles, but does not make it clear whether the former figure includes contributions to cooperative MTS and columns.

[35] SKhG, December 4, 1929.

[36] SZ, 1929, ii, arts. 292, 299.

had 'a menshevik odour (*Voice*: Very interesting)'.[37] In this context, several delegates objected to Markevich's insistence that socialisation within the kolkhozy should at first be confined to arable farming. At a time when giant kolkhozy were increasingly popular, the reluctance of Traktorotsentr to deal with organisations larger than the village also gave rise to grave doubts.[38]

In his speech at the end of the conference, however, Stalin referred impartially to the benefits the kolkhozy would obtain from Machine-Tractor Stations, tractor columns and the acquisition of tractors by the kolkhozy themselves (see vol. 1, p. 393). The central committee resolution of January 5, 1930, was also cautious, merely instructing the MTS under Traktorotsentr, 'in view of the changed conditions' in RSKs, to

> reconstruct their work on the basis of (a) contracts mainly, if not exclusively, with collectives; (b) peasant obligations to cover the cost of the stations within three years.[39]

This ambiguous instruction conveyed no more than a hint of disapproval of the activities of Traktorotsentr. It did not refer to the admissibility or otherwise of the amalgamation of each MTS into a giant kolkhoz embracing a district, and left open the question of whether the MTS, after being paid for by the peasants, would be transferred to the kolkhozy.[40] On February 1, 1930, a decree of STO, announcing that the number of MTS in 1930 was to be increased from 106 to 219, called for the socialisation not only of draught animals and implements, but also of all 'commodity

---

[37] *Trudy* . . . *agrarnikov-marksistov* (1930), ii, 67, 105 (the report was by A. Lozovoi; the speaker from the Lower Volga was A. Gavrilov).

[38] *Ibid.* ii, 108, 160–1, 165–6. In a notorious telegram to the Khoper okrug kolkhozsoyuz signed by Markevich, Traktorotsentr refused to permit MTS to sign contracts with inter-village kolkhozy—the telegram read 'organisation of station precludes inter-settlement kolkhozy[;] must sign contracts with village production unions' (*ibid.* 161; SKhG, December 13, 1929). Some of the criticisms made at the conference were developed at length by M. Golendo, a member of the collegium of Narkomzem, in NAF, 2, 1930, 9–21, and by Karpinsky in SZe, February 11, 1930.

[39] *KPSS v rez.*, ii (1954), 666; clause(b) was clearly a truncated version of the proposal in the draft resolution prepared by the Politburo commission (see p. 22 above).

[40] Later statements (e.g. by Sarkis of the agricultural cooperatives, in P, May 22, 1930, disk. listok 1) to the effect that the resolution involved the *sale* of the MTS to the kolkhozy within three years go beyond its wording.

branches of agriculture' in the area of the MTS, and declared that the state MTS must be a 'fully mechanised large-scale economy, capable of being a model and a school for large-scale collective agricultural construction'; it also again insisted that the construction of an MTS must not begin until 25 per cent of its full cost had been paid in by the peasants.[41] Shortly afterwards, Markevich, conceding that 'basic changes' were needed in the MTS arrangements as compared with Shevchenko, emphasised that MTS must not be treated as a 'tractor hiring point' but as a means of organising 'unified inter-village collective production'; the term MTS should refer to the 'whole kolkhoz-production combine (kombinat)'.[42] This was the farthest point in concessions by Traktorotsentr to the fashionable trend towards kolkhozy much larger than a single village.

While the state MTS were still in process of formation, the abrupt change of policy at the end of February 1930 resulted in a mass exodus from the kolkhozy and the restoration of the viewpoint that the kolkhoz-village should be the basic agricultural unit (see pp. 51–4 below). This change in policy was not always advantageous to MTS operations: tractors now had sometimes to be sent long distances in order to be fully utilised.[43] But on the whole it greatly strengthened the position of Markevich and Traktorotsentr. The scheme of a centrally-managed state network of MTS could now remain intact, modified only by the elimination of the envisaged transitional period in which contracts by the MTS were signed with non-collectivised villages. Markevich's strongly-held opinions that the kolkhoz must be based on the existing village, and that socialisation should not go further than arable farming in the first stage of collectivisation, were now fully restored to party doctrine, supported by the disastrous experience of the excesses of the previous months.[44]

The arguments for keeping the tractor economy in MTS, separate from the individual kolkhozy, now seemed overwhelming. The

[41] SZ, 1930, art. 130; a recommendation of the collegium of Narkomzem of the USSR dated December 31, 1929, using similar wording, is cited from the archives in IS, 4, 1969, 33, and is interpreted as a proposal to establish giant kolkhozy on the basis of the MTS.
[42] P, February 13, 1930.
[43] See IS, 4, 1969, 34.
[44] See his strongly-worded article, or cry of triumph, in P, April 8, 1930 (and see p. 52 below).

break-up of the giant kolkhozy and the drastic reduction in the membership of all kolkhozy had eliminated almost all those which were of sufficient size to control a group of tractors effectively, and the decline in the number of horses and the shortage of tractors in any case made it desirable that each kolkhoz using tractors should be only partially mechanised at first. Moreover, the relaxation in the spring of 1930 of earlier financial pressures on the countryside (see pp. 124–5 below) made it impossible to collect more than a minor part of the cost of the tractors either from kolkhozy or from the peasants direct; this weakened the criticism of the state MTS for failing to persuade peasants to subscribe to tractor obligations.

The case for separating all MTS and tractor columns from the agricultural cooperatives was also now very strong. The agricultural cooperatives continued to form MTS and tractor columns at a remarkable pace in the spring of 1930 (see Table 2(b)); as well as converting existing hiring-points into columns, they must also have received a substantial allocation of new tractors. But, unlike the state MTS, the agricultural cooperatives emerged from the gigantic exertions of the first few weeks of 1930 much weakened, having merged most of their primary organisations with the kolkhozy (see vol. 1, pp. 299–300). The decision in July 1930 to separate the kolkhoz and agricultural cooperative system at every level (see vol. 1, pp. 351–2) deprived the cooperatives of most of their functions in relation to the kolkhozy, and removed the basis of their argument that the existence of Traktorotsentr and the MTS brought confusion to the administrative arrangements by providing a separate line of control over the kolkhozy.

While the separation of local kolkhoz administration from the agricultural cooperatives undermined the position of the cooperatives in relation to the MTS, it left intact the view widely held in the kolkhoz movement that the MTS should be subordinated not to a separate centralised network but to the district kolkhozsoyuzy, so that control over the activities of the kolkhozy was unified. At the party congress in June 1930, some talk took place behind the scenes about transferring the MTS to the kolkhoz system; Khataevich reported that 'comrade Yakovlev told me in a personal conversation that we shall hand over tractors, hand over the whole tractor economy, to the kolkhoz system; but I think that's not enough'.[45] Markevich confidently reported on the activities of

[45] *XVI s"ezd* (1931), 623; the reference here is to a transfer to district kolkhozsoyuzy, not to individual kolkhozy, *pace* IS, 4, 1969, 35. The latter source

'several hundred MTS' with 'twenty thousand tractors', as if the MTS of the agricultural cooperatives as well as those of Traktorotsentr were already under his control.[46] The reports by Stalin and Yakovlev, and the congress resolutions, however, again ignored the question of the relationship between the MTS, the tractor columns and the kolkhozy, and the resolution of the central control commission and Rabkrin of July 9, 1930, on kolkhoz organisation, prepared while the congress was in session, merely recommended the agricultural cooperatives and Traktorotsentr to 'coordinate with the local organisations the plans for the construction of MTS, and their work.'[47]

But matters were now soon resolved in favour of Markevich and the state network of MTS. A month after the party congress, on August 11, a central committee resolution on the Shevchenko MTS claimed that it had 'fully justified the role of the MTS as a powerful lever of the socialist reconstruction and advance of agriculture'.[48] On August 23, Traktorotsentr, which until then had formally retained an autonomous status, was attached to Kolkhoztsentr,[49] presumably in order to allay the strong anxieties within the kolkhoz system that an MTS network independent of Kolkhoztsentr would make control of the kolkhozy difficult and confusing. A few weeks later, on September 10, 1930, apparently without further public discussion, a brief resolution of the party central committee announced that 'all construction and management of MTS must be concentrated in Traktorotsentr'; Traktorotsentr would take over all the cooperative MTS and repair shops, assume responsibility for technical assistance to all tractors belonging to kolkhozy, and, 'on conditions agreed with the kolkhozy', also take over, both from individual kolkhozy and from groups of kolkhozy, all tractor columns capable of being reorganised into inter-village MTS.[50] This resolution greatly strengthened the position of Traktorotsentr, and, in spite of its caution about tractors owned by kolkhozy, effectively cleared the way for their removal to the MTS: the stock of tractors in kolkhozy fell by one-third in the next three months (see

---

reports from the archives that in the Central Volga region in August 1930 tractors were transferred to some kolkhozy big enough to use at least ten tractors.
[46] *XVI s"ezd* (1931), 640.   [47] I, July 15, 1930.
[48] *Kollektivizatsiya . . . 1927–1935* (1957), 316–19.
[49] Miller (1970), 141.
[50] *Kollektivizatsiya . . . 1917–1935* (1957), 322; the decision was first published in I, September 13, 1930.

Table 1), and was again halved in the following year.[51] The resolution of September 10 did not propose any change in the status of Traktorotsentr as a 'joint-stock company', and it said nothing about the all-important question of the relation between the MTS and the district kolkhozsoyuzy. But some recognition was soon given to the need to integrate the MTS system and the kolkhoz system by the appointment of Yurkin, the chairman of Kolkhoztsentr, as chairman of Traktorotsentr as well, with Markevich as his deputy.[52] This was not in any but a formal sense a demotion for Markevich. He continued to act as the effective chairman of Traktorotsentr and as its public spokesman, and at this time he was at last appointed to the collegium of Narkomzem.[53]

In the autumn of 1930, with the resumption of the drive for collectivisation, the MTS were regarded as a major means of attracting individual peasants to kolkhozy, and became an even greater object of public attention. In the various congresses, meetings and publications where the work of the MTS was reviewed, Markevich and his colleagues looked back on 1930 with a considerable sense of achievement. By the spring of 1930, all the MTS planned in the previous autumn had been established, and with a larger stock of tractors, though with a somewhat lower horse-power, than originally planned (see Table 2). In the spring, the MTS cultivated a sown area of 2,000,000 hectares, 510,000 more than the plan (see Table 2) though only eight per cent of the total spring-sown area of the kolkhozy. In the districts served by MTS, 62 per cent of the peasants remained in the kolkhozy, a substantially higher proportion than in neighbouring non-MTS districts.[54] A large harvest was reported from kolkhozy served by MTS. The grain collection plan for these kolkhozy was exceeded by 22 per cent by the end of October and, in all, over half their grain harvest was handed over to the collection agencies; nevertheless, according to Yakovlev, the harvest was so successful in these kolkhozy that their collective farmers still received a larger amount of grain for their own needs than those in other kolkhozy.[55] The autumn sowing plan

---

[51] *Nar. kh.* (1932), 145.

[52] SZe, December 20, 1930, describes them in this way; I have not traced the announcement of the appointment.

[53] SZ, 1930, ii, art. 392 (dated November 1).

[54] NAF, 6, 1930, 112; SZe, October 23, 1930.

[55] *6 s"ezd sovetov* (1931), No. 16, p. 21, No. 17, p. 27; the grain recorded as handed

was also completed successfully.[56] The system of payment in kind, whereby the MTS took part of the harvest (one-quarter in 1930) to cover its expenses, was reported to have provided adequate incentives for both MTS and kolkhoz.[57] Good progress in the training of labour was also claimed. Traktorotsentr established its own network of vuzy, technical colleges and courses; 25,000 tractor drivers were trained during 1930, the vast majority of them collective farmers, and, according to Markevich, a considerable number worked 'not badly'.[58]

While the establishment of the first few state MTS was undoubtedly a solid achievement, the cost was high, and the claims made for them were overdrawn. No systematic investigation was ever published of the operation of the MTS in 1930. But a survey of groups of kolkhozy in North Caucasus and Leningrad regions revealed that, contrary to earlier claims, the gross income per household for a group of kolkhozy served by MTS was in fact slightly lower in 1930 than for a second group, those not served by MTS, though much higher than for a third group of kolkhozy 'with a weak technical base'. Moreover, in the kolkhozy served by MTS, the income distributed to the collective farmers was substantially lower than in the second group. This was also true of the income

---

over to the collection agencies presumably included the payments in grain for the work of the MTS.

[56] SZe, December 30, 1930.

[57] *6 s"ezd sovetov* (1931), No. 17, 23, 25. In cotton, flax and sugar-beet areas, where the harvest was automatically all handed to the state, the MTS charged a fixed amount in rubles per hectare depending on the type of work (*ibid*. No. 17, 23).

[58] *Ibid*. No. 17, 35–6; according to Vyltsan (1959), 22, however, only 17,420 drivers and 2,070 senior drivers were trained by Traktorotsentr in 1930. The decision to send tractor drivers to Central Asia from the central regions was unsuccessful, as 'practice has shown that a European tractor driver on the cotton fields of Central Asia tries to give up the work and leave', so here too members of kolkhozy served by the MTS were to be trained as drivers (*6 s"ezd sovetov* (1931), No. 17, 36; SZe, December 20, 1930). According to a report in NAF, 6, 1930, 122–3, in the spring of 1930, of 322 'leading cadres', 75·1 per cent had been industrial workers, and only 5·9 per cent peasants; 52 per cent were party members; of 21,386 'middle and lower cadres', 5 per cent were party and 19.3 per cent Komsomol members; 15 per cent had been workers, 23·5 per cent batraks, 53·5 per cent poor peasants, and only 21·5 per cent middle peasants; only 5·7 per cent were women. The typical tractor driver was thus a male former batrak or poor peasant. A much higher proportion of the middle and lower cadres than of the collective farmers as a whole were in the party or Komsomol.

distributed in kind: in the North Caucasus the collective farmers served by MTS received 0·7 tons of grain per household, while other collective farmers received as much as 1·1 tons, and had grain to spare to sell on the free market. The lower level of distribution of grain, certainly displeasing to the peasants, was, however, regarded by the authorities as demonstrating the ability of the MTS system to provide better control over the economic activity of the kolkhozy.[59]

In their review of the first experience of the MTS, Soviet officials combined enthusiasm with a fairly frank recognition that they still worked badly in many respects. The MTS, as their opponents had warned, were remote from the kolkhozy. In his survey of the achievements of 1930 at the VI congress of soviets in March 1931, Markevich admitted that the MTS played little part in the work of the kolkhozy as such, sometimes being prevented from doing so by the local authorities.[60] The collective farmers who operated the tractors treated them with indifference:

> In most cases we still have a *barbarous* treatment of the machines not only through ignorance of the machine and inability to deal with it, but also through lack of willingness, carelessness, lack of understanding of the great importance of the machine for the collective farmer in the improvement of his well-being.

Ploughs squeaked through lack of oil, but the tractor driver and the ploughman paid no attention; and in 'hundreds of cases' deliberate damage was done by such acts as putting lumps of metal in the threshers.[61] The MTS, in common with the rest of the economy, suffered from the shortages and low quality of production endemic in the first stages of the industrialisation drive. Yurkin complained of the tradition of supplying sand with the oil, and as far as the kerosene used for fuel was concerned:

> Groznyi kerosene is such that it is capable of crippling a tractor of any system in a single spring, with the exception of the 'International' tractor, which will survive anything.[62]

[59] SRSKh, 8, 1931, 158–9.
[60] *6 s''ezd sovetov* (1931), No. 17, 24.
[61] *Ibid.* No. 17, 37.
[62] SZe, December 20, 1930.

Spare parts were always very scarce; and it took some time for industry to switch from horse-drawn to tractor-drawn implements, so that at the end of 1930 the production of ploughs and seeders was lagging behind the supply of tractors.[63] While tractors were imported in large numbers, lorries and cars were not, and Soviet production was negligible: at the end of 1930 the 158 MTS had in all only 200 lorries and 17 cars.[64] Perhaps the shortage of building materials was the most serious: as a result, new repair shops had been constructed in only half the MTS by December 1930;[65] the rest were presumably using makeshift buildings.

The plans for 1931, debated during the autumn of 1930, envisaged a further vast expansion. With the 13,000 tractors of the cooperatives, and some thousands of tractors transferred from the kolkhozy, the unified MTS system controlled 31,114 tractors by the end of 1930 (see Table 2(b)). The plan for 1931 stipulated that all tractors earmarked for the kolkhoz system were to be allocated to MTS, and none to individual kolkhozy. As a result, MTS were to receive 51·5 per cent of the tractor horse-power allocated, the rest going to the sovkhoz system,[66] and the number of tractors in MTS would rise to over 60,000 in the course of 1931.[67] The number of MTS was to rise to 1,000 in the main grain regions, which would make it possible for 80 per cent of their districts to have at least one MTS, and 405 MTS were to be established elsewhere. This would mean that each MTS would have only enough tractors, in the first year, to work an area of 25,000–30,000 hectares, and even in this area only the heavy work would be carried out by tractors, about 65–70 per cent still being done by horses. This gradual take-over by the tractor was in conflict with Markevich's original proposals of 1929, but would enable the new complement of tractors to provide 'partial tractorisation' of 18 million hectares over a large part of the USSR in the spring of 1931, whereas the alternative scheme would have provided 'full tractorisation' for only 5–6 million hectares.[68]

[63] SZe, December 20, 1930.

[64] SZe, December 20, 1930; *Sots. str.* (1935), 296.

[65] SZe, December 20, 1930.

[66] SZe, December 31, 1930; in addition to the 596,000 h.p. allocated to Traktorosentr, 35,000 h.p. were allocated to 'machine-tractor brigades' and 525,000 to sovkhozy, making a total of 1,157,000 h.p.

[67] P, October 22, 1930.

[68] Markevich's reports on the 1931 plan to the Ekoso of the RSFSR in October 1930, the collegium of Narkomzem in December 1930 and the VI congress of

The resources for this vast programme were to be provided mainly by the state, but in his report to the VI congress of soviets Markevich reminded his listeners that Traktorotsentr was a joint 'state–kolkhoz' organisation, insisted that 160 million of the 540 million rubles required for capital investment must come from the kolkhozy, and sternly warned that when kolkhozy did not pay up new MTS would be re-located to other districts.[69] The planned expansion made it necessary to train a further large number of new workers: the final plan proposed that 200,000 people should be put through courses by the spring of 1931, including 150,000 tractor drivers.[70]

In 1930, 139 of the 158 MTS were 'grain' MTS, and only 17 'cotton' and two 'sugar beet'; the attention of the MTS was heavily concentrated on the grain areas, and they were described at a session of Narkomzem as suffering from a ' "rye and oats" psychology'.[71] In the plans for 1931, a sharp change occurred. Priority was to be given to mechanisation of cotton growing in Central Asia. Markevich claimed that the first experiments with MTS in the cotton areas in 1930 had given 'splendid results', but the task was truly heroic: in some areas 'fuel has to be carried hundreds of kilometres by water and camels', and according to Markevich the MTS created 'scissors' between the technology introduced into agriculture and the general cultural level of the population.[72] In flax areas, marshes would be dried and cleared of roots with the aid of caterpillar tractors, and the 'Stolypin khutors' scattered among the marshes would be 'uprooted with the forests and the bushes'. In these areas other crops would also be mechanised so as to release workers and thus eliminate the 'annual labour crisis' caused by

---

soviets in March 1931 are in SZe, October 23, December 20, 1930; *6 s"ezd sovetov* (1931), No. 17, 27–41. At the session of Ekoso, some speakers suggested that the number of tractors per MTS should be further reduced so as to enable additional MTS to be established.

[69] *Ibid.* No. 17, 41; the original figure for kolkhoz contributions was 200 million rubles (SZe, December 20, 1930).

[70] *6 s"ezd sovetov* (1931), No. 17, 35. A thousand or so directors were to be trained in 1931 for MTS to be set up in 1932; these potential directors were to spend a probationary period as assistant directors at an existing MTS (SZe, December 20, 1930).

[71] *Sots. str.* (1935), 310; SZe, December 20, 1930.

[72] SZe, December 20, 1930; *6 s"ezd sovetov* (1931), No. 17, 36; Markevich called for the gap to be closed by the general education system giving priority to areas served by the MTS.

labour-intensive flax preparation. With sugar beet, the intention was to spread beet cultivation over a wider area, including other crops in the rotation, and then to transport the beet on tractors or horses to single-line narrow-gauge railways leading to the factories. This would enable the factories to be spread out, and thus reduce the shortage of labour and horses in their vicinity.[73] All these proposals, like Markevich's original scheme, were informed with technical competence and ingenuity. But, as with the original scheme, the problem was whether resources and the competent staff would be available in sufficient quantities to gain the enthusiasm of the peasants.[74] And a further trouble menaced the grain regions: grain payments to the MTS were additional to the grain collections required from all kolkhozy. Would the MTS come to seem to the collective farmers not so much a centre of modernisation as an additional agency for exploitation?

[73] SZe, December 20, 1930.

[74] In 1931 the net increase in tractor horse-power in the MTS was 386,000 (*Nar. kh.* (1932), 145), as compared with the 596,000 planned, the main cause of the lag being the failure of the Stalingrad tractor factory to reach its planned level of production. Of the 1,228 MTS established by June 1, 1931, 688 were grain, 153 cotton, 137 flax, 154 sugar beet, and 83 vegetable and potato.

CHAPTER THREE
THE SIZE OF THE KOLKHOZ

(A) THE RURAL SETTLEMENT, THE KOLKHOZ AND THE TRACTOR, MID-1929

The mir was the basic unit of rural economic organisation in the USSR until the end of the 1920s (see vol. 1, p. 6) and was controlled by meetings of all adults in the village, under an elected elder. One or more rural settlements (seleniya) formed a mir, which was legally known as a 'land society', and one or more mirs together formed an administrative village (selo), the lowest unit in the hierarchy of soviets. In the USSR at the end of the 1920s there were approximately 600,000 rural settlements, 319,000 mirs and 72,000 village soviets, so there were on average 1·9 settlements per mir and 4·4 mirs per village soviet.[1] The size of these units varied considerably from one part of the country to another. The basic difference was between the small settlement of Central Industrial, North–Western and Western Russia and Belorussia, with an average of 16–20 households, and the larger settlement of South–Eastern Russia and the Ukraine, with an average of 100–150 households. In the main grain-surplus regions the average settlement was relatively large (100 or more households); the settlements of the Ural and Siberian regions, although somewhat smaller, still contained more households than the grain-deficit areas.[2] The village soviet was an official rather than an economic unit, and its boundaries were changed frequently during the 1920s.

The settlement and the mir were natural units when the horse-drawn plough was the basic agricultural implement: the peasant needed to be able to walk from his cottage and his household plot to his land allotments in the fields of the settlement. But the advent of the tractor challenged this arrangement. At first some efforts were

[1] For the figure for mirs, which may refer to the RSFSR, see SS, xiv (1962/63), 247 (Male) and Male (1971), 11–12; for settlements (approximately equal to 'other inhabited points') and soviets (referring to January 1, 1929) see *Administrativno-*

made to incorporate mechanised farming within the existing land structure, and in the middle 1920s a small minority of peasant households purchased their own tractors. But even at this time most tractors were allocated to sovkhozy and kolkhozy. This immediately raised the question of the size of the kolkhoz. The existing kolkhoz, generally consisting of only part of a settlement, was believed to be too small to cope with mechanised agriculture (see p. 15 above). The study of agricultural developments in the United States, and the energetic experiments and calculations of Markevich, led to the acceptance of a new optimum area for mechanised agriculture, 40,000–50,000 hectares of arable land (see p. 16 above). It was not, however, at first supposed that the unit appropriate for tractor maintenance was also appropriate for field work and other farming activities. Traktorotsentr treated the village as the largest unit of agricultural organisation, even in

---

territorial'noe selenie Soyuza SSR i spisok vazhneishikh naselennykh punktov (8th edn, 1929), 12.

[2] The following table sums up the situation (derived from *ibid.* 24–31):

	No. of settlements per village soviet	No. of persons per village soviet	No. of persons per settlement
RSFSR	9	1540	180
of which:			
Leningrad region (excluding Murmansk okrug)	24	1930	80
Lower Volga region	3	1879	576
North Caucasus region	7	4145	564
Central Volga region	2	1666	747
Siberian region (excluding Krasnoyarsk okrug)	4	1468	405
Ural region (excluding Tobol'sk okrug)	8	2163	257
Central Black-Earth region	5	2312	462
Ukrainian SSR	5	2300	c.500
Belorussian SSR	27	2900	110
Transcaucasian SSR	5	1876	368
Uzbek SSR	6	2000	340
Turkmen SSR	6	2427	440

There is an unexplained discrepancy between the first two columns and the third. There were approximately five persons in each household. For more detailed figures see Male (1971), 92–3.

conditions of comprehensive collectivisation (see p. 24 above).

At the conference of large kolkhozy in July 1929, attended by delegates strongly identified with the need to increase the size of the kolkhoz, a sectional meeting on organisation resolved that 'the size of large kolkhozy is completely adequate for the rational organisation of collective production with high-productivity power and machine bases'.[3] At this time the average number of households in kolkhozy officially classified as 'large' was about 180, equivalent to the population of four or five rural settlements, and about half the size of the average village soviet. The largest kolkhoz then in existence, the Digorskii 'combine (kombinat)', North Caucasus region, included 13 settlements and 1,781 households.[4] At the conference the German expert Püschel argued that the basic unit should have an area of 1,500–2,000 hectares served by 10–15 tractors, which would provide the best possibility of precise supervision and would obviate unnecessary tractor journeys; this was about the size of the average village soviet. He proposed that the larger units which would be required in order to maintain a cultural centre and industrial enterprises could be established either by setting up larger kolkhozy divided into units, or by grouping smaller kolkhozy for common purposes.[5] All this was consistent with the assumption that a village or a larger settlement provided the natural limit for the maximum size of the larger kolkhoz.

Some excitement was caused at the conference by reports that several 'giant' kolkhozy had already been established. The term 'giant kolkhoz (kolkhoz-gigant)' was previously rarely used, and then referred to kolkhozy which embraced a whole village or a whole settlement.[6] These were now designated 'large' kolkhozy, and the term 'giant' henceforth referred to kolkhozy which included a substantial number of villages or even an entire administrative district of thousands of peasant households.[7] The establishment of giant kolkhozy was a startling new development and implied that

[3] ZKK (1929), 141.

[4] ZKK (1929), 91–5, 141, 470–7. For the debate about the definition of the 'large' kolkhoz, see vol. 1, pp. 121–2.

[5] ZKK (1929), 99–100.

[6] See, for example, *Kollektivizatsiya* (Kuibyshev, 1970), 52, 636–7 (a document of September 1928).

[7] The figures given for what is translated as 'giant' kolkhozy in Lewin (1968), 409, refer to 'large (krupnye)' kolkhozy in the wider definition of 2,000 hectares total area and above.

existing rural settlements need no longer be taken as a basis for the agricultural economy. But the giant kolkhozy were still rare exceptions to the general pattern. The movement for large kolkhozy continued to assume that the establishment of both large and giant kolkhozy could be justified only by a substantial degree of mechanisation, and that most kolkhozy would remain small. In July 1929 no-one anticipated the drastic new policies about the size of the kolkhoz which would become more or less orthodox early in 1930.

(B) THE DRIVE FOR GIANT KOLKHOZY, JULY–DECEMBER 1929

From the middle of 1929 onwards, the optimum size of kolkhozy was constantly under discussion, and by the end of the year the assumptions which still prevailed at the July conference of large kolkhozy were swept aside. The view temporarily became dominant that the mechanised kolkhoz must not be a 'large' kolkhoz but a 'giant'. Agricultural policy at this time was strongly influenced by the view that the methods of industry must prevail in agriculture, and industrial policy was increasingly directed towards the implanting of very large new factories using the most advanced United States technology. In this context, two circumstances were of particular importance in encouraging confidence in the viability of very large agricultural units.

First, the new giant sovkhozy set an example. With the support of its American advisers, Zernotrest decided early in 1929 that the optimum sovkhoz should have a sown area of 20,000–50,000 hectares, later raised to 40,000–50,000 hectares; these figures were consistent with Markevich's proposals for the optimum size of an MTS.[8] In the summer of 1929, the first harvest of Gigant sovkhoz in the Sal'sk okrug was thought satisfactory in quantity and yield (see vol. I, p. 148), and this practical success further encouraged the supporters of giant sovkhozy. Kalmanovich reported that he had found only ten farms in the United States 'which on our understanding could be called large', and announced that the minimum sown area for a sovkhoz should be 30,000 hectares.[9] In his article of

[8] Bogdenko (1958), 62.
[9] EZh, October 3, 13, 1929; Kalmanovich was chairman of Zernotrest.

November 7, 1929, Stalin, a strong defender of the new grain
sovkhozy during the discussions of 1928, now felt able to declare:

> The objections of 'science' to the possibility and expediency of
> organising large grain factories of 50,000–100,000 hectares have
> been exploded and turned into ashes.[10]

At the conference of marxist agrarians in December 1929, the
rapporteur on sovkhozy argued that the criterion for deciding their
size should be the 'most rational organisation of the main means of
production, which in grain farming are the internal combustion
engine, the tractor and all the appropriate attachments, and the
repair shops', and concluded that the correct size would be 500
tractors and 100,000–150,000 hectares (this evidently referred to
sown area or arable land);[11] this was already something like twice
the size recommended by Markevich for the MTS.

Even if these vast areas were sensible in the case of the new grain
sovkhozy, they should not have been regarded as necessarily
appropriate for the kolkhoz movement: unlike the kolkhozy, the
new sovkhozy were being established on virgin territory, and with
the aid of very substantial supplies of imported large tractors and
combine-harvesters. During the summer and autumn of 1929,
however, the plans for the sovkhozy created a certain atmosphere in
which the really successful agricultural unit was presumed to be a
huge farm, larger than the biggest in the United States, and worked
with modern machines and a small number of skilled technicians. In
a mood of exuberance and thoughtlessness, the existing settlements
and land structure were often seen as a mere obstacle to the
technical revolution in agriculture; this was already the view taken
of them when they got in the way of providing the sovkhozy with a
continuous land area. At the conference of marxist agrarians, one
speaker argued on the basis of the experience of the sovkhozy that
the agrarian economist Chayanov was advocating a 'biological and
in a sense a private capitalist orientation' when he suggested that the
structure and organisation of the farms should be determined by the

---

[10] P, November 7, 1929. In the version of the speech published in Stalin, *Soch.*, xii
(1949), 129, '50,000–100,000' is replaced by '40–50,000'. He did not indicate in
either version whether he was referring to total land area, arable land, or sown
area.

[11] *Trudy . . . agrarnikov-marksistov* (1930), ii, [i], 201–3 (Anisimov).

territory and type of crop rather than by the needs of the most up-to-date means of production.[12]

The second circumstance encouraging the formation of very large kolkhozy was the belief, vigorously advocated at all levels of the kolkhoz system, that tractors and agricultural machinery should be brought under the control of the kolkhozy themselves, or at least of the kolkhoz system, rather than being managed by a separate state agency such as Traktorotsentr or by the agricultural cooperatives (see p. 20 above). Existing small kolkhozy were at best large enough only for a single tractor, maintenance of which was difficult, and the kolkhozsoyuzy were weak and ineffective. The belief that tractors should not be managed by an agency external to the kolkhoz system thus encouraged the view that tractor and other farm operations should be fused under the unified management of a giant kolkhoz.

In September 1929, giant kolkhozy were still a very minor strand in plans for collectivisation. The grain cooperative organisation Khlebotsentr made a first tentative move towards bringing together tractor and other farm operations under a single management for an entire district. It arranged with Kolkhoztsentr that three districts of the Black-Earth region should be comprehensively collectivised in 1929/30 by extending the facilities of their MTS, which were part of the agricultural cooperative network, to cater for the whole population; in these districts the existing kolkhozy would retain their individual identities, but 'the transfer of the MTS to direct management by the collectivised population' would be accomplished through the establishment of a 'group cooperative union' of the kolkhozy of the district.[13] This plan would have resulted in the establishment of an organisation at the district level intermediate between a giant kolkhoz such as the Ural Gigant, and the district MTS surrounded by kolkhoz villages proposed by Markevich. But Markevich and Traktorotsentr remained sceptical about the prospects for giant kolkhozy. At an all-Union conference of the local officials of Traktorotsentr in September 1929, Markevich envisaged a future stage in which the optimum size of a kolkhoz, so as to enable the 'cheapest, most rational and most exact use of machinery' would

---

[12] *Ibid.* 229–30; Chayanov was working at this time on sovkhoz problems, and was criticised at the conference for being guided by the norms of the American Campbell's capitalist farm (*ibid.* 221); see also pp. 40–1 below.

[13] IS, 4, 1969, p. 32, citing the archives.

be 'thousands or tens of thousands of hectares'; but he continued to presume that in the 'first period' of kolkhoz development, which was evidently to be a lengthy one, the villages served by an MTS would remain separate economic units, with their own economy and crop rotation.[14]

A major shift in attitude followed the central committee plenum in November 1929. The resolutions of the plenum did not specifically refer to the size of kolkhozy or their relation with the MTS, and Molotov appears to have ignored the question in his wide-ranging reports. But Kaminsky in his unpublished report boldly declared that 'life itself is pressing for unification and grouping around the stronger collectives and for a further development via group associations (kustovye ob"edineniya) to large-scale production', and proposed the establishment of kolkhozy which included whole districts, claiming that only kolkhozy of this size could solve the grain and livestock problem by 1930/31.[15] Kaganovich, in his report on the plenum to party activists in Moscow region, pointed out that the land area of ten kolkhozy in the Urals amounted to a million hectares in all, and chose the famous Gigant kolkhoz as his principal example of successful kolkhoz development; this was the largest kolkhoz in the USSR, though so far equipped with relatively few tractors. He depicted—and predicted—in glowing phrases the setting up of a telephone network and a bakery for the whole kolkhoz and of communal kitchens which would deliver food straight to the fields.[16]

The impression that the party leadership was not averse to the establishment of giant kolkhozy equal in size to an administrative district, and that such kolkhozy need not await the arrival of large numbers of tractors, was reinforced by the vigorous campaign conducted at this time against the once powerful group of economists, mainly former Socialist Revolutionaries, who had persistently defended small-scale agriculture as economically more viable. The pressure exercised on these men by the campaign was such that in September 1929 their leading theoretician Chayanov repudiated his earlier defence of the peasant family unit as inappropriate to an age of technical revolution and vigorously advocated large-scale farming and the socialist reconstruction of

[14] EZh, September 10, 1929.
[15] Chigrinov (1970), 48.
[16] P, November 26, 1929 (report of November 21).

agriculture.[17] This change of heart was criticised by official writers as insincere,[18] and the adherents or former adherents of small-scale agriculture were abused on all sides. At the conference of marxist agrarians in December 1929, a work on agricultural settlements was denounced as propaganda for 'Belorussian national-democracy'. Particular scorn was directed at its argument that in the conditions of the Belorussian republic 'everything that is technically and economically progressive finds its maximum expression in settlements of 75–200 hectares' (some 8–20 households), put forward primarily on the grounds that all fields should be easily accessible on foot from the peasant's household plot.[19] A 'bourgeois specialist' who had recently recommended that the optimum area of a kolkhoz should be 1,600 hectares, so that the fields should not be more than two kilometres away from the peasant households, was equally repudiated.[20]

The corollary of this criticism of small kolkhozy was taken to be that the very large kolkhoz had great advantages. Larin, a strong critic of Chayanov, firmly declared at the conference that a single MTS and kolkhoz should be established in each district, and the district soviet executive committee should replace the land society; and he looked forward to a future in which electric vehicles and ploughs would have replaced petrol lorries and tractors, the kolkhozy would become sovkhozy or 'obkhozy' (obshchestvennye khozyaistva—public farms) and the peasants would move into agrotowns.[21] Shlikhter, People's Commissar for Agriculture of the Ukraine, objected to the 'almost dwarf character' of 80–90 per cent

[17] EO, 9, 1929, 39–51, 12, 1929, 95–101; in a letter published in the agricultural newspaper (SKhG, December 12, 1929), he criticised his past defence of individual agriculture as a 'crude reactionary mistake' and announced that a substantial work was now in press on *Organisation of the Large Economy in the Epoch of the Socialist Reconstruction of Agriculture* (his classical defence of the small farm was entitled *The Organisation of the Peasant Economy*).

[18] See for example O. Targul'yan in EZh, December 21, 1929; Milyutin and Gordeev in *Trudy . . . agrarnikov-marksistov* (1930), i, 38, 99–100.

[19] *Ibid.* 176; the work in question was N. Kislyakov, *Poselki* (1928) (100 hectares = 1 sq. km).

[20] *Trudy . . . agrarnikov-marksistov* (1930), i, 185 (1,600 hectares = an area of 4 × 4 km).

[21] *Trudy . . . agrarnikov-marksistov* (1930), i, 65–72; he developed these thoughts in an article in EO, 1, 1930, 41–50. Larin was a former Menshevik who throughout the 1920s consistently advocated more vigorous measures to curb kulaks and private capital.

of kolkhozy, and called for the establishment of inter-village kolkhozy of 50,000–60,000 hectares; these would be appropriate to 'the optimum set or system of machines', would enable land utilisation to be adjusted to the needs of the MTS, and would carry the corollary that the land society (the mir) could be abolished. As alternatives to the giant kolkhoz, Shlikhter also advocated the establishment of 'large integrated agro-industrial combines' (AIKs), and of 'sovkhoz–kolkhoz combines'; the latter would be more appropriate when sovkhozy already existed, or were being established, in places where an MTS was being set up. Both types of combine, according to Shlikhter, should, like the giant kolkhoz, cover an area of 50,000–60,000 hectares.[22]

The brakes were not quite off. In his report to the conference, the agrarian economist Lyashchenko called for central management in the kolkhoz to be 'differentiated' rather than 'integrated', so that the MTS, the processing plant, and so on, would each have different spans of control. He also warned that the transfer of the peasants' household plots into new population centres, which was being 'inexpediently attempted' in some places, involved 'colossal difficulties' and would take a number of years.[23] But the general attitude to the size of the kolkhoz in party circles was now radically different from that prevalent at the conference of large kolkhozy five months before.

(c) GIGANTOMANIA AT ITS PEAK, DECEMBER 1929–FEBRUARY 1930

(i) Policy

In the last weeks of 1929 and the first few weeks of 1930 the campaign in favour of giant kolkhozy was at its most intense, and seemed to form an integral part of the all-out drive for collectivisation. It is true that some directives and statements from the centre continued to assume that giant kolkhozy should be formed only when at least some degree of mechanisation was present. Thus

[22] *Trudy . . . agrarnikov-marksistov* (1930), i, 85–7. For these combines see p. 44, n. 32, below. Sovkhoz–kolkhoz combines (kombinaty) were sometimes known as 'associations' (ob''edineniya): the terms appear to have been interchangeable.
[23] *Ibid.* ii, [i], 56.

in its telegram of January 18, 1930, Khlebotsentr ruled that giant kolkhozy with 50,000–60,000 hectares of arable land should be formed on the basis of its MTS and tractor columns when these held more than 20 tractors (i.e. about 8–10 per cent of the full complement of tractors for an area of this size) (see p. 22 above). In the following month the chairman of Khlebotsentr, on the basis of a proposal by the party central committee in its resolution of January 5, 1930,[24] called for the establishment of 3,790 MKS (Mashinno-konnye stantsii—machine-horse stations) within kolkhozy, stipulating that the area of each kolkhoz should be a minimum of 3,000 hectares;[25] this, though much larger than the average kolkhoz, was very roughly equal in area to the group of rural settlements covered by an average village soviet. The All-Russian Land Consolidation Conference, which met from February 12 to 18, 1930, was also cautious. In his report Shuleikin condemned the widespread proposals to destroy existing rural settlements and to establish agrotowns, and the conference resolved:

> Considering the fact that a whole number of important issues have not yet been worked out, and bearing in mind the need to use capital already invested, elimination of existing settlements should be approached with special care.[26]

But these notes of caution were unusual. In January and February 1930, the central authorities did not commit themselves to specific recommendations about the size of the kolkhozy. But throughout these weeks, the central press and many leading officials made clamorous noises in condemnation of small kolkhozy, and in favour of giant kolkhozy. Thus M. Golendo condemned Markevich in an article in the agricultural journal for his insistence that the size of each agricultural unit was 'determined by the historically established dimensions of the villages', and claimed that, while existing buildings would continue to be used, the sections (uchastki) of most of the giant kolkhozy would not correspond to the boundaries of existing settlements.[27] On January 26, a Sovnarkom decree stated that in 1930 each of the new sovkhozy must undertake a full cycle of work on peasant land with an area of at least 100,000

---

[24] *KPSS v rez.*, (1954), 665.
[25] SZe, February 13, 1930.
[26] SZo, i–ii, January–February 1930, 92–4, 144.
[27] NAF, 2, 1930, 11–12.

hectares.[28] A survey article in *Pravda* reported the formation of giant kolkhozy covering thousands of hectares, and commented 'this is nothing to get cold feet about'.[29] Bukharin, in his enthusiastic defence of collectivisation published on February 19, praised the emergence of kolkhozy embracing a whole administrative district, 'district-kolkhozy', envisaging that each would ultimately be served by an industrial combine.[30] On the same day, Kalinin reported in a speech in Voronezh that the average kolkhoz in the Central Black-Earth region included 20,000 hectares and 20,000 people, but made no criticism of the size of these giant kolkhozy.[31] The view that giant kolkhozy must await mechanisation was now completely abandoned, though it was hopefully assumed that vast quantities of tractors would be available to them within a couple of years.

In this heady atmosphere, far-reaching schemes for establishing giant kolkhozy received much publicity and official acquiescence, and some official support. At the end of December 1929, while the conference of marxist agrarians was in progress, a conference to discuss the AIKs was held under the auspices of the All-Union Council of Kolkhozy. The AIKs were intended as a grandiose development of the association between farming and industrial activities, on a district scale, which had already been attempted by the Tiginskii combine.[32] Ten reports were heard from districts with widely different agricultural profiles, and the chairman asserted that all RSKs were tending to become AIKs. The conference was reported to have looked with disfavour on AIKs of a mere 30,000–40,000 hectares, and to have given its preference to what were described as 'future agricultural Dnieprostrois', evidently on a multi-district basis, of 500,000 hectares. These would include 'dozens of dairy

[28] SZ, 1930, art. 101.

[29] P, February 16, 1930 (V. Feigin).

[30] P, February 19, 1930.

[31] P, March 3, 1930; for the date of this speech see vol. 1, p. 255, n. 232.

[32] See NAF, 1, 1930, 40. The establishment of 'combine enterprises' or units 'of an agro-industrial type' was proposed by Professor V. R. Batyushkov in 1926, and was presented as a partial alternative to industrialisation via large-scale urban factory industry. He envisaged them as involving the collectivisation of agriculture and a considerable degree of mechanisation; they would vary in size from a few hundred to 30,000 hectares of arable land according to the type of production, with an average of 15,000 hectares and 3,000 households, so that there would be 8,000 in the USSR as a whole (PKh, 5, 1926, 107–27; he also published a pamphlet *Postroenie agroindustrial'nykh kombinatov* (1929), which I have not seen; see also article by Oganovsky in SKhG, November 19, 1929).

farms, oil seed and cheese factories, factories to process all other agricultural products, cattlesheds for a thousand animals, electric ploughs, power stations, cultured settlements' and were expected to increase marketed output to 10–15 times its existing level. Most resources for these vast developments were to be provided by the peasants themselves, and the economic newspaper suggested that 'with insignificant help from the state the land in these districts will become a factory'. But even on the wildly optimistic calculations presented at the conference, the cost of establishing these combines would evidently have been some tens of milliards of rubles a year, a substantial proportion of this being borne by the state.[33]

Proposals of this kind continued to appear for some weeks. The famous Khoper okrug in the Lower Volga announced that, with the aid of the Sovkhoz and Kolkhoz Faculty of the Timiryazev Agricultural Academy in Moscow, working all out for three days and three nights, a plan had been prepared for a grain–livestock combine with a single population centre, a 'socialist agrotown', of 44,000 persons, divided into 22 blocks of flats, with communal eating as in the best flats in Europe, not to mention a reading room, library, studies, gymnasium and solarium in each block. This would replace the present situation in which families were isolated from their neighbours and suffered 'boring loneliness under the dark smoky oil lamp in the long snowy winter evenings':

> Eight thousand separate, scattered economic cells, almost defenceless from fire, mass epidemics and other social evils. How much unnecessary waste of energy just to service and light the stoves, prepare eight thousand family dinners, heat water for baths, do the washing, etc.

The agricultural newspaper claimed that this plan was inspired by the spontaneous decision of a group of peasants, previously scattered over a radius of 15–20 km, to move to the centre of their kolkhoz, and commented that the 'local party and soviet agencies, as in the whole development of the process of comprehensive collectivisation, have proved far ahead of our centres, and this time have been the forerunners of a big revolution'.[34] In an article published in January

---

[33] EZh, December 26, 27, 1929; after a brief notice on December 26, *Pravda* did not apparently report the conference further. For a list of estimates made for particular AIKs, see Abramsky, ed. (1974), 278, n. 45 (Davies).

[34] SKhG, January 9, 1930.

1930, Nikulikhin boldly declared that 'all our agriculture will gradually be reorganised along the lines of an AIK'. 'Some comrades', he reported, 'believe it fully possible to have only 50,000 agricultural enterprises by the end of the present five-year plan'; and he envisaged that towards the end of the proposed 'general plan' (i.e. in 10–15 years) the whole of agriculture would be organised into some 5,000 AIKs of 100,000 hectares each.[35] In an address to the Communist Academy on February 22 Larin envisaged the future establishment, once electricity had become the main motive-power for agriculture, of agrotowns with several tens of thousands of inhabitants serving an area of 200,000 hectares; the present villages would become stores on the outskirts of the kolkhoz.[36] The historian sympathetic to industrialisation is almost tempted, as he turns these yellowing pages, to forget elementary economics and commonsense, and identify himself for a moment with these inexperienced urban enthusiasts in those grim January days of 1930, boldly dreaming about rapid progress towards giant mechanised factory farms, cajoling reluctant peasants into kolkhozy, denouncing recalcitrants and driving them out of the villages into the endless snow.

These fanciful programmes were only one strand, though a significant one, in the proposals about the optimum size of kolkhoz prepared in the last few weeks of 1929 and the first few weeks of 1930. In the absence of firm recommendations from the centre, the plans of different regions, or even of different okrugs within the same region, varied considerably. In the Ukraine, as we have seen, there was a general commitment to a kolkhoz–MTS unit of 50,000 hectares. In the Lower Volga region, plans varied from okrug to okrug. Some okrugs, such as Balashov, appear to have favoured giant kolkhozy each covering a whole district: in the Lower Volga, each of these would have been several times as large as the MTS optimum of 50,000 hectares. Others favoured smaller units: in Khoper okrug, the fantastic grain–livestock combine was planned as an experimental exception to the general pattern; for the okrug as a whole, it was proposed to set up 100 kolkhozy each with an area of 12,000 hectares. Gusti, a secretary of the regional party committee in the Lower Volga, argued that a kolkhoz covering a whole district

[35] NAF, 1, 1930, 39, 44; cf. Batyushkov's proposal in 1926 that 8,000 combines should be established with 15,000 hectares of arable land each (see p. 44, n. 32, above).

[36] EO, 3, 1930, 65–6.

would 'at present be almost impossible to manage': in districts served by an MTS, Markevich's optimum was appropriate; for the others districts (which were of course the majority), the regional party committee did not apparently go further than stipulating that each kolkhoz should include at least one village.[37] In the Central Black-Earth region, the regional soviet executive committee approved in one case the establishment of an AIK which included over 11,000 households; this presumably covered a whole district.[38] In the Tambov okrug of the same region, the Kirsanov district endeavoured to establish a single giant commune for the whole district of 198,000 hectares and 23,700 households, explicitly on the model of the Gigant sovkhoz in the North Caucasus; the okrug authorities insisted, however, that the district should limit itself in 1930 to establishing a number of large kolkhozy, and postpone unification until an adequate technical basis was available.[39] In the North Caucasus itself, the authorities appear to have decided to establish one kolkhoz in each *stanitsa*.[40]

At the beginning of 1930, then, policy—or rather policies—towards the size of the kolkhoz fall into the following pattern. It was generally accepted that with the replacement of the horse by the tractor the criterion for determining the size of the kolkhoz should not be the existing land configuration and practices of the peasants but the needs of the machine; and these needs were held to involve the organisation of units of 50,000 hectares of arable land or more. There was also a definite tendency to argue that in districts which were not yet mechanised, the size of kolkhoz should be determined not by the present but by the future level of mechanisation, though this tendency was resisted by some important local authorities. These policy decisions were made in an atmosphere, strongly encouraged by leading members of the Politburo, of 'big means best'; in this atmosphere arguments against giant units were rarely heard, at any rate in public, and wild schemes were rarely publicly rebuffed.

(ii) Practice

Much less was accomplished in practice than might be inferred from

[37] KG, 104, December 30, 1929; SKhG, January 4, 1930.
[38] Decision of January 4, 1930, *cit*, VI, 3, 1965, 14.
[39] SZe, February 23, 1930.
[40] SZe, March 26, 1930, describing the situation in the early part of February; the *stanitsa* was a large Cossack village, usually with a population of several thousands.

these discussions and decisions. Certainly a number of giant kolkhozy were established. The famous Gigant kolkhoz in the Urals was extended to embrace five administrative districts with a population of some 13,000 households and a total area of 275,000 hectares. Land consolidation was said to have been carried out over the whole territory. All animals, farm buildings and even dwellings were declared to have been socialised and transferred to indivisible capital; substantial numbers of cattle were driven into temporary cattlesheds, and an unknown number of peasant households—in addition to those classified as kulaks—were resettled in the course of the effort to establish a single commune over the whole territory. However, even in the case of the highly publicised Gigant the process of forming a single commune was far from complete. The 160 kolkhozy continued their separate existence until the end of January or beginning of February, when they were merged and their elected boards were replaced by 'production sections (uchastki)' of the commune with appointed managers.[41] Elsewhere in the Urals, the kolkhoz for the Shatrovskii district included 215,000 hectares before the end of 1929.[42] Kolkhozy of 354,000 and 259,000 hectares were reported from the Lower Volga region.[43] In Votsk region in the far north, although tractors were very rare, dozens of giant kolkhozy were established, sometimes embracing as many as 300 settlements.[44]

In addition to kolkhozy as large as a district, there were smaller giants which included a substantial number of villages: Kolkhozy including over 30,000 hectares were reported from the North Caucasus and the Central Black-Earth region.[45] In Khoper okrug, a total of 423 kolkhozy established by December 1929, with a total collectivised population of 52,000 households, were replaced early in 1930 by 81 kolkhozy covering 91,760 households, 90 per cent of the rural population of the okrug, as compared with the 100 kolkhozy planned in December 1929.[46]

Some AIKs and sovkhoz–kolkhoz combines were also established. The maximum figure I have found for the number of AIKs is

[41] P, January 12, 1930; SKhG, January 21, 1930; NAF, 5, 1930, 31, 36–7, and 7–8, 1930, 86–7, 92, 95.
[42] I, January 13, 1930.
[43] SKhG, January 4, 1930.
[44] NAF, 5, 1930, 35.
[45] P, December 13, 1929; SZe, February 23, March 9, 1930.
[46] KGN, 98, December 10, 1929, and 32, April 23, 1930.

that early in 1930 some 300 AIKs were 'in the course of being set up (voznikshie)'; in the RSFSR 36 of these were recognised as model combines.[47] Attempts to establish sovkhoz–kolkhoz combines were encouraged by a cautious paragraph in the central committee resolution of January 5, 1930, which welcomed experiments, in areas with a considerable number of sovkhozy, in establishing 'a type of combined economy' based on a sovkhoz and supplying tractor ploughing, machine harvesting and other services to kolkhozy by contract for payment.[48] A combine established round the 'Khutorok' sovkhoz in the North Caucasus included a total area of 150,000–200,000 hectares; a sovkhoz in the Lower Volga region in effect completely absorbed the kolkhozy in its area.[49] But no more than 10 or 20 combines of this kind existed by March 1930;[50] a later Soviet commentator drily commented that 'in practice the directive on setting up kolkhoz–sovkhoz combines was hardly carried out at all'.[51]

In sum, then, giant kolkhozy, varying in size from a whole district to a few villages, and the two kinds of combine were exceptions, even at the height of the collectivisation campaign. Over most of Soviet territory, the general pattern seems to have been that some existing kolkhozy amalgamated, others expanded to include many more members of their settlement or their village, and many new kolkhozy were formed. In the USSR as a whole, the average number of households per kolkhoz rose from 18 to 133 between June 1, 1929, and March 1, 1930 (see Table 3). The figures for households collectivised on March 1, 1930, are certainly over-estimates, so the size of the average kolkhoz is also likely to be overestimated. But even accepting these figures as accurate, the 'average' kolkhoz had a population somewhere between that of a settlement and that of a village. The population of the average kolkhoz was larger than that of the average village only in the Lower Volga region, where there were 481 households per kolkhoz and only about 380 households per village (see p. 35, n. 2, above and Table 3). Even in the Ukraine, where the formation of giant

---

[47] NAF, 1, 1930, 39, 41; NAF, 3, 1930, 47. In SZe, February 5, 1930, Nikulikhin made the extravagant claim that AIKs already included an area of over 30 million hectares.
[48] *KPSS v rez.*, ii (1954), 666.
[49] *Materialy*, vii (1959), 311–21.
[50] NAF, 3, 1930, 49.
[51] *Materialy*, vii (1959), 316n. (Bogdenko).

kolkhozy had explicit official approval, there were 25,000 kolkhozy for 12,000 village soviets.[52] These figures leave out of account the various arrangements for the grouping (kustovanie) of kolkhozy. In the groups the constituent kolkhozy continued to retain their separate identity. Precise figures do not appear to be available, but in the Ukraine at least a substantial proportion of the kolkhozy were members of groups.[53] In some cases the groups controlled tractors and other farm machinery, more rarely some horses as well, in others they were responsible for joint industrial enterprises, dairy farms, silos and so on. But many of the groups were a mere formality.[54]

(D) GIGANTOMANIA IN RETREAT, MARCH–DECEMBER 1930

The size of the kolkhoz was not mentioned in Stalin's article of March 2, or in the party central committee resolution of March 14, and early in March some measures were adopted which seemed to give further encouragement to the formation of large units. On March 4, Sovkhoztsentr announced that it intended to form 12 sovkhoz–kolkhoz associations (ob''edineniya) in 12 regions, varying in area from 30,000 to 500,000 hectares, 1·5 million hectares in all.[55] A week later, a report on collectivisation in the Ukraine treated the village as the basic kolkhoz unit for the time being, but still argued that the village-kolkhozy should be unified, as the MTS developed, into 700–1,000 groups (i.e. one or two groups per district) which would themselves in future become kolkhozy: Markevich's optimum for the MTS thus still remained a goal for the size of kolkhoz.[56] In two long articles on the AIKs published in March, Nikulikhin recognised that the schemes for the immediate establishment of agrotowns were not feasible, but argued that AIKs could be immediately effective if they concentrated on expanding production rather than services for the next four or five years. He claimed that the immense waste of labour resulting from the highly

[52] SZe, March 12, 1930, and source cited in Table 3.

[53] 484 groups had apparently been formed in 22 of the 40 okrugs by the beginning of March, and in 15 of these more than half the kolkhozy belonged to groups (SZe, March 12, 1930).

[54] Minaev, ed. (1930), 239–41.

[55] SZe, March 4, 1930. For these associations or combines see p. 42 above.

[56] SZe, March 12, 1930.

seasonal nature of Russian agriculture could be avoided by establishing a single AIK in each district which would combine agriculture, seasonal industries such as peat and lumber, and simple local factories in which collective farmers would work in the winter months.[57] In this simpler form the proposed AIKs would have resembled the Chinese communes of the 1960s. In the USSR, schemes to handle the seasonality of agricultural labour through the establishment of AIKs were more or less forgotten in the turmoil of the 1930s, but were revived 47 years later.

Simultaneously with the attempts to save the giant kolkhozy strong criticisms of them began to appear in the press. As early as February 26, Odintsev, a deputy chairman of Kolkhoztsentr, criticised the establishment, without proper preparation, of giant kolkhozy of 50,000–70,000 hectares in Kursk okrug in the Central Black-Earth region.[58] On March 9, 1930, a further article by Odintsev was much sharper in tone. He strongly criticised the hasty formation of giant kolkhozy, giving an example, again from Kursk okrug, of a giant with only one telephone in its 16 villages:

Giants are often thought up from above without preliminary work among the masses and without taking into account organisational, technical and economic prerequisites.

He still exempted from criticism, however, both carefully-prepared and long-established kolkhozy such as the Urals Gigant, even though they lacked tractors, and large inter-village kolkhozy in which each sub-unit corresponded to an existing settlement.[59] On March 13, an article in *Pravda* by Khataevich complained that 'super-giant' kolkhozy had been formed in the Central Volga region simply on the basis of instructions from the district kolkhozsoyuzy, endorsed by the boards of the kolkhozy, without the collective farmers knowing anything about it. A few days later, a telegram was published from Narkomzem of the USSR and Kolkhoztsentr which asked local authorities what steps they had taken both to cease further amalgamation and to 'divide up kolkhozy larger than justified by existing machinery'.[60] On the following day, Andreev condemned attempts in the North Caucasus to establish only 100

[57] NAF, 3, 1930, 39–50; B, 6, March 31, 1930, 31–45.
[58] EZh, February 26, 1930.
[59] SZe, March 9, 1930.
[60] I, March 17, 1930.

kolkhozy in each okrug, and pointed out that even a kolkhoz based on a single *stanitsa* containing 3,000 or 4,000 households could be more complicated to manage than any industrial enterprise.[61] On March 24, a conference held under the auspices of the agricultural newspaper 'decisively repudiated' uncritical or exclusive reliance either on giant kolkhozy which were tens and hundreds of thousands of hectares in area, or on small kolkhozy no bigger than a single settlement.[62]

The criticism of giant kolkhozy was now taken up at the highest level. In his article of April 3, Stalin criticised the concentration of attention on 'so-called "giants"', which often developed into top-heavy headquarters on paper, lacking economic roots'; if kolkhoz officials turned their attention to 'the work of kolkhoz economic organisation in hamlets and villages', and were successful, giants would 'appear of their own accord'.[63] A few days later, Markevich bounced back into prominence with a scathing article 'On "Inter-Village Giants"'. He pointed out that a 'large' kolkhoz used to be one with 500 or 600 hectares sown to grain, but 'now a kolkhoz of 20,000–30,000 hectares in no way satisfies the "giant" appetites of our kolkhoz organisers'; one district had even proposed a kolkhoz of 500,000 hectares. This was 'bureaucratic "gigantomania"', in which the collective farmer played 'the passive role of a working unit'. Such giant kolkhozy had no positive side, as they did not result in any new association of labour and implements, and they should be replaced by one kolkhoz corresponding to each village; in such a kolkhoz the peasants knew the work, the animals, and each other, and would understand that the future depended on themselves. No optimum size of kolkhoz could be laid down, as villages varied greatly in size—the search for a standard optimum size was mere '"optimum" ignorance, "optimum" bureaucratisation, and "optimum" lack of comprehension, or lack of desire to comprehend the requirements of kolkhoz construction'.[64] A circular from Narkomzem of the RSFSR on breaking up the giants was also issued at about this time.[65]

Giant kolkhozy were now universally condemned. Astonishing tales were told of the ignorance of their organisers. In one giant

[61] Andreev (Rostov, 1930), 17; speech of March 18.
[62] SZe, March 26, 1930.
[63] *Soch.*, xii, 226.
[64] P, April 8, 1930.
[65] IZ, lxxvi (1965), 35.

kolkhoz each settlement became a field in the crop rotation: Settlement A, rye; B, potatoes; C, grass; D, a year off![66]

Long before the publication of these criticisms, most of the giant kolkhozy had been broken up 'from below'. As early as March 14, *Pravda* reported that in the Borisogleb okrug 'all the "giants" created by proclamation in the past 6–8 weeks are cracking up and disintegrating'. Even the Urals Gigant broke up into separate kolkhozy in the course of March; a district kolkhoz combine (raikolkhozkombinat) was established to handle some common activities, including sales and supplies.[67] During March and April 1930, most of the giant kolkhozy were subdivided or fell apart. Some smaller giants containing several settlements still remained: in May there were still some 200 kolkhozy without tractors and with a sown area in excess of 5,110 hectares,[68] and as late as the summer of 1930 some 'super-giants' of 100,000–200,000 hectares continued to exist.[69] The total number of kolkhozy fell from an estimated 110,000 on March 1, 1930, to 84,000 in May, and the number of households per kolkhoz fell from 127 to 70; in the Lower Volga region, the number of households per kolkhoz fell particularly rapidly, from 481 to 247 (see Table 3 and source there cited). Throughout the USSR the population of the average kolkhoz was now the equivalent of one or two settlements. But the departure of large numbers of peasants from the kolkhozy in a vast number of settlements brought a new problem: the typical kolkhoz now tended to include *part* of the population of each of a number of settlements.[70] Some kolkhozy which contained part of the population of only one settlement now contained only a few households; such very small kolkhozy were condemned by Kindeev as 'an anti-Leninist excess in the opposite direction'.[71] The disadvantages of small size were partly overcome by continuing 'group associations' of kol-

---

[66] SZe, May 30, 1930. Other attacks on giant kolkhozy appeared in I, May 6, 1930 (Khataevich); SZo, June 1, 1930 (A. Lisitsyn); NAF, 3, 1930, 10–11 (Gaister), 30–1 (Vareikis); Minaev, ed. (1930), 237–8.

[67] NAF, 7–8, 1930, 88, 100.

[68] Minaev, ed. (1930), 238.

[69] PKh, 7–8, 1930, 100 (Kindeev).

[70] 54·5 per cent of all kolkhozy contained 35 households or less (*Kolkhozy v 1930 g.* (1931), 78–9).

[71] PKh, 7–8, 1930, 100; he was a Rabkrin specialist on kolkhozy. For 'dwarf' kolkhozy of a few households formed at this time, see also SZe, June 1, 1930 (Lisitsyn).

khozy (see p. 40 above) for the joint use of tractors, horses and other services; 20,219 kolkhozy belonged to the associations in May 1930, most of them in the Ukraine.[72]

In July 1930, the more modest approach to the size of kolkhoz was endorsed by the XVI party congress, which roundly condemned 'the creation as so-called "giant" kolkhozy of lifeless bureaucratic organisations, designed on the principles of orders from above'.[73] The kolkhoz-village was now treated everywhere as the basic unit for further development.[74] The Rabkrin report on the kolkhozy, completed at the time of the congress, warned that 'even now some kolkhozy are too large, although they formally include only one village, and some are too small'. The report attributed such mistakes to the 'absence of precise directives (ustanovki)' on kolkhoz size, and called upon Kolkhoztsentr to prepare 'model sizes' for different regions.[75]

Much remained unresolved. In districts where agricultural machinery was relatively unimportant, the village would certainly remain the basic economic unit. But what would be the effect of mechanisation? How were the tractor and the existing land structure to be reconciled? Was the sole criterion for organisation to be the needs of the tractor and the machine, as was generally believed between the end of 1929 and the middle of 1930? Considerable differences of opinion remained. An article published in the planning journal immediately before the XVI party congress continued to assume that giant kolkhozy of 50,000–60,000 hectares would be formed when enough modern machinery was available; on the other hand Grin'ko, writing in the same journal, looked forward to the establishment of as many as 50,000 MTS (which would mean 10 or 15 per administrative district) and several hundred thousand kolkhozy (which would presumably mean one per settlement rather than one per village).[76]

The issue was resolved by the sudden decision in September 1930 to concentrate tractors in large state-owned MTS, each of which served a substantial group of kolkhozy (see p. 27 above). This

[72] *Kolkhozy v 1930 g.* (1931), 260.
[73] *KPSS v rez.*, iii (1954), 53.
[74] See the control figures for the economic year 1930/31, published in SZe, July 27, 1930.
[75] SZe, July 13, 1930 (resolution of presidium of central control commission and collegium of Rabkrin, dated July 9).
[76] PKh, 5, 1930, 79 (Kraev), 16; for Grin'ko see vol. 1, p. 169.

almost automatically set broad limits to the size of the kolkhoz. In conformity with Markevich's original scheme, the problem of the efficient unit for the management, maintenance and use of the tractor was separated, at least in part, from the problem of the efficient management of the farm. The needs of both management and production now pointed in the direction of keeping the order of magnitude of the production unit the same as that of the traditional rural settlement. Moreover, though this point was rarely mentioned, the kolkhoz based on the rural settlement or village was a workable unit, close to the peasant, for the collection of grain and other state exactions. The lure of giant agricultural units did not completely lose its savour in the summer and autumn of 1930; the existence of kolkhozy with over 1,000 households was reported in the last few months of 1930.[77] But such attempts to retain kolkhozy which included more than one village were now dogmatically criticised. While intermittent attempts were made to establish giant kolkhozy during the next quarter of a century, the compromise solution that the MTS should serve many kolkhozy while the kolkhoz was based on the traditional rural settlement or village remained more or less intact for a period of nearly 28 years between the summer of 1930 and the abolition of the MTS in 1958.

---

[77] SZe, August 3 (Yelan', Urals), December 16 (Far East), 1930.

CHAPTER FOUR

THE STRUCTURE OF THE KOLKHOZ

Like the mir, the typical small kolkhoz of the 1920s was a self-governing association both legally and to a large extent in practice. According to successive model Statutes, in all three types of kolkhoz the supreme organ was the general meeting of members—equivalent to the skhod. In the kolkhoz, unlike the mir, the model Statutes usually provided that the general meeting should elect a small executive council(sovet) or board(pravlenie) to run its affairs, but for many of the small kolkhozy in the 1920s such boards were hardly necessary, and they were often not established. In nearly all kolkhozy, as in mirs, the general meeting elected one of its members as its head. The head of the kolkhoz—at first known as the 'elder (starosta)' as in the mir, and later as the 'chairman'—in practice shared power with the general assembly. He (it was almost invariably a man and not a woman) sometimes possessed great powers. An authoritative textbook of the mid-1920s stated that 'he alone is in charge in the farm, allocates labour and manages the work'.[1] Model internal rules for artels adopted in 1929 also made the chairman responsible for all executive work, including the allocation of labour.[2] But he could always be replaced by the decision of the general meeting.

Before the revolution, the constituent members of the mir were the peasant households, represented at the skhod by the head of the household, normally the oldest man in the family. In the post-revolutionary mir, all the adults in the household, male and female, were supposed to be full members, and this principle was naturally followed in the kolkhozy. In practice, however, the household for many purposes remained the main economic and social unit, in the kolkhoz as well as in the mir. The main non-collectivised agricultural activities of collective farmers were carried out by the

---

[1] Bauer *et al.* (1925), 54; see also Wesson (1963), 135–8.

[2] *Pravila vnutrennego rasporyadka sel'skokhozyaistvennoi arteli* (8th edn, 1929), clauses 1–3, 30; these rules were a development of the model Statute prepared by Kolkhoztsentr in 1928.

household on the household plot; and in TOZy and artels the household, using its own horses and implements, often remained the basic unit of labour for a substantial part of collectivised farming. Women played only a minor role in kolkhoz management: only 6·8 per cent of the members of the administrative organs in the kolkhozy on June 1, 1929, were women.[3]

During the mass collectivisation drive of the winter of 1929–30, many millions of peasant households were forced into the kolkhozy against their will. Nevertheless, strenuous efforts to win the support of the peasantry were an integral part of the collectivisation process, and official propaganda loudly proclaimed that this support had in fact been secured. Against this background, both the February 6 and the March 1 versions of the model Statute of the artel fully retained the principles of self-government:

> Clause 19. The general meeting (or the meeting of plenipotentiaries) shall be the supreme organ of administration of the artel, shall decide the most important questions on the activity of the artel, shall elect a board and a commission of inspection and shall adopt an instruction about their work.[4]

The Statute did not formally provide for the election of a kolkhoz chairman; this omission seems to have been without significance, as the post of chairman was universally regarded as the senior position in the kolkhoz.[5]

Not surprisingly, the principles of self-government were frequently ignored. During the retreat from collectivisation the giant kolkhozy were strongly criticised on the grounds that their boards and their principal officials were not elected, but appointed from above.[6] The more flexible kolkhoz organisation established (or re-established) in the spring of 1930 did not avoid the crucial conflict between the rival principles of self-government and subordination to the state. In the winter of 1929–30 many of the traditional leaders

---

[3] *Kolkhozy v 1929 godu* (1931), 154–5.

[4] P, February 7, March 2, 1930; *Kollektivizatsiya . . . 1927–1935* (1957), 286–7. 'Plenipotentiaries' in this context had no connection with the urban workers sent in to the villages in support of collectivisation; they were peasant representatives elected by each settlement in the case of artels which had many members or were territorially scattered (clause 18); see p. 61 below.

[5] In the model Statute of February 17, 1935, clause 20(b) stated that the chairman as well as the board should be elected by the general meeting.

[6] See, for example, NAF, 1930, 39–40 (Tsil'ko).

of the village community fled or were exiled as kulaks or 'kulak henchmen'. The general meetings of the kolkhozy were now expected to elect boards or chairmen who were acceptable to the state and prepared to bend the kolkhoz to its will. The 'elected' officials included many workers and others sent from the towns to take up leading positions in the kolkhozy. By the summer of 1930, 44·4 per cent of the 25,000-ers, all previously unknown to the collective farmers, had been 'elected' as chairmen of kolkhozy, and a further 15·3 per cent as members of their boards.[7] Some workers sent into the kolkhozy were no doubt welcomed by those collective farmers who remained after the exodus, themselves primarily batraks and poor peasants. But this cannot have been general. Nevertheless, the traditions of rural self-government were not extinguished, and the tension between the powerful state and party authorities and the residual democracy of the kolkhoz general meetings became a permanent if secondary feature of kolkhoz organisation throughout the Stalinist period.

The mass kolkhozy of 1930 continued the traditions of the 1920s in another important respect: the peasant household as a unit continued to be an integral part of the kolkhoz. The household was nowhere mentioned in the model Statute of February 6, prepared at the height of the campaign for socialisation. But the Statute of March 1 recognised the right of the members of the artel to their own livestock, minor agricultural implements, and *usad'ba*. All this implied the organisation of the non-collectivised sector of the kolkhoz on a household basis. The term '*usad'ba*' is translated in the present book as 'household plot', and although the word 'household' (dvor or khozyaistvo) was not used in connection with the *usad'ba* in the Statute, all the discussion about *usad'ba* lands assumed that they would be allocated to households and not to individuals. And the Statute formally recognised that households and not individuals would own non-socialised livestock, stating that 'in one-cow households(khozyaistva) dairy cattle shall not be socialised'.[8]

In the discussions and experiments in 1929–30 relating to the internal structure of the kolkhoz the crucial question was the

---

[7] Selunskaya (1964), 78; the percentages are based on records of the posts occupied by 17,888 of the 25,000-ers.

[8] *Kollektivizatsiya . . . 1927–1935* (1957), 283 (clause 4).

relation of collective farmer—yesterday's individual peasant—and kolkhoz administration. During NEP the individual peasant household, with help or hindrance from the arrangements made by the mir, was directly responsible for its own production, and sold its own crop on the market or through an intermediary. But the collective farmer of 1930 worked on the collective lands under the instructions of the kolkhoz, which also undertook the sale of the collective product. Management of the work of the collective farmer by the kolkhoz, and the associated rewards and penalties provided, now replaced joint work as a family and the stimulus of the market. Efficient labour organisation was recognised by all concerned to be essential to the success of the kolkhoz.

While internal organisation was not a serious problem for the average kolkhoz in the middle of 1929, with its membership of only 18 households, it was a major issue for the large kolkhozy. By July 1929 it was already normal practice for the large kolkhoz of 200–400 households to be subdivided into temporary or permanent work units of 15–30 households, variously referred to as 'brigades', 'departments (otdeleniya)', 'operational groups', etc. The term 'brigade', which soon became the standard expression for the basic kolkhoz work unit, was regularly and widely used in Siberian communes in the 1920s.[9] In one kolkhoz in the North Caucasus, the brigades were further subdivided into groups.[10] A brigade was sometimes formed on an *ad hoc* basis, but at first more often consisted of all the collective farmers living in a particular settlement; when the large kolkhoz was an amalgamation of smaller ones, each of the smaller kolkhozy, usually the whole or part of a particular settlement, was formed into a brigade. Brigades based on neighbourhood were frequently required to undertake additional field work elsewhere in the kolkhoz, or to send some of their members on other jobs; the brigade thus acted as a kind of bridge between the old and the new rural organisation. The brigade leaders met regularly with the chairman and senior administrators of the kolkhoz to receive work-orders(naryady), and this group in many cases acted as the council or working leadership of the kolkhoz.[11] Summing up

[9] For these terms and for reports on the organisation of large kolkhozy, see ZKK (1929), 22, 51–2, 55; SZe, April 2, 1930.
[10] ZKK (1929), 54.
[11] The above account is based on reports to the conference from representatives of large kolkhozy in the Siberian, Lower Volga and North Caucasus regions (ZKK (1929), 19–25, 48–55, 62–3).

this experience, the organisation section of the conference of large kolkhozy recommended that 'the cultivated land mass of a large kolkhoz should be divided into sections(uchastki) depending on the land relief, the quality of the soil, the crop rotation etc.' and that 'the cultivation of each section (or part of a section) should be entrusted to a brigade'; among examples cited were a field brigade with 23–28 members (including 20–24 men) and a nursery garden brigade with 25 members (including 23 women).[12] In the discussion, the rapporteur drew attention to an 'issue of principle': should field brigades be responsible for all the work in a particular area (ploughing, sowing, harvesting) or instead be separately organised for each agricultural process? He recommended the former arrangement for the time being, as it was less complicated.[13]

In the upheavals of the next 12 months, little further progress was made towards devising a rational kolkhoz structure. In the absence of a firm lead from the central authorities, a Kolkhoztsentr official complained that 'every kolkhoz is organising its administration as seems best'.[14] The giant kolkhozy which emerged between October 1929 and March 1930 were confronted with acute problems of internal organisation. Their large size made it necessary for them to be subdivided into a three- or four-stage hierarchy.[15] A kolkhoz group in the Central Black-Earth region, effectively organised as a single kolkhoz, was divided into ten 'economies (khozyaistva)'; each 'economy' had 120–200 households, and was in turn divided into brigades of 20 households, each headed by an appointed brigade leader (brigadir), generally known as the 'administrator of the link (admzveno)'.[16] In his vigorous criticism of giant kolkhozy, Markevich summarised their organisational complexity: typically the kolkhoz would be divided into 'economies (ekonomii)' of 5,000–10,000 hectares which were in turn divided into fields and sections (uchastki) without regard to the existing villages—the aim was to achieve a 'fully depersonalised optimum land area', and, as people, animals and implements were located randomly and unevenly, some 'economies' had two or three populated points and others had none.[17] On the industrial or military analogy, the subdivisions of the

[12] ZKK (1929), 161.
[13] ZKK (1929), 147.
[14] SZe, March 26, 1930.
[15] SZe, March 26, 1930; for an example see SZe, February 3, 1930.
[16] SZe, February 3, 1930.
[17] P, April 8, 1930; for this article see p. 52 above.

kolkhoz were even called 'shops' or 'detachments'; a party secretary of a North Caucasian kolkhoz suggested it should be divided into 'battle sectors' and 'battle columns' headed by 'commanders'.[18] The number of members, and the distances involved, also made general meetings impossible, so special delegate meetings were introduced, such as the 'institution of plenipotentiaries' in the North Caucasus region.[19]

Beneath these artificial structures, the settlement or the village remained the basic unit, except in those few cases where the population was transferred into a makeshift central 'agrotown' (see p. 48 above); and, even at the peak of the all-out drive, the average kolkhoz was in any case no larger than two or three settlements (see pp. 49–50 above). Both in the large and in the small kolkhoz, the neighbourhood or 'territorial' brigade, consisting of a group of neighbouring households (brigada-dvorka) tended at this time to be the primary unit of agricultural organisation.[20]

When the all-out collectivisation drive was put into reverse in March 1930, and the village or group of settlements emerged as the basis for the non-mechanised kolkhoz, the brigade of 15–35 households, or an equivalent number of individuals, was soon recognised as the basic unit within the kolkhoz (the brigades were in some cases grouped into sections of the kolkhoz concerned with particular activities, usually called 'ekonomii'). Much was uncertain: the membership of the kolkhoz was unstable, and its boundaries were often unclear; the division of the land between individual peasants and kolkhozy was not settled until the eve of the spring sowing (see vol. 1, pp. 291–3). These confusions and complexities made stable work units difficult to establish. Nevertheless, brigades were widely introduced as the main work unit in the course of the spring sowing,[21] and they become the main form of organisation everywhere by the time of the harvest.[22] It was often claimed that the brigade system had become so popular that individual peasant households very frequently copied them by combining in work teams (supryagi) to bring in the harvest;[23] it is more likely, however, that these *supryagi* were merely a resumption

[18] See, for example, B, 5, March 15, 1930, 48–9.
[19] SZe, March 26, 1930.
[20] Anisimov, ed. (1931), 29; P, February 25, 1930 (Lower Volga).
[21] P, April 18, 1930.
[22] VTr, 7–8, 1930, 37.
[23] VTr, 7–8, 1930, 37; SZe, June 22, 1930.

of the arrangements which were widespread among individual peasants in the 1920s.

Agreement was soon reached that the primary work unit should not be very large. The autumn ploughing in 1929 had already shown the disadvantages of large glamorous columns ploughing the whole field simultaneously: if one plough broke down the others were held up or had to go round, leaving gaps in the ploughing.[24] In large brigades record-keeping was complicated and supervision difficult. Brigades with 10, 12 or at most 25 ploughs or harrows were said to be more efficient than those with 70.[25]

While it was agreed in the spring of 1930 that the brigade, as a sub-unit within the kolkhoz, was an essential element in labour organisation, the way in which the brigades should be organised was quite unclear. As we have seen, the 'territorial' (neighbourhood) brigade seems to have predominated in the large kolkhozy in 1929. The main rival to the territorial brigade to emerge in the winter of 1929–30 was the 'production' brigade, a term which apparently covered all varieties of brigade in which the needs of agriculture rather than the territorial location of the workforce were the guiding principle of organisation. Production brigades were either permanent or temporary. Some permanent production brigades were, like the territorial brigades, responsible for all the agricultural work on a particular land area, and differed from the territorial brigades only in not drawing their membership from neighbouring households; they were known as 'mixed' or 'combined' brigades. Other permanent production brigades were 'specialised', dealing with, say, nursery gardening or livestock farming. Temporary production brigades, on the other hand, were usually formed to deal with a particular agricultural process or sub-process, such as sowing or reaping; they were thus specialised by function, though they did not necessarily include highly skilled personnel.[26]

Discussions about the best form of brigade continued throughout 1930 and after. The case for the territorial brigade rested on the natural or traditional character of a unit based on neighbours with the habit of working together. But it soon fell into disfavour. Its opponents argued that with such an arrangement the number of horses and the amount of land per household varied enormously in

---

[24] P, March 1, 1930; for later criticisms of so-called 'ploughing in one furrow' see *6 s"ezd sovetov* (1931), No. 17, 5–6 (Yurkin) and P, May 18, 1931.

[25] P, March 1, 1930; *6 s"ezd sovetov* (1931), No. 16, 13 (Yakovlev).

[26] VTr, 7–8, 1930, 37; P, February 25, April 5, 1930.

different parts of the same kolkhoz, depending on historical accident;[27] in the North Caucasus territorial brigades tended to turn into 'dwarf kolkhozy', a 'kolkhoz within the kolkhoz'.[28] Behind these objections lurked the fear that work units organised on a territorial basis would preserve or acquire the strength of the mir, and a potential source of resistance to the policies of the state would be re-established. In the spring of 1930, territorial brigades predominated in the North Caucasus, where the traditional village, the *stanitsa*, contained a large number of settlements, and the average kolkhoz contained some 200 households (see Table 3). Here the brigade normally consisted of 35, 50 or 100 households: the brigade was responsible for all the farming activities on the land allocated to it, and was itself divided into small work groups.[29]

In most other regions, the various forms of production brigade apparently predominated;[30] and from the spring of 1930 onwards the discussion focused on which type of production brigade should be preferred. Combined production brigades shared important advantages with the territorial brigades without their disadvantages. Handling the whole of the agricultural process on a particular land area from sowing to threshing, they could be held responsible for deficiencies and rewarded for successes; they could also take permanent charge of specific working animals and implements. They were compatible with a substantial measure of decentralisation of kolkhoz management: the work-orders from the kolkhoz board could be fairly simple and cover a substantial period of time. They could be divided into specialised groups, the nature of which could vary according to the stage of the work. Their principal disadvantage was their inflexibility. The amount of work on a particular land area varied considerably during the agricultural season, but the number of members of the brigade remained constant: it was difficult to transfer members of the brigade temporarily to jobs elsewhere in the kolkhoz. At the same time it was feared that in those parts of the country where labour was in surplus the establishment of permanent combined brigades would permanently exclude many collective farmers from agricultural work.

The alternative argument in favour of permanent specialised

---

[27] *6 s"ezd sovetov* (1931), No. 17, 6.

[28] SZe, December 13, 1930, January 19, 1931.

[29] SZe, April 2, 1930; *6 s"ezd sovetov* (1931), No. 17, 6; P, May 18, 1931; Anisimov, ed. (1931), 26–8.

[30] SZe, June 22, 1930 (Kudinov).

brigades was strong in the case of clear-cut and independent functions such as livestock breeding. But, within field work, brigades specialising in particular processes obviously had to be temporary in nature. Specialised temporary production brigades set up to undertake particular jobs made it possible to allocate labour more flexibly within the kolkhoz, and enabled collective farmers to develop special skills. On the other hand, their grave disadvantage was that responsibility for the final product was divided, with the consequence that the kolkhoz board had to issue its work-orders in great detail, sometimes on a daily basis.[31]

At the beginning of 1932 it was finally agreed that in field work the advantages of the permanent combined brigade outweighed the disadvantages. In 1930, the central kolkhoz authorities were concerned to emphasise their own lack of experience, and the importance of experiment, in the organisation of kolkhoz labour, and did not issue binding regulations. At first they indicated a definite preference for the establishment of combined brigades. A Kolkhoztsentr instruction published in February 1930 proposed that all collective farmers should be attached to definite work for at least a whole season as part of brigades for field work, livestock, etc.[32] At the end of May 1930 the instruction approved by Kolkhoztsentr proposed that brigades should each have responsibility for a certain area, though it assumed that new brigades would be formed at each main stage of agricultural work (harvesting, sowing of winter grains, and so on); this was a kind of temporary combined brigade.[33] But after the 1930 harvest the kolkhoz authorities, as well as taking a firmer line in opposition to the territorial brigade, now tended to favour the establishment of specialised brigades. At the kolkhoz conference in January 1931, Tataev, a deputy chairman of Kolkhoztsentr, argued that while permanent brigades could exist in special branches of farming, the brigade in general should be a 'mobile working nucleus'.[34] The resolution of the conference on labour in kolkhozy in January 1931 called rather

---

[31] For discussion of various types of production brigade see P, April 5, 1930, May 9, 1931; SZe, April 2, June 22, 1930; VTr, 7–8, 1930, 37–41; Anisimov, ed. (1931), 51–9.

[32] SZe, February 14, 1930.

[33] SZe, May 31, 1930; Jasny (1949), 335, is thus mistaken in supposing that 'the brigade itself appeared in a resolution of a central agency for the first time in the Party decision of February 4, 1932'.

[34] SZe, January 19, 1931.

unhelpfully for the establishment in field work of brigades of 40–60 members, divided into groups, which could be combined or specialised, permanent, seasonal or temporary.[35] At the VI congress of soviets in March 1931 Yurkin suggested that in the spring sowing combined brigades for all types of work, with 40–50 members, and specialised brigades for separate processes such as ploughing, were both possible forms of organisation; but he favoured the establishment of separate specialised brigades during the harvest period for each of the major processes of stacking (skirdometanie) and threshing.[36] The resolution of the congress failed to mention the brigade at all: flexibility was evidently still the order of the day.

Much also remained unclear about the relation between the brigade and the kolkhoz of which it formed a part. Should the brigade, like the kolkhoz, be a self-governing organisation, the leader of the brigade being elected by those who worked in it? One of the main objections to the giant kolkhozy was that those in charge of the work units were appointed by a remote board, not elected by the peasants.[37] A meeting convened by the agricultural newspaper proposed that all responsible officials of the kolkhozy, presumably including the brigade leaders, should be elected, not appointed (except for agricultural specialists): production conferences of the brigades, similar to general meetings, could propose several candidates, and the kolkhoz board could make the final choice.[38] This Utopian scheme had no practical outcome. From the point of view of the authorities, the election of brigade leaders may have appeared, like the establishment of territorial brigades, to encourage the infiltration of the principle of the mir into kolkhoz organisation, and was certainly incompatible with the notion of brigades which changed frequently in size and composition in response to agricultural needs. At the end of May 1930, without explanation, but presumably with these considerations in mind, an instruction endorsed by Kolkhoztsentr ruled that brigade leaders were to be appointed by the 'field-work organiser (polevod)', who was in charge of them all.[39] How far the instruction was carried out

[35] SZe, February 8, 1931; this resolution was endorsed by Kolkhoztsentr.
[36] *6 s"ezd sovetov* (1931), No. 17, 6–7.
[37] NAF, 3, 1930, 9–11.
[38] SZe, March 26, 1930; the meeting was held on March 24.
[39] SZe, May 31, 1930; the instruction was prepared by the grain cooperative organisation Khlebotsentr, but apparently applied to all kolkhozy.

in practice is not known. But the issue was not yet quite settled. In the autumn of 1930 an article in the Narkomtrud journal proposed that brigade leaders should be elected by the collective farmers and approved by the kolkhoz board; this would avoid the appearance of 'ordering about' and inspire confidence.[40]

Another bone of contention was whether the brigade leader should simply be a supervisor, like the charge-hand in a factory (the Russian term—*brigadir*—was the same), and not take part in agricultural work himself. The party agricultural journal reported in the summer of 1930 that in the Central Volga region collective farmers complained to the brigade leaders:

> You just give us instructions, order us about and shout at us—you should come and work with us.[41]

On this issue the authorities sympathised with the collective farmers; Yurkin argued that large brigades, in which the brigade leader did not work, should be reduced in size.[42]

Behind all these discussions lay the uncomfortable fact that the post of brigade leader was a strange novelty in almost all Soviet villages. In the summer of 1930, trained brigade leaders were completely lacking. At the XVI party congress in July 1930, Yakovlev, characteristically comparing the brigade leader with the foreman in a factory, reported that about $1\frac{1}{2}$ million needed to be trained, together with a million tractor drivers, and half a million agronomists with secondary education and 90,000 with higher education.[43] The shortage was made more acute by the tendency of the authorities to promote poor peasants and batraks, who were less agriculturally competent but presumed to be more reliable. At the party congress, Yakovlev complained that middle peasants were frequently removed even from positions such as group leader (zvenevoi) or head of the cattle yard, and were rarely admitted to membership of the kolkhoz board. The resolution of the congress urged 'the systematic involvement of *middle peasants in kolkhoz management*'. But the ambiguity of official attitudes was reflected in the support by the congress for continuation of the practice of

[40] VTr, 7–8, 1930, 38 (Reznikov).
[41] NAF, 7–8, 1930, 110.
[42] P, May 12, 1931.
[43] *XVI s"ezd* (1931), 596.

organising poor peasant groups in the kolkhozy, and in Yakovlev's assurance to the congress that while the middle peasant should participate in management, 'management will of course be in the hands of (budet za) the working class, the poor peasant and the batrak'.[44]

[44] *XVI s"ezd* (1931), 590; *KPSS v rez.*, iii (1954), 53, 60.

CHAPTER FIVE

SOCIALISATION WITHIN THE KOLKHOZ

(A) THE BACKGROUND

The three major types of kolkhoz—the commune, the artel and the association for joint cultivation of land (the TOZ or SOZ)—were defined primarily by the extent to which their means of production were socialised. In the commune, all land was supposed to be worked in common and all animals, implements and production buildings were collectively owned; in many communes members also shared living quarters and prepared and ate their food together. In the intermediate type of kolkhoz, the artel, arable farming was socialised: thus land was worked in common, except for the household plot (usad'ba), and draught animals and agricultural implements were owned collectively. Other branches of agriculture, however, remained partly or wholly private. In the TOZ, some land was worked in common, and major agricultural machines, if any, were owned collectively, but all animals, including draught animals, and most implements, remained in private possession.

No detailed official definition of the different types of kolkhoz was prescribed at an all-Union level; and the definitions adopted at different stages of kolkhoz development and in different regions varied considerably.[1] Frequently kolkhozy did not correspond to their official registration, or failed to change their registration when their degree of socialisation changed. In some communes only part of the land was cultivated in common. This was also true of artels, and in artels the proportion of implements and animals owned collectively also varied considerably. Societies for the joint use of machines and land-improvement societies were also sometimes

---

[1] A kolkhoz handbook in 1925, for example, stated that in artels the household plot and all means of production, including all animals, were held in common, and that 'all labour is devoted to the general economy' (Bauer *et al.* (1925), 11–12, 19); this was not the case either in principle or practice in the later 1920s.

classified as kolkhozy, though they appear in the official statistics as cooperatives.[2] At the XVI party conference in April 1929, Gusti, a secretary of the Lower Volga regional party committee, drew attention to an important factor which added to the prevailing confusion:

> Incentives are incentives, but they are given in collective farms simply on the basis of their name, and not according to the actual content of their work. Associations for joint cultivation of land get one level of tax reduction, artels another, and communes a third. But we all know that there are communes which are operating like associations for joint cultivation of land.[3]

Such arrangements obviously encouraged kolkhozy to register in a higher category than that to which they were entitled. The Central Statistical Administration, in a well-meaning attempt to make the record more realistic, confused matters further in some of its publications by disregarding the category in which kolkhozy were legally registered, instead classifying a kolkhoz as a TOZ, artel or commune according to the degree of socialisation of its means of production and its sown area.[4] But, in spite of all the exceptions, means of production were generally more socialised in communes than in artels, in artels than in TOZy.

In the official view, the movement from TOZ to artel and from artel to commune was a progression from 'lower' to 'higher' forms of production and distribution. The rise of the TOZy and the decline of the communes and artels between 1921 and the summer of 1928 thus indicated a persistent movement away from 'higher' towards 'lower' forms of collectivisation (see Table 4). The increase in the number of TOZy was nevertheless accepted and even encouraged by the authorities as a useful temporary concession to peasant psychology in the conditions of NEP, though this was regarded as a purely tactical requirement. Higher forms of production were believed to be much more efficient as well as socially desirable. In particular, the socialisation of livestock would make it possible to

[2] For the varied definitions and practices in 1921–8 see Lewin (1968), 109–12, 530, 533–4; Carr (1958), 219; and Carr and Davies (1969), 160–1.

[3] *XVI konf.* (1962), 419.

[4] NAF, 4, 1929, 95; kolkhozy were deemed to be artels if 90·1–100 per cent of their sown area and 60·1–95 per cent of means of production were socialised (NAF, 10, 1929, 117; see also Wronski (Paris, 1957), 16).

build adequate cattlesheds, employ specialists and organise a modern kolkhoz dairy industry.[5]

The trend towards lower forms of kolkhozy was reversed during the rapid expansion of the kolkhozy between October 1928 and June 1929. The proportion of artels and communes increased.[6] This was not simply a change in formal arrangements: draught animals in collective ownership increased from 27·7 to 44·0 per cent of the total number in the kolkhozy, and cows from 16·8 to 24·0 per cent.[7] Whether this remarkable new trend was brought about by direct pressure from the central authorities is not known. But it certainly corresponded to a change in official attitude. In the autumn of 1928, the long-standing tactical support for the TOZ and the prevalent toleration of a low level of socialisation in all types of kolkhozy were discarded. The plenum of the central committee in November 1928 criticised the 'inadequate growth of socialised means of production and capital' in the kolkhozy of the North Caucasus;[8] and the XVI party conference in April 1929 drew the attention of party organisations to the need for increased socialisation in TOZy, and for their transformation into artels and communes.[9] A month later the V congress of soviets added two further strands to the proposed pattern of development. It specifically approved the proposal in the final draft of the first five-year plan that 85 per cent of peasant households should become members of simple production cooperatives during the course of the five-year plan; and it looked forward to 'undeviating transformation' of associations of simple cooperatives into large kolkhozy.[10] Thus in the spring of 1929 the agreed strategy was to recruit the vast majority of peasant households into simple production associations during the next few years; a

[5] See for example Krot-Krival' (1926), 7–14; this is a typical pamphlet on collective farming.

[6] See Carr and Davies (1969), 945; these figures are evidently calculated on a different basis from those in Table 4 below.

[7] *Kolkhozy v 1928 g.* (1932), 48–51; *Kolkhozy v 1929 godu* (1931), 116–17; *Nar. kh.* (1932), 130–1; the figures for both 1928 and 1929 refer to June 1.

[8] *Kollektivizatsiya* (Krasnodar, 1972), 123.

[9] *KPSS v rez.*, ii (1954), 587. A version of the first five-year plan drawn up by the cooperative movement assumed, however, that 3·5 of the 4·4 million households in kolkhozy in 1932/33 would be in TOZy (Lewin (1968), 354).

[10] *Resheniya*, ii (1967), 71; the final draft of the five-year plan completed a month previously proposed that 85 per cent of households should be in *all* types of cooperatives and only 25 per cent in simple production associations (*Pyatiletnii plan*, ii, i (1930), 281).

substantial minority of these would be transformed into kolkhozy; existing small kolkhozy would be amalgamated; and the degree of socialisation in them would steadily increase.

By encouraging the artel at the expense of the TOZ the authorities hoped to bring about the socialisation of horses and implements, and thus provide the basis for collective production of grain. The socialisation of livestock apart from draught animals was rarely mentioned, and, when it was considered at all, was envisaged as a further stage subsequent to the consolidation of socialised arable farming. The authorities were aware that the general livestock situation had deteriorated,[11] but they were preoccupied with the far more urgent, and less intractable, grain problem. At the XVI party conference in April 1929, Eikhe complained that the five-year plan contained no precise recommendations about the development of collective livestock, and that current policy was 'murderous for livestock in the kolkhoz sector'.[12] During the next few months no change in policy took place as far as the mass of small kolkhozy was concerned. Mikoyan and Kalinin referred to the livestock shortage in major speeches, and attributed it to the absence of large-scale farming, but did not offer a practical solution.[13] The campaign for large kolkhozy, however, assumed that they would be advanced in organisation as well as technology, and among the first large kolkhozy the proportion of artels and particularly of communes was relatively high.[14] At the conference on large kolkhozy in July 1929, Kaminsky declared in his opening statement:

The large kolkhoz—and this is entirely clear to everyone—must in its type be a production economy similar to *our socialist factories and state farms.*[15]

---

[11] See Carr and Davies (1969), 100.

[12] *XVI konf.* (1962), 90.

[13] P, June 27, 1929 (Mikoyan); P, July 19, 1929 (Kalinin).

[14] According to the report to the organisation section of the conference of large kolkhozy in July 1929 only one-third of the 147 large kolkhozy which then existed were TOZy as compared with 53 per cent of all kolkhozy (ZKK (1929), 124); the Kolkhoztsentr report to the central committee in September 1929, probably using information from the same date, reported that the 147 large kolkhozy included 48 TOZy, 37 artels and 15 groups with common arable farming, and as many as 47 communes—a much higher proportion than in the case of the ordinary kolkhozy (*Materialy*, vii (1959), 22).

[15] ZKK (1929), 7.

At the organisation section of the conference, the Kolkhoztsentr representative argued that the process of socialisation should be rapid and complete in the large kolkhozy, and that they should accordingly have a special unified Statute, thus obviating the need to re-register them whenever their degree of socialisation increased. He was, however, vigorously opposed by speakers from the grain areas, who were not persuaded that the mass of the middle peasantry would be prepared to accept a high degree of socialisation. Some speakers even challenged the view that horses should be socialised in all large kolkhozy, arguing that this might antagonise the middle peasants.[16] The socialisation of livestock other than draught animals was not specifically mentioned by Kaminsky in his main report, and little was said about it at the conference. Some speakers called for the socialisation of livestock in more advanced kolkhozy,[17] and Kolkhoztsentr endorsed an announcement from the Ural Gigant kolkhoz that its productive animals would be socialised by January 1, 1930.[18] But the Urals, with long-established communes, was recognised to be an exceptional area; the central kolkhoz authorities, in spite of their support for socialised arable farming, continued to believe that, except in specialised livestock-farming areas, and in the minority of communes, collective farm households should continue to work their own household plot, and to own a modest number of cows, pigs, sheep and poultry. The theses presented to the conference did not go beyond the proposal that land, agricultural machines, draught animals and means of transport should be socialised in large kolkhozy. Moreover, the conference did not take any decision about the proposed unified Statute for large kolkhozy, and it was not mentioned in the subsequent decree of Kolkhoztsentr.[19] For the moment, a cautious attitude to advanced forms of socialisation prevailed in official circles, even in relation to the large kolkhozy.

(B) THE FIRST PHASE, JULY–SEPTEMBER 1929

During the next few months, a significant increase took place in the socialisation of some large kolkhozy and areas of comprehensive collectivisation which were the objects of special attention from the

[16] ZKK (1929), 133–5, 152.   [17] ZKK (1929), 145–52.
[18] ZKK (1929), 38, 437.
[19] ZKK (1929), 160–3, 465; the decree was dated July 25, 1929.

central authorities. The Gigant kolkhoz in the Urals already included 25 communes and 34 artels as against only 25 TOZy in July 1929;[20] by September there were 31 communes, 44 artels and only 17 TOZy—this was a far smaller proportion of TOZy, and a far higher proportion of communes, than in the country as a whole.[21] Khoper okrug in the Lower Volga region, which in September 1929 became the first 'okrug of comprehensive collectivisation' (see vol. 1, p. 131), announced as early as June that 100 per cent of draught animals and 35 per cent of cattle in the kolkhozy would be socialised,[22] and the local press reported that existing kolkhozy were being re-registered as communes, usually after amalgamation.[23] On August 27 the okrug party bureau resolved that all the large kolkhozy in the okrug should achieve 'full socialisation' of their means of production by November 1, and that all existing large kolkhozy should be re-registered as artels or communes by the time of the spring sowing.[24] In September, an inter-departmental okrug conference described in enthusiastic if rhetorical terms the transformation of Khoper into an 'okrug-commune of gigantic dimensions'. A survey carried out in the okrug in October or November reported that 95 per cent of draught animals, 40 per cent of cows, 57 per cent of sheep and 16 per cent of pigs were already socialised; socialisation was incomplete, however, as the animals were left with their former owners owing to the lack of common cowsheds and pigsties.[25] It is uncertain how far the upsurge of socialisation in these special areas was due to the spontaneous enthusiasm of the local officials, and how far it was inspired from Moscow.[26] But certainly it was not resisted by the central party authorities, and the activities of Gigant, abundantly publicised in *Pravda*, were presented as if they were of more general relevance.[27]

---

[20] ZKK (1929), 433.

[21] KG, 74, September 24, 1929.

[22] *Krasnyi Khoper*, June 6, 1929.

[23] *Povol'zhskaya pravda*, July 24, August 21, 1929; *Krasnyi Khoper*, August 13, 29, September 15, 1929; SKhG, August 31, September 4, 1929.

[24] *Krasnyi Khoper*, September 17, 1929; for the date of this resolution see vol. 1, p. 130, n. 83.

[25] In *Krasnyi Khoper*, December 12, 1929, the survey is said to be dated November 1 and to refer to 23 kolkhozy with 8,000 households; in P, January 13, 1930, the survey is said to have been general and to have taken place in October.

[26] For a general discussion of this question see vol. 1, pp. 124–31.

[27] Favourable reports appeared in the issues of August 22, September 12 and

In the mass of small kolkhozy the situation was quite different. Between June 1 and October 1, 1929, the new trends of the previous eight months were again reversed, and the TOZy increased more rapidly in numbers than the artels (see Table 4). But in view of the rapid expansion of the membership of kolkhozy, which almost doubled during these four months, this switch to the TOZ was not incompatible with the systematic but gradual progress from lower to higher types of kolkhoz which was envisaged by Kolkhoztsentr.

In extensive publicity in *Pravda* during August in favour of mass collectivisation and RSKs, little was said about the type of kolkhoz, or about socialisation generally, except in the case of the large kolkhozy.[28] Figures for the socialisation of draught animals and livestock in this period do not appear to be available. The continued decline in total livestock numbers gave rise to much anxiety, however, and was reported at length.[29] On August 22, a significant editorial in the economic newspaper, entitled 'For Large-scale Socialised Livestock Farming', attacked the Narkomzem five-year plan, which proposed that only seven per cent of all meat output should come from the socialised sector, for its 'completely obvious underestimation of the importance of livestock'. The editorial attributed the decline in livestock to the predominance of individual peasant farming, and condemned 'archaic ideas' that livestock breeding required 'careful individual handling', citing West European and American experience to demonstrate the superiority of large-scale mechanised livestock farming. It recommended the use 'in the main of the methods with which the grain problem was solved': large livestock sovkhozy should be established and livestock farming in the kolkhozy should undergo 'energetic socialisation'.[30]

For the moment this striking change of approach did not command general support. Throughout September the authorities remained cautious about proposals to extend socialisation beyond arable farming, except in the case of large kolkhozy. The Kolkhozsentr report to the central committee of September 7, 1929, called for increased socialisation in large kolkhozy, and provided information about the socialisation of cows in the kolkhozy of the RSKs, but on

---

October 1, 1929; at this time publicity in the central daily press for developments in Khoper seems to have been confined to the agricultural newspaper.

[28] See for example the editorials on August 7, 16, 23.

[29] See, for example, EZh, August 14, 1929 (A. Lositskii); for the decline in livestock in 1928/29 see vol. 1, pp. 44–6.

[30] EZh, August 22, 1929.

the whole it paid little attention to the question.[31] In a simultaneous article in *Pravda* Kaminsky specifically mentioned livestock only in relation to the non-grain areas, and in reiterating the earlier proposal that a unified Statute should be adopted for the large kolkhozy (see p. 72 above) he was careful to suggest that the maximum requirement was the socialisation of arable farming.[32] Later in the same month, at a Moscow regional soviet congress, Syrtsov drew attention to the lag of livestock behind grain, attributing it to the situation in which the kolkhozy owned 165,000 and the sovkhozy 82,000 cows as against the 30 million owned by the individual peasants, and called for the introduction of a 'zoominimum' to supplement the 'agrominimum'; but he also stopped short of making specific proposals for the socialisation of livestock.[33] Moreover, the assumption still persisted at this time that collective farmers would be compensated for relinquishing their livestock. The kolkhozy would purchase some animals from them outright, with the assistance of state loans and grants, and others would be transferred to the kolkhoz on the understanding that the state would support livestock farming in the kolkhoz by loans to construct collective cattlesheds, or by the allocation of breeding animals.[34] In the mass of small kolkhozy, the socialisation of livestock was to be cautious and relatively painless.

(C) THE DRIVE FOR SOCIALISATION,
OCTOBER 1929–FEBRUARY 1930

From the beginning of October, the central kolkhoz authorities rapidly drifted into new waters. On October 6, 1929, *Pravda* published an appeal signed by Kaminsky as chairman of the All-Union Council of Kolkhozy in connection with the forthcoming Day of Harvest and Collectivisation (see vol. 1, p. 132), which made a significant favourable reference, applying to all the kolkhozy, to 'full socialisation':

In the kolkhozy there are still strong groups which fasten on the remnants of their individual economy, and struggle against truly-

---

[31] *Materialy*, vii (1959), 230–5.
[32] P, September 12, 1929.
[33] P, September 25, 1929.
[34] EO, 9, 1929, 33 (I. Gershman); this issue was published in September 1929.

kolkhoz strivings for full socialisation and real socialist reconstruction of the whole village.

This was intended as more than a conventional exhortation. A few days later, the plans of Kolkhoztsentr for the economic year 1929/30 were revealed, and included the socialisation of 60 per cent of draught animals and 50 per cent of productive animals in the kolkhozy by October 1, 1930; the corresponding percentages for the large kolkhozy were 80–100 and 80, and in respect of the large kolkhozy this was stated to be a government directive.[35]

In the same month in which these ambitious plans were published, a report submitted to the presidium of Gosplan strongly criticised the practice of providing loans from state funds to kolkhozy to enable them to purchase animals from collective farmers:

> If we followed this path, in the next few years we would have to spend hundreds and thousands of millions of rubles and hand them over to collective farmers who are socialising their sown areas, thus increasing the monetary resources of the countryside without being able to supply a corresponding quantity of consumer goods.[36]

The published volume of control figures took the same line, and also insisted that kolkhozy should carry out 'a huge amount of work' to

[35] P, October 13, 1929. The published volume on the control figures, prepared in the early autumn and eventually approved by Sovnarkom, gives somewhat lower figures (horses 55, cows 50, sheep 41 and pigs 40 per cent) (*KTs . . . na 1929/30* (1930), 124). NAF, 10, 1929, 64, reported that in large kolkhozy in the RSFSR and the Ukraine 80 per cent of cows, sheep and pigs were to be socialised, and in the Belorussian SSR 90 per cent.

[36] EO, 10, 1929, 51 (M. Golendo); the report stated that at most 120,000 out of the more than 1·5 million additional cattle planned for the socialised sector of the kolkhozy in 1929/30 would be paid for by the state. Golendo previously took a moderate line on agricultural problems (see Wheatcroft (1974), 166). Golendo, born in 1894 in a poor peasant family, joined the party in 1917 and became a political commissar in the Red Army; he was appointed deputy chairman of the agricultural section of Gosplan in 1924 (SKhG, December 19, 1929). According to Larin, the budget commission of TsIK, at its session in November 1929, discovered that kolkhozy had been spending state credits on the purchase of livestock and equipment from their members; he argued that all such expenditure within the boundaries of an RSK was impermissible (*Trudy . . . agrarnikov-marksistov* (1930), i, 65).

build cattlesheds, again primarily using their own labour, money and materials.[37] The peasant newspaper, in a special page devoted to the importance of livestock, argued that even TOZy should begin to establish collective cattlesheds, and that over the next two years all peasant dairy cooperative associations should build collective cattlesheds and turn into large dairy kolkhozy.[38] Thus the increasing pressure of industrialisation on state finance was believed to rule out the provision of economic incentives to socialisation in the kolkhozy by the injection of resources from outside. Instead the collective farmers themselves were expected to provide resources for their own kolkhozy and move them forward by their own efforts. How they were to be persuaded to accept these new arrangements was hardly mentioned and never satisfactorily explained. This was a further move towards a system based on exhortation and administrative order.

It was not yet, however, a commitment to the all-out drive for socialisation which was to take control at the end of 1929. In October 1929, it was still assumed that the proposed increase in socialisation within the kolkhozy should be only a fairly small element in the total livestock programme. The kolkhozy were expected to include 10 per cent of all households by October 1, 1930, so that by that date, even if the ambitious plans of Kolkhoztsentr were realised, only 1.6 million of the 31 million cows in the USSR would be in the socialised sector of the kolkhozy. Livestock development would thus still primarily depend on the individual peasants.[39] Moreover, opinions continued to be divided about the wisdom of the immediate socialisation of livestock. An official of Kolkhoztsentr called for a two or three year programme in the RSKs which would be marked by 'gradualness and a systematic approach in socialising means of production in conformity with the new technical base'.[40] In Khoper okrug, the local party newspaper strongly defended the artel and the TOZ against the commune, evidently encouraged by the caution of the visiting commission of Kolkhoztsentr:

---

[37] *KTs . . . na 1929/30* (1930), 124; the text of the volume was drafted in about October 1929.
[38] KG, 84, October 22, 1929; a *Pravda* journalist visiting Odessa okrug praised local party and soviet organisations which put pressure on a TOZ to establish a socialised cattleshed (P, October 10, 1929).
[39] *KTs . . . na 1929/30* (1930), 124.
[40] EZh, October 13, 1929.

Our officials and the masses, not having measured their forces, not testing the ground under their feet, not strengthening the foundations enough, often in a burst of creative ecstasy decide to adopt the Statute of the commune.[41]

A few days later, in a letter to *Pravda* Sheboldaev, while defending the rapid pace of collectivisation in Khoper okrug, at the same time conceded that TOZy and artels rather than communes should predominate.[42]

The November plenum of the party central committee paid little attention to the question of socialisation within the kolkhoz. A few days before the plenum Stalin, in his article of November 3, conferred his approval impartially on 'joint cultivation of land, machine-tractor stations, artels and kolkhozy based on new technology, and giant sovkhozy equipped with hundreds of tractors and combine-harvesters'. He did not mention the commune in this list, and the only reference to it in his article was in his quotation of Lenin's famous statement that the middle peasant would say he was 'for the commune (i.e. for communism)' if provided with 100,000 first-class tractors.[43] At the plenum Kaminsky was more enthusiastic about socialisation; he recommended that preparation should be made for the transformation of large TOZy into communes and called for the solution of the livestock as well as the grain problem as early as 1930/31 through the establishment of large kolkhozy.[44] In contrast Molotov made no reference to different types of kolkhoz, and ignored the socialisation of livestock. But he stressed the need to increase the 'socialised Funds' in the kolkhozy, primarily by 'mobilisation' of the physical resources of the peasantry such as their implements. According to Molotov, these 'Funds' were particularly important because the state, 'in view of our poverty', was unable to provide much financial support for the kolkhozy.[45] This section of Molotov's speech was influential; it was henceforth abundantly clear that kolkhozy must depend on their members for their capital, and would get little help from the state.

The resolutions of the plenum were cautious about socialisation. The resolution on Kaminsky's report drew attention to the

[41] *Krasnyi Khoper*, October 17, 1929; for the commission, see vol. 1, pp. 152–3.
[42] P, October 22, 1929; for other aspects of this letter see vol. 1, p. 154.
[43] *Soch.*, xii, 125.
[44] VIK, 1, 1964, 36; Chigrinov (1965), 48.
[45] B, 22, November 30, 1929, 15–17.

importance of the socialised Funds of the kolkhoz, and sternly warned that animals and implements must not be sold by peasants before joining the kolkhozy, but it made no other reference to the livestock issue. And although the resolution on Ukrainian agriculture stressed that large kolkhozy as well as sovkhozy must organise livestock production, it merely mildly referred to the necessity of 'socialising in SOZy and artels the main instruments of production and animal draught power', and failed to mention other kinds of livestock.[46]

In spite of all this public caution by the central committee and by leading members of the Politburo, the effect of the plenum, with its atmosphere of urgency and self-confidence, was to foster the movement towards socialisation; and at the time of the plenum and during the following weeks a vigorous campaign was mounted in favour of higher types of kolkhozy and the immediate socialisation of livestock. In the campaign, increasing attention was paid to the problem of social inequality in the lower forms of kolkhozy, and the risk of kulak influence which this entailed. While the November plenum was in session, *Pravda* published an article by Azizyan, head of its department of agricultural affairs, which argued that kolkhozy with a small degree of socialisation provided 'conditions for the emergence and preservation of economic inequality'; this could be avoided only by further socialisation. According to Azizyan, the 'tendencies of small proprietors to develop individual accumulation' would remain even if the kulaks were driven out of the kolkhozy; such tendencies were strongly supported by the kulaks, who wanted the kolkhoz to become a 'joint-stock capitalist enterprise':

> *The ossification of the kolkhoz in the lower stages of socialisation is a fundamental element in all the tactics of the kulak within the kolkhoz.*[47]

This argument, far-fetched as it seems in the light of later developments, was obviously taken very seriously at the time. Trotsky, observing collectivisation from exile, argued a few weeks later that even when kulaks were expelled from the villages, 'preventing the re-emergence of the kulak within the kolkhoz is

---

[46] *KPSS v rez.*, ii (1954), 642–53, 658–9.

[47] P, November 11, 1929; he enlarged upon this view in B, 21, November 15, 1929, 53–8, and 22, November 30, 1929, 56–64 (for other aspects of these articles see vol. 1, pp. 183–4).

much more difficult'; the kolkhozy could become '*a new form of social and political disguise for the kulak*'. But Trotsky, unlike Azizyan, argued that only 'an industrial and cultural revolution' could avoid this danger.[48]

The more practical motive for intensifying the campaign for socialisation was the rapidly worsening livestock crisis in the autumn of 1929. The events of the previous autumn and winter were repeated on a larger scale. Much more grain was collected by the state, and this limited the availability to the peasants of a major source of fodder; part of the pasture was sown for grain; the harvest of hay and other fodder was poor; and the price of fodder rose.[49] And the enormous new complication was that peasants everywhere were selling their horses and other livestock before joining the kolkhoz. As early as August 1929 dozens of messages were sent from local soviets in the Black-Earth region urging livestock cooperatives to buy up animals to prevent their destruction, and in Stavropol' okrug in the North Caucasus 'kulaks drove herds of oxen, dairy cows, horses and sheep from district to district'.[50] At the November plenum, Petrovsky sounded a note of alarm:

> From all sides information is received that peasants write to their acquaintances and relatives: 'I am going into the collective, I have sold the cow, sold the horse, etc. . . . ' This is very dangerous and it is necessary for us to guard against it in advance, in order not to find ourselves in a very difficult position.[51]

By this time the market was flooded. A year later Mikoyan told a plenum of the party central committee that between October 1929 and March 1930 'the supply of animals was huge', so that delivery agencies had not needed to exert any effort in order to fulfil their plan.[52] The price of animals fell; and the peasants, instead of selling their cattle, pigs and sheep, now killed them in large numbers for home consumption or for sale as meat. In the Lower Volga region the meat collection agencies could not cope with the increased

[48] BO (Paris), ix (February–March 1930), 4–5 (article dated February 13, 1930).
[49] The alternative series for fodder production by Bryanskii and Nifontov both show a marked decline in 1929/30 (Gaister, ed. (1930), 58; Nifontov (1932), 127). See also NAF, 2, 1930, 5 (Vol'f); SO, 6, 1930, 16 (Gosplan survey); PKh, 9, 1930, 121–4 (Kindeev).
[50] SZe, February 1, 1930.
[51] Chigrinov (1965), 49.
[52] B, 1, January 15, 1931, 15.

numbers, the bazaar price of a milk cow fell from 93 rubles in September to 74 rubles in November 1929, and animals were 'driven from the bazaars unsold and killed at home, the meat being sold at bazaars or salted down'. The fall in the number of animals in the region between the spring of 1929 and the end of the year was estimated at 18 per cent, being as high as 25 per cent in Khoper okrug.[53] The price of meat also fell: in some places in the North Caucasus, it was cheaper than bread.[54] And rumours of imminent collectivisation led peasants to sell up their animals even in areas in which collectivisation was not taking place, or was taking place on a modest scale.

The crisis was an urgent one, and the anxiety of the peasants could have been brought to an end only by a very firm statement from the highest authorities that livestock would not be socialised in the kolkhozy. Instead, the authorities tried to gather livestock into the socialised sector of the economy as rapidly as possible, and became much more sympathetic to grandiose plans for the immediate establishment of giant communes. In an article published while the November plenum was in progress, Shlikhter, People's Commissar for Agriculture in the Ukraine, declared that a *'revolution in livestock farming'* was required, but was hindered because 'young animals in considerable quantities are going under the knife':

> Saving young animals from the knife, we must concentrate them exclusively in the socialist sector, in large sovkhozy and kolkhozy.[55]

He was soon followed by Ryskulov, who declared during his visit to Khoper okrug that the TOZ was out of date: higher types of kolkhozy should be organised immediately and the model Statutes should be re-examined. The crucial issue was livestock: 'We must immediately engage in the socialisation of product livestock, which are being sold right and left'.[56] On November 21, Kaganovich, in his report on the plenum to Moscow regional activists, included a

[53] *Nizhnee Povol'zhe*, 1, 1930, 32–4.
[54] SZe, February 1, 1930.
[55] P, November 16, 1929; in P, November 11, 1929, Shlikhter published another article, perhaps written before the plenum, which much more modestly set out a four-year socialisation programme for three Ukrainian RSKs.
[56] *Krasnyi Khoper*, November 19, 21, 1929; he visited some 20 kolkhozy on

long passage in praise of the Ural Gigant kolkhoz, though, like Stalin, Molotov and Mikoyan in these months, he made no specific mention of the socialisation of livestock in his published statements.[57] At a joint meeting of Sovnarkom and Ekoso of the USSR on November 27, Syrtsov was much more explicit:

> We cannot in this sphere leave to the will of fate the spontaneity which we can observe at present. *We must now, at once embark on the collectivisation of livestock.*[58]

An editorial in *Pravda*, while calling for the encouragement of livestock breeding by the individual peasant, placed its main emphasis on '*large-scale livestock farming in kolkhozy and sovkhozy*'; 'the stormy rate of growth of collectivisation' made it possible to embark on the rapid socialisation of livestock in kolkhozy.[59] At an all-Union conference of kolkhoz and cooperative officials under the auspices of Kolkhoztsentr of the USSR, the rapporteur returned to the theme that the livestock problem must be approached 'with the tempos and the methods used for work on the solution of the grain problem'.[60] At the session of TsIK which met at the beginning of December, the chairman of the Lower Volga regional soviet reported that most kolkhozy in his region were 'artels with socialised productive labour', but urged delegates not to fear higher forms of collectivisation: in the conflict within each peasant between his role as individual property owner and his role as master of the new collective economy, victory for the latter was assured: 'The general formula "aim for communes (itti na kommuny)" is completely correct'.[61] A delegate from Siberia, optimistically describing collectivisation as 'a more or less well-trodden path', and merely an 'initial stage', urged that it should be followed by socialisation of all means of production.[62] At a conference on collectivisation of members of TsIK held at this time Ryskulov, reporting on his visit to the Lower Volga, again urged a movement towards the artel and

---

November 16 and 17, and gave his report on November 19. For the term 'product livestock', see p. 89 below; for Ryskulov, see vol. 1, pp. 178–9, 187, 199.

[57] P, November 26, 1929; see also p. 40 above.
[58] SKhG, November 29, 1929.
[59] P, November 29, 1929.
[60] SKhG, December 1, 3, 1929.
[61] *TsIK 2/V* (1929), No. 6, 3.
[62] *Ibid.* No. 6, 19.

the commune.[63] Andreev, in an interview in *Pravda*, claimed to have observed in the North Caucasus a 'direct transition to purely kolkhoz forms, more complex and with a greater degree of socialisation than earlier in the kolkhoz movement'.[64] More ambitious plans for socialisation were now prepared in the localities. Tyumen' okrug in the Urals, for example, planned to socialise all animals by the end of 1930, and reported that in one district of the okrug 56 per cent of cows were already socialised.[65]

The plans for the spring sowing campaign prepared at this time were strongly influenced by the growing pressure for socialisation. At the beginning of December 1929, the plan of Narkomzem and Kolkhoztsentr proposed that by the end of the spring sowing 25 per cent of kolkhozy in the RSFSR should be TOZy, 50 per cent artels and 25 per cent communes. This proposal involved a very big change from the proportions actually prevailing on October 1, 1929 (62·3, 30·8, 6·9), a return, for a far higher level of collectivisation, to the kind of proportions which had prevailed at the end of war communism in 1921 (15, 65, 20) (see Table 4). The plan also proposed that 80 per cent of productive cattle, pigs and sheep should be socialised in RSKs, and 60 per cent in small kolkhozy.[66] These percentages were not much different from those in the plan for 1929/30 prepared in October, but they were now to be reached in six months instead of a year, and referred to kolkhozy which would include 37 per cent of households instead of the 10 per cent planned in October. In the October plan, 1·6 out of 31 million cows in the USSR were to be socialised by September 1930; in the December plan, 4·24 out of 23 million in the RSFSR were to be socialised by the spring of 1930. On December 11, a decree of Sovnarkom of the RSFSR endorsed the plan; it specificially approved the proposal that 'at least 70 per cent' of kolkhozy should be artels and communes, and declared January 1930 to be a 'Livestock Month'.[67] Meanwhile, on December 10, a telegram from Kolkhoztsentr of the USSR to its local organisations proposed similarly high figures for

[63] EZh, December 6, 1929.
[64] P, December 13, 1929.
[65] P, December 24, 1929.
[66] *Plan kollektivizatsii v vesennyuyu sel'skokhozyaistvennuyu kampaniyu 1930 g.* (1930), 16–17; Nemakov (1966), 89–90; the plan may be dated by an unsigned article in P, December 6, 1929, which gave the planned percentages of TOZy, artels and communes.
[67] SU, 1929, art. 910; the Narkomzem plan in fact proposed 75 per cent.

the socialisation of livestock in RSKs and large kolkhozy.[68] Not to be outdone, a conference called by the grain cooperative organisation Khlebotsentr proposed that 88 per cent of cows should be socialised in kolkhozy by the spring.[69]

While these detailed instructions were prejudging the issue, socialisation within the kolkhozy was a major preoccupation of the Politburo commission on collectivisation; one of the eight subcommissions set up at its first meeting on December 8, 1929, dealt with 'the type of economy of collectivised districts' under the chairmanship of Grin'ko.[70] Before the subcommission could meet, Ryskulov, in an article in *Pravda*, again insisted that the new kolkhozy must mainly be artels and communes: 'The higher the form of the kolkhoz, the better its economy is managed'. He added that the charters of artels and communes should be revised so as to bring about an increased degree of socialisation. Thus the Indivisible Fund should be increased (see p. 120 below), and productive animals should be socialised in both artels and communes; the attention of the collective farmer would then no longer be divided between collective and individual interests.[71] The Grin'ko subcommission took a similar line. In a report to the meeting of chairmen of subcommissions held on December 14 and 15, it proposed that 'the artel type should be the minimum, with obligatory collectivisation of all arable land, all implements, all draught animals, all cattle, at least three-quarters of the pigs, at least half the sheep, etc., taking into account local circumstances', and that kolkhozy should be transformed into communes as soon as possible.[72] But these proposals were resisted in the main commission. Yakovlev stated:

> We have events, although they are not so many, when attempts are made to construct a directly Evangelical socialism in which everything to the last hen is socialised, and an immediate transition is made to the commune Statute without a sufficient base for it.[73]

[68] Danilov, ed. (1963), 41; Kolkhoztsentr proposed that 100 per cent of cows, 80 per cent of pigs and 60 per cent of sheep should be socialised in RSKs and large kolkhozy, and a further decree of December 24 proposed that 73–74 per cent of productive livestock in *all* kolkhozy in the RSFSR should be socialised.

[69] P, December 20, 1929.

[70] IISO, [i] (1964), 266–7, 274; for Grin'ko see vol. 1, p. 169.

[71] P, December 9, 1929.

[72] IISO, [i] (1964), 274–5.

[73] Nemakov (1966), 92; the date of the statement is not given, but it was

At this point in the proceedings, an editorial in *Pravda* insisted that the 'kolkhoz public and especially the kolkhoz activists' in RSKs were collectivising draught animals and productive livestock 'on their *own initiative*', and that the 'broad masses of poor and middle peasants' were striving for 'maximum socialisation of draught animals and productive livestock'; to cope with this, peasant buildings should be adapted as cattlesheds and pigsties.[74] In spite of this rallying-cry, in the draft decree forwarded to the Politburo on December 22 the main commission proposed that in view of the 'hesitations' of the middle peasants, who constituted the majority of collective farmers in okrugs of comprehensive collectivisation, the artel should be the 'main form of organisation at the present stage', and that in the artel the main means of production, including land, implements, working animals and 'commodity production animals' should be collectivised but there should be *'private property of the peasant in minor implements, small animals, milk cows, etc. where they serve the consumer needs of the peasant family'*.[75] The draft also warned:

Each further step towards socialisation on the road to the commune must rely on the direct experience of the peasant collective farmers, on the growth of their belief in the stability, profitability and advantage of collective forms of management of the economy. Special care must be taken in the sphere of everyday life (byt), where the prejudices of the ordinary peasant are most profound.[76]

At this point in the deliberations, the conference of marxist agrarians, which met from December 20 to December 27, 1929, provided an opportunity for reflection on the nature of the kolkhoz and its place in the Soviet economy. Larin defined 'socialist economy in the true meaning of this concept' as one in which 'the economy is not the property of a particular group of individual owner-shareholders working in it, but of the state', and members of society work for the whole society and not for themselves. Hence kolkhozy, even in RSKs, were not socialist but transitional types of

---

presumably made either at the meeting of December 14 and 15 or at the meeting of the main commission on December 16 and 17.

[74] P, December 17, 1929.
[75] IISO, [i] (1964), 276; VIK, 1, 1964, 36; in the first source the phrase is italicised, in the second source it is not.
[76] VI, 3, 1965, 12.

economy, in which some features assisted the movement to socialism and others were a basis for struggle against it.[77] In the kolkhozy, peasant families had no personal connections with a particular piece of land, plough or horse, but the means of production and farm output belonged to them collectively as 'a group of private persons'; a clash of interests was therefore possible between the kolkhoz and the state, both over state prices, which could lead the kolkhoz to try to sell its production on the private market, and over the type of crops grown. Kolkhozy would become a 'consistently-socialist type of economy' only when they were transformed into sovkhozy, though Larin conceded that 'in conditions of the dictatorship of the proletariat the transformation of *all means of production* into the indivisible capital of the kolkhoz would approach close to this'.[78] Larin's analysis supported his call for the conversion of kolkhozy, within a few years, into state enterprises, and for a rapid advance of socialisation.[79]

In the debate, Kalinin, while ignoring the theoretical issue, agreed that 'the kolkhoz, *taken by itself*, at the present stage still does not save us from the fact that it may carry on a capitalist policy', and contrasted the 'two souls' of the peasant, 'the soul of the proprietor and the soul of the labourer'; it was accordingly necessary to 'sharpen to a certain stage the struggle between the socialist and private capitalist tendencies inside the kolkhoz'. Collectivisation should be spread to 'fruit, eggs, milk and meat' as well as grain farming, appropriate forms of organisation being set up for each branch of farming.[80] Other speakers at the conference also called for more socialisation: a Moscow delegate presciently warned that a delay in socialisation would lead the peasant to settle into the kolkhoz with his cow and garden.[81] Larin's discussion of the nature of the kolkhoz was a major theme of the debate. Most speakers, while conceding to Larin that the kolkhozy were not yet economies of a 'consistently socialist' type, insisted that they were already 'socialist'

---

[77] *Trudy . . . agrarnikov-marksistov*, i (1930), 70, 63; according to a later speaker at the conference (*ibid.* i (1930), 107) and to P, December 25, 1929, Larin described comprehensive collectivisation as 'large-scale cooperative private economy production', but these words do not appear in his report as printed.

[78] *Trudy . . . agrarnikov-marksistov*, i (1930), 64, 70.

[79] For other aspects of Larin's report, see p. 4 above and vol. 1, pp. 195–7.

[80] *Trudy . . . agrarnikov-marksistov*, i (1930), 95–7; the divided interests of the peasant were a familiar theme at this time (see p. 79 above and p. 94 below).

[81] *Ibid.* ii (1930), 163–4 (G. Chernyi).

or 'transitional-socialist'. No agreement was reached on whether kolkhozy would become 'consistently socialist' with tractorisation, or only when they transferred their means of production to the state and thus became sovkhozy.[82]

On the last day of the conference, December 27, Stalin, in a dramatic intervention, vigorously attacked 'one of the speakers' (he did not deign to name Larin) who had 'uncrowned the kolkhozy'; the view that kolkhozy had 'nothing in common with the socialist form of economy' had 'nothing in common with Leninism'.[83] According to Stalin, the kolkhoz was 'a form of socialist economy' because its main instruments of production were socialised, land belonged to the state, and there were no exploiting and exploited classes within the kolkhoz. There were 'contradictions' within the kolkhozy, and 'individualistic and even kulak survivals', but these would 'fall away' as the kolkhozy grew stronger and were mechanised. Stalin admitted that 'elements of the class struggle' existed within the kolkhozy, resulting from the 'survivals of individualistic or even kulak psychology', and from 'a certain inequality in material position which still remains'; but he vigorously attacked ' "Leftist" phrasemongers' who equated this with the class struggle outside the kolkhozy.[84] A notable feature of Stalin's speech, otherwise distinguished for the vigour of its support for the collectivisation drive and dekulakisation, was his failure to mention all practical questions of socialisation in the kolkhozy, and his stress on the 'considerable amount of work' which would be required to 'correct the individual psychology' of the peasant collective farmer.

During the last few days of December 1929, the draft central committee resolution prepared by the Politburo commission on collectivisation was considered by members of the Politburo. When the draft was sent to Molotov, he objected to its treatment of the degree of socialisation of peasant property.[85] Ryskulov, in his note on the draft (see vol. 1, p. 199) criticised the restriction of

---

[82] *Trudy . . . agrarnikov-marksistov*, i (1930), 107–8 (Lozovyi), 109, 111 (Karpinskii), 149, 151 (Nazimov).

[83] *Soch.*, xii (1949), 161, where the word 'Leninism' which appeared in the verbatim report is replaced by the word 'reality'; Stalin's speech was first published in P, December 29, 1929.

[84] *Soch.*, xii, 162–5; for Stalin's criticism of Larin's attitude to the kulaks see vol. 1, p. 198.

[85] VI, 3, 1965, 6; no archival source is given.

socialisation to 'commodity livestock', and attacked the proposal to make a firm statement that small implements and other livestock should remain in private ownership as 'a clearly incorrect slogan' which would 'drag events backwards', and help the 'strong' or 'upper' middle peasant in his struggle against the 'poor peasant and the poor middle peasant'.[86] According to a Soviet source, these criticisms were approved by Stalin and Molotov,[87] though, as has been shown, in his only published statement at this time Stalin made light of class antagonism within the kolkhozy and ignored the question of livestock. At all events, Stalin sent back the draft resolution and proposed that it should be much abbreviated by referring questions relating to the Statute of the kolkhoz for inclusion in the forthcoming model Statute.[88] The final resolution of January 5, 1930, appeared to be a compromise between the main commission and the Grin'ko subcommission:

> Insofar as, in place of the association for joint cultivation of the land, in which, together with the socialisation of labour, private property in the means of production is maintained, experience of comprehensive collectivisation at the present stage of kolkhoz development is promoting the agricultural artel, in which the *main* means of production (implements and draught animals, farm buildings and commodity-product animals (tovarno-produktovyi skot)) are collectivised, the Central Committee of the CPSU(b) instructs Narkomzem of the USSR to work out as quickly as possible, involving kolkhoz organisations on a broad scale, a model Statute of the agricultural artel, as a form of the kolkhoz transitional to the commune, bearing in mind that it is impermissible for kulaks to join the kolkhozy.[89]

The draft resolution of December 22 had described the artel as the 'main form of organisation' and did not include the phrase 'transitional to the commune'; thus the revised wording in the resolution of January 5 removed the implication of the draft that kolkhozy could remain artels indefinitely into the future, and

[86] VI, 3, 1965, 12–13; IISO, [i] (1964), 280–1.
[87] IISO, [i] (1964), 282–4.
[88] See vol. 1, p. 199, and n. 206; on December 23, the collegium of Narkomzem instructed Kolkhoztsentr to prepare a draft Statute; a draft was submitted on December 28, but rejected as unsatisfactory (Ivnitskii (1972), 177).
[89] *KPSS v rez.*, ii (1954), 666.

promoted the status of the commune.[90] The cause of socialisation was also promoted by the omission from the resolution of the explicit acknowledgement in the draft of December 22 of the existence in the artel of private property in small animals and milk cows for consumption purposes.[91] This increased the ambiguity inherent in the term 'commodity-product livestock', which was nowhere defined.[92]

The ambiguity remained unresolved during the next two months. A few days after the decree, the agricultural newspaper reported unhelpfully that a Statute for the artel, 'just approved and published' by Kolkhoztsentr of the RSFSR, stated that 'pro-

[90] For these changes see VI, 3, 1965, 13.

[91] See p. 85 above. All these changes were already incorporated in Yakovlev's revised second draft submitted to the Politburo on January 3. As compared with the resolution of January 5, the draft of January 3 did not mention the TOZ, and stated that '*so far only* the main means of production . . . are collectivised' (my italics—RWD) in the artel (Ivnitskii (1972), 175–6). These changes appear to be editorial in character; 'so far only' was redundant when 'transitional to the commune' was added.

[92] The term was an unusual one. In the normal terminology, animals were officially divided into *rabochii skot* (working or draught animals, i.e. grown horses and oxen) and *pol'zovatel'skii skot* (all other animals). In the statistics, horses, *krupnyi rogatyi skot* (literally, 'large horned livestock'—i.e. oxen, bulls and cows) and *melkii skot* (literally, 'small livestock'—i.e. sheep, goats and pigs) were shown separately (EO, 10, 1929, 46). *Produktivnyi skot* (productive livestock) was a very frequently used term which sometimes appears to have referred to all 'large horned' and 'small' livestock except oxen, and sometimes only to cows: Kalinin later referred to 'dairy cattle (molochnyi skot) or, as they call it, productive livestock (produktivnyi skot)' (P, March 3, 1930). *Tovarno-produktivnyi skot* (commodity-productive livestock), a term often used at this time, presumably referred to that part of the dairy cattle, or of all the livestock, which was sold on the market, or whose products were sold on the market. But the term in the resolution of January 5 was *tovarno-produktovyi skot* (commodity-product livestock) which taken literally would mean all livestock sold on the market as a commodity or transferred to the state as a product: the term 'product livestock' reappeared in Yakovlev's speech published on January 24, where it was simply used to mean 'large horned' but not 'small' livestock (see p. 90 below; it was also used by Ryskulov on November 19 (see p. 81 above). It was replaced in the Statutes of February 6 and March 1 by the familiar term 'commodity-productive livestock'. Perhaps the term was simply a typing error. But whatever its nuances may have been, it certainly implied that the collective farmer could not retain in his own possession livestock, particularly cattle, for the primary purpose of selling them or their products, whether to the state or on the market. Any sale of meat or dairy produce by a collective farmer was thereby in jeopardy. It was, however, quite unclear how far the term covered, for example, cows in households which owned a single cow, sold a small part of the milk, and consumed the rest.

ductive animals (all or part)' were to be socialised.[93] A few days later, Yakovlev, addressing Moscow workers who were leaving to work in the kolkhozy, appeared to revert to the position of the Politburo main commission about the socialisation of livestock, while simultaneously encouraging the growth of communes:

> Last year the overwhelming majority of newly-organised collectives were associations for joint cultivation of land . . . From the summer and autumn of 1929, the collective movement has proposed as the main type of kolkhoz for the present moment the agricultural artel, *in which not only labour but all the main means of production and commodity-product animals are socialised. This is not yet a commune*, because socialisation does not yet include that part of product livestock which is kept for consumption, part of the small livestock, and the sphere of everyday living, *but it is undoubtedly a gigantic step towards the commune, a transitional stage to the commune.*

This determines the main features of the new model Statute of the agricultural kolkhoz artel worked out by Narkomzem of the USSR in accordance with the directives of the party central committee of January 5, 1930.

The Statute, envisaging the immediate socialisation only of the commodity part of the product herd, and the socialisation of household plots only to the extent of and in conformity with the creation of socialised vegetable gardens which are able to satisfy both the needs of the collective farmers and give commodities for the market, *warns against any excessive haste*, rushing ahead, warns in others words against forcing the transition from the agricultural artel to the next higher stage, the commune, artificially and by administrative means.[94]

However, the model Statute of the artel which was approved on February 6, 1930, did nothing to resolve the controversial issues. While insisting on the collective use of all the land allotments (nadel), it did not mention the household plot (usad'ba) and said

---

[93] SKhG, January 11, 1930. The model Statute of February 6, 1930, contained no such statement (see p. 91 below); it was approved by the new Narkomzem of the USSR and by Kolkhoztsentr of the USSR, and the latter had a common staff and a common chairman with the Kolkhoztsentr of the RSFSR. A draft model Statute, submitted by Kolkhoztsentr of the USSR on January 13, was 'approved in the main' (Ivnitskii (1972), 177); the Statute was referred to in an editorial in P, January 19, 1930.

[94] I, January 24, 1930.

nothing about excessive haste. In the clause on the means of production Yakovlev's qualification that 'only' commodity animals should be socialised was omitted; the clause hardly departed from the resolution of January 5, apart from the use of the word 'productive' instead of 'product':

There shall be socialised all draught animals, agricultural implements, all commodity-productive animals, all stocks of seed, fodder resources in the amount needed to maintain the socialised animals, all farm buildings necessary for managing the economy of the artel, and all enterprises for reworking agricultural products.[95]

According to a contemporary Soviet source, secretaries of regional party committees, after the publication of the model Statute, appealed to the central committee and to Stalin to give a ruling on the extent to which livestock, small implements and household plots should be socialised, but received no answer; Vareikis commented that they had to act 'at their own risk and fear'.[96]

During the first six weeks of 1930, leading officials continued to demand the immediate socialisation of productive livestock. At the conference of RSKs which met from January 11 to January 14, 1930, Vrachev, a member of the board of Kolkhoztsentr, explained how the plan to socialise 80 per cent of the total number of cattle, pigs and sheep in each RSK during the spring campaign should be carried out. In higher forms of kolkhoz, all the animals would be socialised, but the more widespread arrangement would be to leave some of the animals with the collective farmers for consumption purposes, while using socialised fodder and common pastures. To house the socialised animals, existing buildings should be adapted and simple cattlesheds and pigsties should be constructed; socialised poultry and rabbit farms should be established in the kolkhozy.[97] Vrachev's proposals were wildly extravagant in comparison with the most extreme notions of a few months before, and with what came to be regarded as realistic three months later. It was

---

[95] I, February 7, 1930 (for the date of the Statute, see VI, 3, 1965, 12); those concerned with the British Labour Party may like to note that this was clause four . . .

[96] IISO, [i] (1964), 282–3 Vareikis was Central Black-Earth region party secretary.

[97] P, January 14, 1930; a long article by Vrachev, evidently the advance text of his report, appeared in SKhG, January 11, 1930, and has also been used here.

characteristic of the feverish excitement of those weeks, however, that, according to the newspaper report, 'particularly many objections were raised' to Vrachev's proposal that only 80 per cent of livestock should be socialised; delegates to the conference argued that this would deepen inequality in the kolkhoz and restrict production for sale, and proposed instead that all livestock should be socialised by the spring of 1930, using the existing cattlesheds of households until new ones had been constructed.[98] A representative from the Central Black-Earth region who proposed that the model Statute should recognise that the collective farmer should have his own household plot, milk cows and small animals for family needs was a lone voice, and was not reported in the press.[99] On the day the conference ended, an editorial in the agricultural newspaper insisted that fewer animals were killed or sold up in areas where collective livestock farming was taken seriously and collective cattlesheds were under construction; it urged the okrug press to pay more attention to socialisation, and called for the immediate cancellation of local decrees which delayed it, such as the decision in the North Caucasus that collective herds should contain only certain varieties of cattle.[100]

Legislation adopted in the first six weeks of 1930 continued to support a high level of socialisation. Instructions from the all-Union authorities were primarily directed towards securing the socialisation of draught animals and the collection of seed, urgently required before the spring sowing. In January a letter from Narkomzem urged the formation of horse and mixed horse-tractor bases in all kolkhozy, and the transfer of all horses, including those of expropriated kulaks, to the kolkhozy, as well as implements and fodder; pressure was to be exerted on those who refused, including if necessary explusion from the kolkhoz.[101] In February, the authorities complained that the progress of the socialisation of draught animals was 'completely unsatisfactory' and must be completed everywhere by April 1, and called for buildings and fodder to be made available.[102] Further decrees called for the collection of 'seed funds' (see vol. 1, pp. 238–9, 252–3).

Other legislation insisted on the socialisation of productive

[98] P, January 14, 1930.
[99] IISO, [i] (1964), 285; VI, 3, 1965, 7.
[100] SKhG, January 14, 1930.
[101] SKhG, January 7, 1930.
[102] SZ, 1930, art. 127 (Sovnarkom decree of February 11); Kolkhoztsentr decree

livestock. As late as February 13, 1930, a decree of Sovnarkom stated that in the course of the economic year 1929/30 cattle in sovkhozy and kolkhozy must reach 30 per cent and sheep and pigs 20 per cent of the total in the USSR, with the number of dairy cattle in kolkhozy reaching 11 million during the year, and again called for the organisation of socialised cattlesheds to accommodate them, and for the collective production of fodder.[103] This implied no reduction of the rate of socialisation proposed in December 1929, even though the expected level of collectivisation had more than doubled since December. In the RSFSR, a decree of Sovnarkom, whose chairman Syrtsov and vice-chairman Ryskulov were keen protagonists of the socialisation of livestock, planned to double the total number of hens by 1933, and to increase the proportion in the socialised sector to 70–80 per cent of all hens, with 60–70 per cent in the kolkhozy, and 10 per cent in the sovkhozy.[104] On February 11, a further decree of Sovnarkom of the RSFSR complained that Livestock Month had been 'completely unsatisfactory' in most regions, and instructed that it should be extended to March 1 in grain-surplus areas and March 15 in grain-deficit areas, by which time the slaughter must end and the 'necessary degree of socialisation' be achieved.[105]

In the middle of February the party central committee made its one published pronouncement since January 5 relevant to the socialisation of livestock. In its resolution about the Central Volga region of February 15, it urged the regional party organisation to improve 'production indicators and quality' in kolkhozy by 'more and more socialisation of means of production and processes of production in kolkhozy, more and more growth and strengthening in them of socialised indivisible capital'.[106] The Central Volga region was by no means backward at this time in its efforts to socialise livestock (see p. 100 below), so the Politburo had evidently not yet wavered in its enthusiasm about socialisation.

The flow of instructions was supplemented by visits from authoritative officials. Alarmed by the failure of the seed collections to keep pace with the growth of the kolkhozy, the Politburo

---

of February 11, in SZe, February 13, 1930 (the completion date given in the latter is April 30, but this must be a misprint).
[103] SZ, 1930, art. 141.
[104] SKhG, January 28, 1930.
[105] SZe, February 20, 1930.
[106] PS, 3–4 (5–6), 1930, 91–3.

sometime early in February despatched a number of members of the central committee to the provinces for ten days to enforce its decisions.[107] Exhortatory visits from representatives of the commissariats were also frequent. A brigade from Narkomzcm of the USSR, for example, after touring Stavropol' okrug in the North Caucasus, complained in strong terms that dairy cattle and draught animals were not being socialised.[108] A plenipotentiary of Kolkhoztsentr in the Western region complained that village soviets had failed to organise groups of batraks and poor peasants against the kulaks, with the result that the kulaks, using the women, had prevented the socialisation of animals and implements.[109]

Further measures sought to prevent the destruction of livestock by peasants joining the kolkhozy. On January 16, a decree of TsIK and Sovnarkom condemned the destruction of animals, which it admitted was taking place 'in a number of places', as due to 'kulak wrecking'; kulaks who maliciously destroyed animals, or inspired others to do so, could be banned from all use of land, their animals and implements could be confiscated, and they could be sentenced to up to two years' deprivation of liberty with or without exile. The decree also endorsed the ruling of Kolkhoztsentr that peasants who destroyed or sold their animals should not be admitted to kolkhozy, and instructed local soviets to ban the killing of young animals.[110] As the expropriation of the kulaks was already taking place in many places, the penalties added little to their plight, and to be effective needed to be used against middle peasants as well as kulaks. On the day after the publication of the decree, a *Pravda* editorial returned in connection with the slaughter of livestock to the theme of the two peasant souls. It distinguished the kulak, who had only the soul of a proprietor, from two types of middle peasant. The middle peasant in whom the soul of a proprietor predominated killed and salted down his calves and piglets before joining the kolkhoz, but there was also another type of middle peasant whose prime motive was to join the kolkhoz and for whom selling his livestock was a 'tribute paid by the "soul" of the labourer to the "soul" of the proprietor'.[111] Within a few days the legislation was widened to cope with poor and middle

---

[107] P, June 3, 1930 (Mikoyan).

[108] SZe, February 1, 1930.

[109] SZe, February 5, 1930.

[110] SZ, 1930, art. 66; the draft prepared by Narkomzem did not include the provision about deprivation of liberty (SZe, January 16, 1930).

[111] P, January 18, 1930 (see also p. 86 above).

peasants whose proprietorial souls led them to behave like kulaks. A new sub-clause added to the criminal code of the RSFSR, unlike the decree of January 16, made no mention of kulaks, merely stating that 'malicious slaughter of livestock, deliberate damage to it and inciting others to do this', were criminal offences punishable with deprivation of liberty if they were undertaken 'with the objective of disruption of the collectivisation of agriculture and preventing its advance.'[112] At the XVI party congress in June 1930, Krylenko complained that in practice this clause was applied to middle peasants, and referred to 'strict party directives' that it should be applied only to the kulak; he also objected to the practice of applying it retrospectively to animals sold months before.[113]

Financial penalties and incentives were also introduced in the hope of encouraging socialisation. A new decree on the agricultural tax, dated February 23, 1930, relating to the tax to be collected in the following autumn, imposed a much higher rate of taxation on the income of the collective farmer from his 'personal economy' than on kolkhoz income; the rate was even higher than on individual peasant households. The decree also increased the discrimination in favour of the commune as against other types of kolkhoz.[114]

Thus pressure from the centre for increased socialisation was extremely strong, though the ambiguities of the central committee resolution of January 5 and the model Statute of February 6, the silence of Stalin and his close political associates, and the cautionary remarks of Yakovlev all provided some room for manoeuvre. The extent to which this pressure was reflected in local instructions varied considerably, and practice varied still more. Such key areas as the Ural Gigant and Khoper okrug were already committed to a full-blooded socialisation policy (see p. 73 above). By January, all the 100 or so kolkhozy in the Ural Gigant had been converted into communes, and in that month they were formally merged into a single commune. Enthusiastic reports improbably claimed that the peasants, formerly 'conservative and immobile', now looked on their houses as living quarters provided by the commune, and willingly moved house, or even village, to improve their conditions or in the interests of farm management. In one commune, everything was socialised except the hens.[115] In Khoper okrug, all

---

[112] I, January 24, 1930; the new sub-clause was 79¹.
[113] *XVI s"ezd* (1931), 352.
[114] SZ, 1930, arts. 143–4.   [115] SKhG, January 21, 1930.

TOZy were abolished, 82 per cent of the kolkhozy were 'artels with a higher Statute' (i.e. with a greater degree of socialisation), and 18 per cent, including some of the largest, were communes.[116] In Khoper, the fanciful plans for establishing an agrogorod envisaged the conversion of a whole district into a giant commune (see p. 45 above). The campaign for agro-industrial combines (AIKs) was now at its height (see p. 46 above); its adherents saw them as a move towards *'unified large-scale agriculture of a higher type'*, in which all branches of agriculture were fully socialised. This was seen as the only way to 'eliminate all petty-proprietorial incentives': with the introduction of AIKs, all animals, gardens and vegetable plots could be 'completely depersonalised'.[117] Giant communes were established in many places, even in national minority areas. In Votsk autonomous region, giant kolkhozy 'normally absorbed everything in their huge territory, turning into a kind of Great Universal Stores'; their Statutes were later said to be 'closer to a commune than to an artel'.[118]

Some regional authorities enthusiastically endorsed the socialisation of livestock. In the Central Volga region, Khataevich responded to the encouragement provided by the central committee resolution of February 15 (see p. 93 above) by declaring that 43 per cent socialisation of productive livestock was not enough.[119] In Belorussia, the party central committee called in January 1930 for a maximum switch to the commune, and for the socialisation of animals in general, without making it clear that animals kept for consumption purposes should not be socialised.[120]

Other regions were more modest. In the Lower Volga region, a secretary of the regional party committee recommended that the normal type of kolkhoz should be an 'artel of a higher type', which implied that all productive animals would be socialised, but added that the TOZ or the commune must be allowed if the artel was not accepted;[121] and Sheboldaev later claimed that the regional party bureau recommended on January 11, 1930, that not more than 40 per cent of milk cows should be socialised.[122] In the Central Black-

---

116 SKhG, January 3, 1930; KGN, 2, January 7, 1930.
117 SZe, February 5, 1930 (Nikulikhin).
118 NAF, 5, 1930, 30, 35.
119 P, February 16, 1930.
120 P, May 19, 1930.
121 SKhG, January 4, 1930 (Gusti).
122 P, April 27, 1930.

Earth region collectivisation was undertaken at a frantic pace, but pressure for socialisation was less intense. In a series of articles in *Pravda* at the end of 1929, Vareikis did not go further than calling for the socialisation of draught animals.[123] At the conference of RSKs in January, a representative of the region called for the retention in the personal possession of the collective farmers of milk cows and small livestock (see p. 92 above). The instructions issued by the rural department of the Tambov okrug party committee in this region in January 1930 to workers involved in mass collectivisation merely told them to arrange for the socialisation of seeds, implements and draught animals, and stated that all means of production would not be socialised at first.[124] In the North Caucasus, in a report to a congress of comprehensive collectivisation on January 9, Andreev, while calling for the immediate socialisation of 'animals and large implements' argued that communes could not be established in the initial stage: 'for a certain period some elements of individual farming will remain within the framework of the kolkhoz—the household plot, the nursery garden, small livestock, poultry and various other branches of the economy'.[125] This left unclear what was to be done with the peasants' cows, but did at least set certain limits to socialisation; and in practice there does not seem to have been any pressure from the North Caucasus authorities for the establishment of communes or AIKs. The situation in the Ukraine seems to have been similar. Ukrainian officials later claimed that they had permitted the establishment of a much higher proportion of TOZy than elsewhere in the USSR.[126] However, there was strong pressure in the Ukraine to socialise livestock including, in a number of districts, small domestic animals and birds.[127]

During the all-out drive, changes in the definitions of different types of kolkhozy also encouraged further socialisation. New model Statutes for the TOZ were introduced in the Ukraine and in the RSFSR. In the Ukraine, the model Statute proposed that productive animals and poultry should be socialised;[128] in the RSFSR,

---

[123] P, December 28, 31, 1929.   [124] *Materialy*, vii (1959), 341.

[125] P, January 10, 15, 1930.

[126] *XVI s"ezd* (1931), 603 (N. Demchenko); the proportion of TOZy in the Ukraine on June 1, 1930, was 42.5 per cent as compared with 17.3 per cent for the whole USSR (*Sots. str.* (1935), 320–1).   [127] SZe, February 23, 1930 (Tsil'ko).

[128] Slin'ko (Kiev, 1961), 202 (Statute dated December 7, approved by Narkomzem and Kolkhoztsentr of the Ukraine).

the Statute more vaguely favoured 'all measures to develop kolkhoz livestock and socialise the livestock of the members'.[129] Similar changes were made in the regions. In the Lower Volga, the party committee called for the revision of the regional Statutes so that in the TOZ draught animals, seeds, fodder and breeding cattle should be socialised; in the artel, all productive animals; and in the commune, all property, living arrangements and feeding, with all property transferred to the Indivisible Fund. The Statute for the artel approved by the regional kolkhozsoyuz required the socialisation of '*all* productive and dairy animals'.[130] Such shifts in definition were widespread. An agricultural journal later complained:

> Frequently the association for joint cultivation of land became in essence what was called an agricultural artel a year ago, and the agricultural artel, in the form in which it was introduced in the localities, was in essence something close to a commune.[131]

(D) RESULTS OF THE DRIVE, SPRING 1930

No general picture of the relative importance of the different types of kolkhozy during these months of rapid change can now be reconstructed. Figures showing the proportion of TOZy, artels and communes nominally or actually established during January and February 1930 were rarely published for particular regions, and not published at all for the USSR as a whole; they may not have been collected. In the confusion and haste of the whole process, in many villages peasants were simply nominally inscribed in a kolkhoz without an up-to-date Statute being available: the model Statute for the artel was not published until February 7, when over 8 million households were officially supposed to belong to the kolkhozy (see vol. 1, Table 16).

Socialisation was taken furthest in the case of draught animals and seed. Here the intentions of the central authorities were unambiguous, and the urgency of completing the campaign in time for the spring sowing was obvious to all concerned. Between

---

[129] *Ustav tovarishchestva po obshchestvennoi obrabotke zemli* (16th edn, 1930, clauses 2–3 (Statute dated December 21).

[130] I, April 19, 1930 (A. Kiselev).

[131] NAF, 5, 1930, 30.

January 1 and March 1, socialised draught animals increased from 17·4 to 78·3 per cent of the total number in kolkhozy.[132] The tendency of the first phase of mass collectivisation in the summer of 1929 was thus dramatically reversed. Great efforts were made to collect socialised horses into common stables, for which purpose existing stables, particularly those previously belonging to kulaks, were taken over and converted.[133] The scheme to establish a central machine-horse station in each kolkhoz did not prove viable. Available stables were too small, and experience of managing large stables was completely lacking. With central stables, the journey from peasant cottage to stable to field was lengthened, and personal responsibility diminished.[134] In the Ukraine, only 85,000 of more than 1 million socialised horses were located in machine-horse stations on February 10.[135] A delay often occurred between formal socialisation and the transfer of the horse to a common stable.[136] But evidently most horses were transferred: in later discussions it was taken for granted that horses had already been removed from the household of their former owner.[137]

The seed campaign was at first less successful, and gave rise to much anxiety among the authorities (see vol. 1, p. 239). But by March 10 enough seed was collected to enable sowing to take place on 80 per cent of the land nominally collectivised at this peak moment in the collectivisation drive (see vol. 1, p. 253); this was more than adequate for the land which remained in the kolkhozy after the huge exodus of peasants in March and April.

---

[132] The following figures for draught animals were reported in I, March 9, 1930 (millions):

	January 20 [? January 1]	February 1	February 10	February 20	March 1
Total in kolkhozy	2·11	5·16	8·43	10·53	11·93
Total socialised	0·37	2·76	5·67	8·55	9·35

[133] See, for example, P, January 13, 1930 (Khoper okrug).
[134] See SZe, June 22, 1930 (I. Kudinov).
[135] P, February 22, 1930.
[136] See for example Shatskin in P, March 1, 1930 (referring to Lower Volga region); at this point he was still calling for complete transfer to common stables four weeks before field work began.
[137] See for example SZe, March 30, 1930, in which Tsil'ko describes the temporary transfer of the horse to its former owner as 'a very dangerous experiment which might lead to the break up of the kolkhoz', and also I, April 19, 1930 (Kiselev); NAF, 6, 1930, 103, 107, 110.

No precise information is available about the extent to which socialisation of cattle and other livestock was actually carried out. The claims of some RSKs look very impressive: Shatrovo district in the Urals claimed that 56 per cent of cows were socialised as early as December 1929, and Khoper okrug reported that in seven large kolkhozy as many as 70 per cent of cows, 64 per cent of sheep and goats and 69 per cent of pigs aged more than one year were socialised.[138] These areas were certainly not representative: in the Central Volga region as a whole, 43 per cent of productive animals were reported to have been socialised by January 15;[139] in the Ukraine, percentages varied between 5 and 30 in different okrugs on February 10.[140] An even lower percentage was recorded by Khlebotsentr, which reported that in the kolkhozy which belonged to grain cooperatives, which included 3·3 million households, only 600,000 productive animals were socialised, a mere 11 per cent of the plan.[141] All these are far below the equivalent percentages for the socialisation of draught animals. Even so, like the figures published at this time for the number of households in kolkhozy (see vol. 1, pp. 443–4), they often record transactions which took place purely on paper. As in the case of draught animals, the central authorities encouraged collective farmers to construct common animal sheds,[142] and at first they also urged that all socialised animals should be transferred to such makeshift buildings (see p. 91 above). In view of the harm caused by hasty transfer, however, they eventually agreed that the former owners of the animals should keep them for the time being, and many animals were therefore simply listed as belonging to the kolkhoz without being transferred to collective buildings.[143] A spokesman for the Lower Volga region at the conference of RSKs in January 1930 reported that

hundreds of thousands of horses, oxen, cows, pigs, and small animals have already been brought into collective stables,

[138] P, December 24, 1929, January 13, 1930.
[139] P, February 16, 1930 (Khataevich).
[140] SZe, February 23, 1930 (Tsil'ko).
[141] SZe, February 22, 1930.
[142] See for example the article by G. Krumin launching Livestock Month, P, January 1, 1930, the editorial in SKhG, January 1, 1930, and SKhG, January 11, 1930 (I. Vrachev).
[143] See, for Khoper okrug, *Krasnyi Khoper*, December 14, 1929, and P, January 13, 1930.

cowsheds, sheep farms and pigsties, and for hundreds of thousands of other animals retention notes (okhrannye zapiski) have been issued.[144]

Throughout these months, sale and destruction of livestock by the peasants continued, in spite of the legislation to prevent it. As the drive for socialisation intensified, so did the destruction of animals. At a meeting of members of TsIK in December 1929, Mikoyan spoke of animals being thrown on the market in masses.[145] On January 9 Andreev described 'really rapacious squandering (razbazarivanie)' in the North Caucasus of 'simply dangerous dimensions', from which it would take four or five years to recover.[146] Vol'f also admitted that 'the losses to our livestock from kulak agitation cannot be immediately cured'.[147] Those animals which survived often entered the kolkhozy in a pitiable state. A speaker at the first conference of women collective farmers in December 1929 acidly remarked:

It is necessary to put pressure on collective farmers that animals should be fed as they were before entering the kolkhoz. Otherwise the several million horses which are to be socialised will go into the kolkhozy in a state in which they won't be able to drag their own legs, let alone a plough.[148]

After socialisation, problems and losses continued. In the makeshift collective stables, cattlesheds and pigsties, the animals were badly looked after.[149] Organisation was poor and incentives were inadequate.[150] Cows were shifted from one household to another when they were on the point of calving, and a considerable number died as a result.[151] After investigating the Lower Volga region in March, a senior government official reported:

---

[144] P, January 12, 1930.
[145] EZh, December 7, 1929.
[146] P, January 10, 15, 1930.
[147] NAF, 2, 1930, 5; all official plans, however, expected complete recovery within a year.
[148] P, December 24, 1929.
[149] PKh, 9, 1930, 120 (K. Kindeev).
[150] See for example I, January 24, 1930 (Yakovlev).
[151] B, 5, March 15, 1930, 51 (Syrtsov).

The management of livestock in several kolkhozy is simply *repulsive*. Cows are almost up to their knees in dung, and horses are not looked after properly either, which in general is leading to a fairly considerable *death rate* of draught animals. Pigs and poultry are also perishing in some places.[152]

In those kolkhozy in which poultry were collectivised, they were often kept in insanitary conditions, and sometimes fatal epidemics broke out.[153] And when cows and other livestock were left with the household which originally owned them, the peasant had little interest in looking after them. Speaking in Voronezh on February 19, Kalinin argued that to leave collectivised cows with their former owners until the autumn would risk considerable losses.[154] The fodder situation, generally difficult in the winter of 1929–30 (see vol. 1, pp. 44–5), was worse for collectivised livestock. No measures similar to those used in the seed campaign were taken to obtain fodder. Kindeev claimed that the planned expansion of socialised livestock did not take the question of fodder into account: even the inadequate existing plans for grasses and root crops had not been met, plans to store fodder in silos had hardly been carried out at all, and the results had never been checked.[155] Socialised fodder was badly managed: owing to the absence of feeding standards socialised animals often at first 'stood up to their stomachs in hay', but by sowing time nothing was left to feed the horses.[156] Touring RSKs in March, Preobrazhensky reported that fodder was the main problem; if it was not solved by improving crop rotation in the spring of 1930, the towns would remain on hunger rations in 1931.[157]

(E) THE RETREAT FROM SOCIALISATION, FEBRUARY–JUNE 1930

Socialisation was one of the major issues in the radical reconsideration of policy which took place in the last three weeks of

---

[152] I, April 19, 1930 (Kiselev); in his reply on this point, Sheboldaev merely grumbled that this line of argument helped the Right wing (P, April 27, 1930).

[153] SZe, February 26, 1930.

[154] P, March 3, 1930; the date of this report is given in Kalinin, ii (1960), 628.

[155] PKh, 9, 1930, 121–2 (Kindeev).

[156] NAF, 5, 1930, 37 (Tsil'ko).   [157] P, March 18, 1930.

February 1930,[158] and vacillation and confusion were amply displayed in the press. The statements in favour of the socialisation of livestock in the Sovnarkom decree of February 13 and the central committee resolution of February 15 (see p. 93 above) were the last to be made at the highest level. But an article in *Pravda* on February 17, and an editorial on the following day, made no reservations in their references to further socialisation of 'commodity-productive' livestock, and as late as February 26 the agricultural newspaper still assumed in a small item in its columns that 60–80 per cent of poultry in kolkhozy would be collectivised in the spring of 1930.[159] During the previous fortnight, however, such a radical change in policy had taken place that this already seemed to be the extravagances of a far-off era. On February 11, Syrtsov, formerly an enthusiastic protagonist of socialisation (see p. 82 above), and now turning into an even more vigorous advocate of caution, recommended at the Sovnarkom of the RSFSR that cows, while remaining in kolkhozy in social ownership, should be left in the household if improved common cattlesheds were not available.[160] On February 14, Mikoyan published an article on the 'meat problem' which managed to avoid the whole question of the socialisation of peasant cows.[161] On the following day, the agricultural newspaper reported without comment that it was now planned to socialise 6 million milk cows, all of which must be provided with warm stalls and fodder, in the whole of 1930; this was a substantial reduction on the plan of 11 million announced only three days earlier.[162] By this time Kalinin, Ordzhonikidze and Kaganovich were in the provinces investigating the situation on behalf of the Politburo (see vol. 1, p. 267). On February 16, Kalinin told collective farmers in the Central Black-Earth region that in his opinion they could be allowed to retain their own pigs and poultry, temporarily and as an exception, but did not apparently mention cows.[163] Three days later, on February 19, he reported his meetings with collective farmers to the regional soviet executive committee and the Voronezh soviet:

---

[158] For other aspects of this reconsideration see p. 51 above and vol. 1, pp. 261–7.

[159] SZe, February 26, 1930.

[160] SZe, February 11, 1930; this recommendation was embodied in the decree of the Sovnarkom of the RSFSR dated February 11 (SZe, February 12, 1930).

[161] SZe, February 14, 1930.

[162] SZe, February 15, 1930 (A. Demchenko); for the earlier figure see p. 93 above.   [163] IISO, [i] (1964), 283.

If comrade Birn and I had not expressed our opinion and had relied on the natural development of the debate, then most probably collective farmers in all cases would have resolved to collectivise hens and piglets.

According to Kalinin, this enthusiasm came primarily not from the peasants but from party members, who were afraid of being accused of Right deviation. Kalinin now mentioned the socialisation of dairy cattle, arguing that it called for 'tremendous tact', and that it was necessary to move more slowly for reasons of expediency.[164] The following day, February 20, *Pravda* carried an article by Milyutin stressing the importance of socialisation, but arguing that '*to do it in a hurry, or only for show*' was '*completely impermissible*'; in the first stage kolkhozy specialising in grain and not livestock should not attempt to socialise cows. This seems to have been the first published statement at this time to urge moderation in the socialisation of cows. While no Politburo decision on this matter has been reported, this article obviously had the backing of higher party authorities: Milyutin was not the kind of man who would act independently on such an issue. The views of Yakovlev, who persistently resisted excessive socialisation, had now begun to prevail: the shift in policy was made easier because Stalin had never publicly endorsed the immediate socialisation of animals. On the same day Syrtsov, in a strongly-worded speech to the party cell of the Institute of Red Professors, which was not published until nearly a month later, anticipated many of the major points in Stalin's article of March 2 and in the central committee resolution of March 14. He described the 'reduction of the forces of production' in such sectors as livestock as 'very serious', though partly 'the inevitable overheads of revolution', and he attacked hasty efforts to turn kolkhozy into communes, which sometimes 'even' involved the socialisation of poultry and small animals:

> *The main issue now is not to drag as many cows and hens as possible into the kolkhozy but to organise people and horses correctly for work in the kolkhoz.*[165]

[164] P, March 3, 1930; for the date of this speech see vol. 1, p. 255, n. 232. This text of the speech was published after Stalin's article of March 2 and the new Statute of March 1, and may therefore have been tampered with.

[165] B, 5, March 15, 1930, 47, 51; this speech was not published until after Stalin's article and the resolution of March 14, and may also have been tampered with.

On February 21, on Ordzhonikidze's recommendation, the party central committee in the Ukraine resolved that the socialisation of 'small productive livestock' (i.e. sheep and pigs) should cease; cows were apparently not mentioned.[166] Thus far emphasis was placed on ceasing the socialisation of pigs and sheep and on reducing, but for the time being only, the rate of socialisation of cows. On February 21, however, a *Pravda* editorial, presumably prompted by the Politburo meeting of the previous day, went much further: it condemned the socialisation of any animals, including cows as well as pigs, sheep and poultry, which were not 'commodity in character', coolly reminding its readers that the Statute of February 6 had required the socialisation 'only' (the word does not appear in the Statute) of draught animals and productive livestock:

> Peasant livestock which is not commodity-productive in charac-
> ter, and dairy cattle, the socialisation of which will not help to
> increase marketed production (tovarnost') must remain in the
> personal use of collective farmers.

Numerous articles on these lines now followed. The need for caution in the socialisation of livestock was one of the major themes of Stalin's article of March 2. Stalin insisted that the grain problem was the '*main link of the kolkhoz movement*', the solution of which was a prerequisite for the solution of the problems of livestock and industrial crops. The artel was the best type of kolkhoz for solving the grain problem, and therefore must predominate at present. Stalin restored the original definitions of the three types of kolkhoz. In the TOZ, now a 'past stage', means of production were not yet socialised; in the commune, for which 'conditions are not yet ripe', distribution was socialised as well as production. In the artel:

> The main means of production are socialised, mainly those for
> grain farming: labour, land utilisation, machines and other
> implements, draught animals, farm buildings. The following *are
> not socialised*: the lands of the household plot (small nursery
> gardens, orchards), dwellings, a certain part of the dairy cattle,
> small livestock, poultry, etc.

Socialisation of small livestock and poultry was being carried out by

166 IZ, lxxvi (1965), 26.

'the issuing of bureaucratic decrees on paper' when conditions were not ripe; this was 'stupid and harmful rushing ahead'.[167] The new version of the model Statute, also published on March 2, followed the same lines. It recommended that one cow should be retained per household; sheep and pigs should be socialised only in areas of 'developed industrial farming of small livestock', and even then collective farmers should retain some animals. Poultry should not be socialised at all. The Statute also recommended that households should retain implements with which to work their household plot.[168] The resolution of March 14 added that artels could in future be re-registered as communes only with the approval of the okrug soviet or kolkhozsoyuz,[169] and on the same day Narkomzem ordered that such re-registrations must cease immediately.[170] Finally, on April 2 Stalin further undermined the position of the communes by declaring that while a number of long-established communes were 'splendid', they should nevertheless be turned into artels; he added for good measure that it would be a long time before conditions were ripe for the transformation of existing artels into communes.[171]   The reasons for these more cautious policies were stated fairly frankly. First, the middle peasants were not ready for this degree of socialisation, and were antagonised by it. Forced socialisation was treated in Stalin's article of March 2 as a major cause of peasant dissatisfaction 'useful only to our accursed enemies'.[172] An editorial in *Pravda* claimed that socialisation of livestock kept by peasants for consumption purposes had been used by kulaks to stir up anti-Soviet agitation.[173] An article on the role of women in the kolkhozy frankly admitted that those who 'strive to socialise everything straightaway' were 'ignoring the feelings of what is sometimes a significant part of the population', and reported that 'anti-Soviet demonstrations of peasant women' had occurred 'in a number of places'; in a village in Khoper okrug an illegal meeting called by kulaks had resolved 'not to give hens, cows and children to the kolkhoz'.[174] Peasant destruction of livestock was

[167] *Soch.*, xii, 195–8.
[168] P, March 2, 1930 (clause four, as in the previous Statute—see p. 91, n. 95 above).
[169] *Resheniya*, ii (1967), 196.
[170] SZe, March 14, 1930.
[171] *Soch.*, xii, 223–4.
[172] *Ibid.* 197–8.
[173] P, February 21, 1930.
[174] P, February 22, 1930.

usually attributed not to forced socialisation but to the influence of the deliberate campaign sponsored by the kulaks.

Secondly, forced socialisation was criticised for distracting attention from the grain problem, and in particular from preparations for the spring sowing:

> One might think [Stalin wrote] that the grain problem is already solved in the kolkhozy, that it is already a past stage, that the main task at the present moment is not the solution of the grain problem, but the solution of the problem of livestock breeding and poultry raising.[175]

Thirdly, socialisation, and the removal of the market regulators of the economic activity of the peasantry, was said to have encouraged 'an explosion of consumptionist tendencies'.[176] *Pravda* now admitted that hasty socialisation resulted in a fall in productivity, and pointed out that this did not make animals 'commodity-productive', but merely eliminated commodity production, including the supply of milk to the market.[177]

In March and April 1930, 8 million households left the kolkhozy, taking with them some 7 million draught animals (see Table 5), and an unknown number of socialised livestock. Within the kolkhozy which remained, a dual process occurred: the socialisation of draught animals continued and was almost completed, but the collective farmers removed from socialisation a large number of other animals which were previously socialised either nominally or in fact. The census of May 1930 revealed that as many as 95·1 per cent of draught animals were socialised, as compared with 78·3 per cent on March 1 and only 44·1 per cent on June 1, 1929 (see Table 5). Socialised draught animals in kolkhozy amounted to 16 per cent of the total number of draught animals in the USSR, as against only 1 per cent on June 1, 1929.[178] A far smaller percentage of cattle and other livestock was socialised by May 1930. But the absolute increase as compared with June 1, 1929 was impressive;[179] and, in spite of all the fluctuations in policy, the proportion of kol-

---

[175] *Soch.*, xii, 197; see also P, February 22, 1930.
[176] B, 5, March 15, 1930, 47 (Syrtsov).
[177] P, February 21, 1930.
[178] Calculated from Table 5 and vol. 1, Table 2.
[179] The following are the percentages of total numbers in the USSR socialised in kolkhozy in May 1930 (percentages for June 1, 1929 in brackets): cattle 5 (0.6), sheep and goats 5 (0.5), pigs 6 (0.6) (for the statistics on which these percentages are based see Table 6 and vol.1, Table 2).

khoz animals which were socialised increased substantially: the percentage of socialisation increased from 24·0 per cent of all cows in kolkhozy on June 1, 1929, to 33·9 per cent in May 1930.[180] The main type of kolkhoz was now the artel: in May 1930 73·7 per cent of kolkhozy were in artels, and only 17·3 per cent in TOZy, as compared with 33·6 and 60·2 per cent on June 1, 1929 (see Table 4).

The increase in socialisation took place against the sombre background of a decline in the total number of draught animals and of all kinds of livestock. In less than twelve months all the increases of 1925–8 had been wiped out (see vol. 1, Table 2); and the decline was particularly substantial in the case of animals less than one year old. At least in the case of horses and cows it was physically impossible for the losses to be replaced for at least the next 18 months.

The new arrangements announced during March cleared up some of the most obvious ambiguities in official policy, but left lesser ones unresolved. First, while the right of the kolkhoz household to own a cow, sheep, pigs and poultry, and to work its own plot, was assured, a certain vagueness remained. The size of the household plot was not regulated. The right to own calves as well as a cow was not mentioned in the model Statute, and peasants continued to kill off their calves until this point was cleared up.[181] The boundary between 'commodity' and 'consumption' livestock remained somewhat indefinite. Although the model Statute permitted only one cow per household, Vareikis held that collective farmers had a complete right to keep their own cows unless they were of a *'purely commodity-industrial* character'; in his opinion, only the surplus sheep and pigs of the richer part of the peasantry should be socialised, and even then compensation should normally be paid.[182] Others were less prepared to return completely to past practices, and much discussion took place on the familiar question of the relationship between the size of the family, the number of animals and the size of the household plot. The prevailing view was that households with more than four or five members should be permitted to retain more

---

[180] *Nar. kh.* (1932), 130–1; 300,000 of the 1,400,000 cows in the socialised sector of the kolkhozy, or some 7 per cent of all cows in kolkhozy, were stated to have been expropriated from kulaks (PKh, 7–8, 1930, 66).

[181] Chigrinov (1970), 55–6.

[182] P, March 4, 1930; a writer in the agricultural newspaper wanted cows to be socialised only in areas of *'developed commodity-productive* livestock' (SZe, June 10, 1930).

than one cow, and should be allocated a larger household plot.[183]

Secondly, while collective farmers had an unrestricted right to take their products to market (see p. 160 below), it remained unclear whether they were required to sell part of the products of the household plot to the state. This was to remain a sensitive issue for the next 40 years. In March and April 1930, however, it was mentioned only cursorily.[184]

Thirdly, the official endorsement of the continued existence of a 'dual economy', the individual and socialised sectors of the kolkhoz, gave rise to new problems. A survey in the North Caucasus revealed that the socialisation of arable farming encroached drastically on the normal functioning of the individual household. The peasant customarily used his horse to fetch water, to take grain to the mill, to go to the hospital and the bazaar, to visit relatives and to go fishing. Now some kolkhozy required their members to give notice a day or two in advance, and to queue, before they could borrow a horse. Some peasants, with influence with the groom, got an unfair advantage; others, who did not use the horses much, still had to contribute to their maintenance; keen collective farmers did not have time to queue.[185] Nor was it clear whether the collective farmer was entitled to use kolkhoz horses on his household plot. An article in the agricultural newspaper insisted that for the collective farmer to take his horse home until the harvest would be 'a very dangerous experiment which might lead to the break-up of the kolkhoz'; on the other hand, it would annoy the collective farmer to observe his former horse standing idle.[186] Eventually it was agreed that horses and implements should be made available for the household plot; a small charge for this was to be arranged by the general meeting or meeting of plenipotentiaries of the kolkhoz, to be deducted from earnings at the end of the economic year.[187]

Equally contentious problems arose with livestock in individual possession. In some kolkhozy, cows were deprived of pasture, all the

[183] SZe, April 11, June 10, 1930 (N. Nikol'skii, I. Urmanskii); P. July 10, 1930, disk. listok 30.

[184] According to Vareikis, in P, March 4, 1930, sales would be 'at the personal discretion' of the collective farmer; according to SZe, April 11, 1930, the disposal of the 'marketable surplus' from the household plot should be determined by the kolkhoz board and general meeting, which would make contracts with the agricultural cooperatives.

[185] B, 11–12, June 30, 1930, 108–9 (survey of Eisk district).

[186] SZe, March 30, 1930 (Tsil'ko).

[187] SZe, April 11, 1930.

land surrounding the village being sown to grain, and the distant land, occasionally 20 or 30 kilometres away, lacked a well. Frequently collective farmers, accustomed to taking their poultry with them into the steppe to feed, could do so no longer, and therefore killed and ate them.[188] The problem of fodder for both socialised and individually-owned animals in the autumn and winter of 1930–1 loomed before the collective farmer. A writer in *Pravda*, reporting that the newspaper had received numerous queries on this subject, suggested that the kolkhozy should make contracts for products from the individual economy of their members, including manure, in return for supplying them with fodder.[189]

The household plot and the individual ownership of livestock undoubtedly fostered inequality within the artel. Poor peasants had relinquished their only means of production, their horse and plough, and depended entirely on the socialised sector for their income, while middle peasants still retained one or more cows and various other animals; in the Central Volga region, some batraks and poor peasants left the kolkhozy as a result.[190] Long-standing members of kolkhozy also had no cows of their own, and had to buy milk.[191] More generally, those who worked diligently for the kolkhoz did not have enough time to cultivate their household plot, and their income declined as a result: in the spring of 1930 reports already appeared of collective farmers who neglected the kolkhoz fields, or left them after a morning's work, in order to cultivate their own plots [192] The tension between household plot and collective work remained a permanent feature of the kolkhoz, usually resolved by the collective farmer in favour of his own plot.

Yakovlev's theses to the XVI party congress, published on May 19, 1930 (see vol. 1, p. 323) provided an occasion for a general review of the disastrous experience of the previous nine months. Past practices in socialisation were again bluntly condemned:

> To require peasants, when they enter the artel, to renounce immediately all individualistic habits and interests, the possibility of carrying on, in addition to the social, a personal economy

---

[188] B, 11–12, June 30, 1930, 107, 109.
[189] P, May 9 (O. Popova), 31, 1930.
[190] *XVI s"ezd* (1931), 619.
[191] Hindus (1934), 151; P, May 31, 1930.
[192] P, May 1, 31, 1930. ᐟ

(a cow, sheep, poultry, the vegetable garden of the household plot) and the possibility of themselves using earnings on the side, etc.—this is to forget the ABC of marxism – leninism.[193]

The theses further confirmed that the establishment of communes must await the further development of technology and experience, and commended the establishment of TOZy, as a transitional stage, in certain non-grain areas and in the national republics of the East. But they did not propose a return to the individual peasant economy, whether within or outside the kolkhoz, as the primary, or even the major, means of solving the livestock problem. While admitting the existence of a 'crisis of livestock farming', they also stressed the bright prospects opening up after the success of the spring sowing campaign: the solution of the grain problem would in itself result in an improvement in industrial crops and livestock, and demonstrated that other branches of agriculture could, like grain farming, be developed through collectivisation and state farming. Particular emphasis was placed on the establishment of livestock sovkhozy modelled on the grain sovkhozy, and the 'mass establishment of special farms (fermy) with a high degree of marketability' within the kolkhozy.[194]

In the pre-congress discussions of the next few weeks, the unease felt by many party members was reflected only in a few outbursts by bold critics. Mamaev, in the course of his indictment of the party authorities, firmly blamed them for 'repressive measures' in consequence of which the middle peasants had 'barbarously destroyed' marketable and breeding animals and a food crisis had resulted.[195] From the opposite extreme, another contributor to the discussion urged that without the immediate socialisation of all means of production, including cows and pigs, the kolkhozy would remain 'weak and pitiful'; while the individual economy remained, the collective farmer would continue to devote more attention to it.[196] Both deviations were vigorously condemned by other contributors, as was a more modest proposal that in the national areas collectivisation, even in the form of TOZy, should not be embarked upon until land consolidation was complete.[197]

[193] *KPSS v rez.*, ii (1954), 52.
[194] *Ibid.* 55–6.
[195] P, June 10, 1930, disk. listok 9; for other aspects of this article see vol. 1, p. 325.
[196] P, June 2, 1930, disk. listok 6 (P. Medvedskii).
[197] A. Avtorkhanov in P, June 22, 1930, disk. listok 17. Avtorkhanov was

The livestock problem, and the wider question of the degree of socialisation in kolkhozy, were both prominent themes in the proceedings of the party congress, which met from June 26 to July 13, 1930. The official speakers, while continuing to condemn excessive socialisation, emphasised the universal advantages of large-scale economy. In the political report, Stalin recited statistics of the decline in livestock and in marketed meat output and attributed the decline to 'the instability and economic unreliability of small-scale economy and of economy with a low level of marketability'; the way forward was to 'follow the road which we followed in solving the grain problem', namely to organise sovkhozy and kolkhozy.[198] Yakovlev, in his report on the kolkhoz movement and the development of agriculture, also stressed the importance of large-scale socialised special livestock farms within the kolkhozy, claiming that large-scale pig breeding and the improved feeding of cattle would enable the consumption of meat and milk to be doubled during the five-year plan. In a sub-section on 'Inequality among Members of the Artel', he turned to a theme which underlay many of the anxieties expressed in previous discussions. While rejecting any notion that class antagonism between the poor peasant and the middle peasant was a feature of the kolkhoz, he admitted that 'inequality of property' resulted from the continued existence of an individual peasant economy within the kolkhoz:

> The inequality which subsists between factory workers in the USSR is in the main a result of the varying quantity and quality of labour, the varying skills of the workers. But in the artel, in which the output of the socialised economy is in the main distributed according to the quantity and quality of labour, there is this inequality and also an additional inequality, resulting from the varying property position, the varying dimensions of the supplementary individual economy of the middle and the poor peasant.

---

denounced in P, June 26, 1930, disk. listok 21 (K. Tabolov) and June 30, 1930, disk. listok 25 (L. Gotfrid), and recanted in P, July 4, 1930; he reported after emigrating that he had been threatened with expulsion from the party because of his article, and was eventually removed from the Institute of Red Professors and sent to work in the press bureau of the central committee (Avtorkhanov (Munich, 1959), 167–75).

[198] *Soch.*, xii, 275–6, 333.

The solution was to increase the socialised income of the kolkhoz systematically, thus reducing the proportion of this income which the collective farmer received from the individual sector, 'not hurrying unnecessarily or getting nervous'.[199]

A temperate but definite emphasis on the paramount importance of the socialised sector in solving the livestock problem also pervaded the congress debates. A speaker from the Northern region contended that in the North, Siberia, Kazakhstan and elsewhere socialised cattlesheds and fodder should be the central feature of the artel.[200] Lominadze, asserting that class distinctions and political differences would continue as long as private property remained within the kolkhozy, urged that their poor peasant groups should continue and that the elimination of economic inequality should 'not proceed all that slowly'.[201] Only Kalinin stressed that a successful pig-breeding programme must involve the individual economy of the collective farmer, and warned that the arguments about the need to eliminate petty-bourgeois tendencies might result in a harmful reduction in the size of the individual economy within the kolkhoz.[202]

(F) SOCIALISATION RESURGENT, JULY–DECEMBER 1930

In the course of the next few months, the rival themes of the expediency of providing proper facilities for the individual economy of the collective farmer, and the desirability of encouraging the socialised sector, continued in uneasy harness. While the party congress was still in session, a resolution of the central control commission and Rabkrin called upon the kolkhozy to provide enough animal power and implements to enable non-socialised vegetable gardens, melon plots and orchards to be cultivated, and, at least in principle, settled the conflict about the provision of kolkhoz fodder to non-socialised productive animals by ruling that it should be provided, but as part of payment for work on the kolkhoz.[203] A few weeks later, an explanatory note of Narkomzem and Kolkhoztsentr declared that the model Statute did not limit the

[199] *XVI s"ezd* (1931), 579–80, 591–2.
[200] *Ibid.* 171.
[201] *Ibid.* 195–6.
[202] *Ibid.* 635.
[203] SZe, July 13, 1930.

right of collective farmers to rear calves or to buy and breed cattle and other livestock; it thus in effect extended the permitted size of the personal economy.[204] Simultaneously, however, plans were announced for a steady increase in the socialisation of kolkhoz animals. By the spring of 1931, the socialised dairy herd in kolkhozy was to expand from 1·5 million to 3·3 million, 1·5 million of these being located in special livestock farms within the kolkhozy. In the same period, the number of collective farmers was planned to double, so the proportion of socialised cows was to increase; other socialised livestock was planned to expand even more rapidly.[205] At a conference of planning officials in September 1930 Vol'f stressed the urgency of carrying out socialisation so that additional meat and dairy supplies were available by the spring of 1931.[206]

During the autumn of 1930, the authorities, in preparing for the further collectivisation drive, frequently stressed the importance of socialised livestock in kolkhozy and the inadequacy of the preparations for it. After a tour of the Central Black-Earth region and the Ukraine, Yurkin, the head of Kolkhoztsentr, condemned the 'complete inactivity' of the kolkhozy in this respect.[207] Andreev, in a report to the Politburo at the end of November 1930, claimed that in the North Caucasus socialised cattlesheds and poultry farms were being constructed on a substantial scale, and emphasised that kolkhozy should increase the socialised sector of the non-grain branches of their economy generally; all this would reduce the role of the individual economy, and 'eliminate duality'.[208] At this time the central agencies acquired greater powers to purchase livestock from all sectors of the economy, and a centralised system for vegetable deliveries was introduced (see vol. 1, pp. 362–8). With these levers of control, even if the personal economy of the collective farmer and the individual peasant could not be socialised immediately, it would be brought under stricter state control. At the same time, part of the livestock purchased by the state from peasants and collective farmers would be sold to kolkhozy to build up their socialised farms. Of the credit to kolkhozy of 1,000 million rubles planned for 1931, at least 400 millions were earmarked for livestock farming;[209] and Andreev urged kolkhozy to raise money from their

---

[204] SZ, 1930, art. 446 (dated August 25).   [205] SZe, July 27, 1930.
[206] PKh, 7–8, 1930, 58; he was the chief agricultural planner in Gosplan.
[207] SZe, October 15, 1930.
[208] Andreev (Rostov, 1931), 17, 22.
[209] SZ, 1930, art. 442 (Sovnarkom decree of August 11).

members for the purchase of livestock for their socialised sector.[210]

The joint plenum of the party central committee and central control commission in December 1930 heard a report from Mikoyan on the meat question. Attributing the difficulties of the past year to the 'kulak manoeuvre' which resulted in the destruction of large numbers of animals in the spring, he urged the development of specialised livestock kolkhozy in association with the large livestock sovkhozy; this, together with the establishment of 100–200 'livestock MTS', would make livestock farming as advanced as grain farming. Rejecting all suggestions that the pressure of the new system of official livestock collections would lead the peasants to reduce their livestock still further, he confidently predicted that the meat problem would be solved in 1932.[211] Although the authorities temporarily permitted the establishment of a clearly defined individual sector within the kolkhozy, and now intended to eliminate it gradually by example rather than immediately by persuasion, they were fully persuaded that the economic advantages of large-scale mechanised farming were so considerable that the individual sector would rapidly dwindle into insignificance. They had no conception of the magnitude of the further livestock crisis which would develop during the next two years.

---

[210] Andreev (Rostov, 1931), 22.
[211] B, 1, January 15, 1930, 14, 21–3; this is described as the 'shortened stenogram of the report'.

CHAPTER SIX

KOLKHOZ INCOME AND CAPITAL

The kolkhoz, like the individual peasant economy, was to a considerable extent a subsistence farm: part of the gross production of its socialised sector was used in kind to feed its members and its livestock, to provide seed and so on. This part of production thus became an income in kind, which did not involve a monetary transaction. The rest of kolkhoz production was sold to the state or on the market, and provided the major part of kolkhoz money income. Income in kind and money income were frequently combined and confused in the statistics, which did not always distinguish clearly between the *money* income of the kolkhoz, and the substantially larger total income *in money terms*, which included an estimate of the value of the kolkhoz income in kind.

The main sources of kolkhoz income in this wider sense were as follows:

(1) Membership fees in money and in kind, paid by peasants when joining the kolkhoz.
(2) Agricultural and other production retained in kind within the kolkhoz.
(3) Kolkhoz production sold to the state or on the market.
(4) Other payments by the peasants to the kolkhoz—e.g. a proportion of their money income from otkhodnichestvo.
(5) Money grants and loans from the state.

Kolkhoz expenditure in the wider sense similarly consisted of two major parts: the utilisation or expenditure within the kolkhoz of its income in kind, and the expenditure of its money income.

Income in kind was allocated in two principal directions:

(1) Collective requirements. These included working capital for further production—e.g. fodder for animals, which might be set aside in a Fodder Fund. Similarly some products might be allocated to a Fund to maintain the sick and elderly, etc.

(2) Individual requirements. Production was distributed in kind to collective farmers as remuneration for their work, for use as food, or as fodder for their personally owned animals (part of the distributed production might subsequently be sold by the collective farmer on the market).

Money income was allocated as follows:

(1) To pay taxes and repay loans.
(2) To various Funds for investment and other purposes.
(3) To collective farmers as remuneration for their work.

The fixed capital of the kolkhoz also included both capital in kind—its collectively owned equipment, animals and buildings—and capital held as money in its collective Funds (when it had any).

The pattern of kolkhoz income and expenditure was affected by two major issues, or decisions. The first, discussed in chapter 5, was the extent of socialisation within the kolkhoz. The shifts in the degree of socialisation affected the proportion of the total economic activity of the kolkhoz which formed part of its collectively managed, or socialised, income and expenditure, both in kind and in money.

The second major issue was the division of the income of the kolkhoz between collective and individual needs. The longer-term collective interest in investment and the immediate personal interest in consumption were perpetually in conflict. In the weak kolkhozy with low incomes characteristic of the 1920s the collective interest suffered.

Initially, most of the land and much of the capital equipment of the kolkhozy were obtained, via the state, from private estates confiscated after the revolution which were not divided up among the peasantry. This land and equipment was legally state property. In 1927 it was formally placed at the disposal of the kolkhozy 'in perpetuity'; on transfer, it was valued, and its value was treated as a 'permanent interest-free loan to the fixed (indivisible) capital of the agricultural collective'.[1] The term 'indivisible' implied that the property or money concerned could not be returned to members if they left the kolkhoz. As early as 1925, a system had already been established whereby members of kolkhozy paid small non-returnable 'membership fees (vstupitel'nye vznosy)', contributed

---

[1] Vlasov and Nazimov (1930), 17; SU, 1927, art. 605 (decree of August 22, 1927).

part of their property to the kolkhoz as 'share payments (pai)', and loaned another part of it to the kolkhoz as a 'deposit (vklad)' on which they were paid interest. By this time some kolkhozy were also already paying a regular share of their income or profits into their indivisible capital.[2] From 1926 onwards, the kolkhoz authorities made much greater efforts to encourage kolkhozy to establish their own 'indivisible capital' for investment purposes by setting aside part of their current money income.[3]

The injunctions to the kolkhozy to establish collective Funds were at first couched in very general terms: a report in 1929 complained that the kolkhozy 'received almost no specific instructions from leading agencies, and therefore have so far groped their way, sometimes simply thinking up different devices out of their heads'.[4] In the spring of 1929 the collective Funds of the kolkhozy were still very weak. Only 48·2 per cent of kolkhozy had formally established Funds of 'indivisible capital', and only 39·4 per cent of this capital was derived from kolkhoz income, almost all the rest being capital loaned by the state in perpetuity. In many kolkhozy, Funds of divisible capital in fees and deposits were also lacking: 67·6 per cent of kolkhozy had established a Fund of membership fees and fees levied on members by the kolkhoz general meeting, but a Fund of returnable 'deposits' of implements, animals, products or money loaned by members existed in only 30·9 per cent of kolkhozy.[5] No information has been traced about the extent to which either indivisible or divisible capital were money savings for future investment rather than merely an evaluation in money terms of property owned or used collectively, but money savings are likely to have been very small. The weak development of collective capital in the spring of 1929 is shown by the fact that, taking all the capital Funds together, in both money and kind, they were smaller than

---

[2] Bauer *et al.* (1925), 20–1. A model Statute current at the time provided that this should be not less than one-fifth of profits (*ibid.* 61); how profits were to be calculated was not stated.

[3] Vlasov and Nazimov (1930), 18–19.

[4] *Ibid.* 27.

[5] *Kolkhozy v 1929 godu* (1931), 136–7; 'deposits' and 'fees' were not always distinguished, and the compilers of the kolkhoz census pointed out that 'owing to the poor development of accounting in many kolkhozy the data on collective funds suffer from a certain incompleteness' (*ibid.* p. xlvi). 'Fees' presumably include 'share payments'. Other sources stated that membership fees, as distinct from other fees and share payments, were not returnable.

outstanding kolkhoz debts.[6] Collective Funds were of course much more strongly developed in artels and in communes than in TOZy: 83·5 per cent of communes, 55·2 per cent of artels and only 39·2 per cent of TOZy possessed indivisible capital, and the amount per kolkhoz was much higher in the communes and artels (see Table 7).

On the eve of comprehensive collectivisation, opinions about the feasibility of substantially enlarging the indivisible capital or Funds of the kolkhozy were divided.[7] At a seminar held in the Communist Academy in the summer or autumn of 1929 an official of the Kolkhoz Council of the USSR reported that proposals to incorporate all the savings of the kolkhozy in their Indivisible Funds had 'very many' supporters in the kolkhoz movement,[8] and at the seminar some speakers proposed that the size of deductions to Funds from kolkhoz income be fixed by central regulations, and not left to the whim of kolkhoz general meetings.[9] But the prevailing mood among the assembled officials was one of caution. An official of the Kolkhoztsentr of the RSFSR pointed out that any increase in the level of the Indivisible Fund could be obtained only by reducing personal income; with an excessive Indivisible Fund 'the economy grows, means of production increase—and members go hungry and have no trousers'.[10] Speakers from the Kolkhoz Council, Gosplan and the agricultural newspaper all recommended caution. One speaker pointed out that 'deductions to these Funds are far from evoking feelings of tenderness and delight among kolkhoz members', while another reported that some artels admitted that

---

[6] The figures are as follows (million rubles):

Indivisible capital	72·0
Deposits	24·6
Fees	38·1
Total collective Funds	134·7
Total outstanding debts	152·9

(*Kolkhozy v 1929 godu* (1931), 126–7); debts were almost all outstanding loans from the state and the cooperatives.

[7] In 1929 the term 'capital' began to be regarded as inappropriate for collective or state property, and to be replaced by the term 'Fund'.

[8] Vlasov and Nazimov (1930), 167; the date of the seminar is not given, but from internal evidence it seems to have taken place before the November plenum.

[9] *Ibid.* 146, 154.

[10] *Ibid.* 132.

payment into the Funds was like a 'sickle cutting the heart'.[11] The spokesman for the Kolkhoz Council of the USSR described a Ukrainian Kolkhoztsentr proposal to increase the size of the Indivisible Fund at the expense of the divisible Funds as 'simple, but not always good politics'.[12] Even the representative of Rabkrin, while insisting on the importance of the Indivisible Fund, agreed that 'it is wrong to force its creation'.[13]

The widespread hesitations were swept aside after the November plenum, at which Molotov strongly insisted that kolkhozy must rely on their own resources and not expect much help from the state (see p. 78 above). In December 1929 the Politburo commission on collectivisation recommended that monetary membership fees for kolkhozy should be fixed at between 5 and 50 rubles for most peasants, while well-to-do middle peasants should pay 100 rubles; the commission calculated that this would yield at least 80–100 million rubles in 1929/30.[14] In addition, at least 10 per cent of the assessed value of the socialised property of members should be allocated to the Indivisible Fund.[15] Ryskulov himself proposed that as much as 50 per cent of socialised capital in artels and 60 per cent in communes should be designated as part of the Indivisible Fund, and therefore not returnable on leaving;[16] it is not known whether the commission made any recommendations on this point.

The model Statute for the artel of February 6, 1930, went much further than the commission in respect of membership fees. It provided that between 2 and 10 per cent of the value of the socialised and non-socialised property of the peasant, except domestic goods and goods for personal use, should be paid into the Indivisible Fund as a 'monetary membership fee'; batraks, however, would pay only five rubles.[17] Membership fees on this scale could be expected to contribute a substantial sum: the value of fixed capital in the autumn of 1929 was about 660 rubles per household, excluding housing, so with fees of 2–10 per cent of property, the 6½ million households which joined kolkhozy in February 1930 were

[11] *Ibid.* 136–7, 148–9, 152–3, 158.
[12] *Ibid.* 167.
[13] *Ibid.* 195 (Kindeev); for Rabkrin see p. 5 above.
[14] VI, 1, 1964, 38; according to this source, entry fees were to be used for *working* capital.
[15] VI, 1, 1964, 38.
[16] P, December 9, 1929.
[17] I, February 7, 1930 (clause 8).

due to pay between 85 and 450 million rubles.[18] The Statute also went some way to meet Ryskulov's proposal by a provision that 25–50 per cent of the socialised property of collective farmers should be allocated to the Indivisible Fund, the higher percentage being applicable to wealthier households. The remaining 50–75 per cent of socialised property would be designated a returnable 'share fee (paevoi vznos)', but would be returnable 'as a rule only after the end of the economic year'. These allocations of socialised property between Indivisible Fund and share fees were of course, unlike the membership fees, transactions in kind; the lumping-together of socialised property and money accumulation in the Funds resulted in much confusion, both for the collective farmers and for future historians.

A further clause of the Statute, clause 11, concerned the proportion of kolkhoz income which was to be allocated to the various Funds, and evidently also covered income both in kind and in money. It read as follows:

11. Expenses for economic purposes and those related to the economy shall be covered from the incomes of the artel received by the end of the economic year, as shall expenditure to maintain those not capable of work; deductions shall be paid into the Indivisible and social Funds (from 10 to 30 per cent into the Indivisible Fund, from 5 to 15 per cent into other social Funds) and due payments to labour (raschety po oplate truda) shall be made.[19]

The wording of clause 11 seemed to imply that the deductions should be made from gross income even before products or money had been set aside for seeds, fodder and other necessary economic expenditure.[20] This would have been an impossibly crippling burden. But even if made from net income these deductions, like the membership fees, were very large, and reflected the extent to which the authorities were committed to socialisation and to forcing the kolkhozy to expand their own investment at their own expense.[21]

---

[18] For fixed capital in individual agriculture see *KTs . . . 1929/30* (1930), 446–9.

[19] P, February 7, 1930.

[20] This interpretation of the model Statute was accepted by Gei, a member of the board of Kolkhoztsentr (SZe, June 24, 1930), but rejected in NFK, 6, 1930, 39.

[21] The model Statute of the commune, approved on December 21, 1929, and still in force throughout the spring of 1930, proposed that 20 per cent of income should

The eagerness of the authorities to introduce a high level of monetary membership fees and deductions from current kolkhoz income was partly due to the large amount of money held by the peasants. Their cash holdings had been increasing relentlessly since the autumn of 1927: rural purchasing power rose rapidly, owing partly to increases in the market prices of agricultural products, and partly to increased rural earnings for seasonal work; and the supply of industrial consumer goods fell far short of the increase in demand (see vol. 1, p. 81). The middle peasants who joined the kolkhozy in the autumn of 1929 certainly held several hundred million rubles in cash, and added to the hoard by selling their animals before joining (see pp. 80–1, 101 above).

The authorities, as well as attempting to increase the Indivisible Funds and working capital of the kolkhozy, also conducted a vigorous campaign to 'mobilise the resources of the countryside' for the general purposes of industrialisation. At first sight, the kolkhozy were treated generously. In accordance with the central committee resolution of January 5, 1930, the plan for agricultural loans to kolkhozy in 1929/30 was increased from 275 to 500 million rubles, primarily by transferring credits originally intended for individual peasant households.[22] But simultaneously the issue of loans was made conditional on the contribution of a proportion of the required resources by the kolkhozy themselves; 'compulsory returnable contributions' to the agricultural credit system were introduced, payable on the same basis as self-taxation.[23] Other measures were also directed towards transferring money from the peasants to the state. On January 8, 1930, a decree called for compulsory collection prior to the due date of loans received by

---

be deducted to the Indivisible Fund and 10 per cent to the Cultural and Welfare, Bonus and other Funds; this Statute did provide that 'income' was what remained after depreciation and taxes had been deducted and economic needs covered, so communes were in a less ambiguous position than artels (NAF, 6, 1930, 39). The model Statute of the TOZ, adopted on the same date, provided that 30 per cent of income, again after economic expenditure had been met, should be allocated to Funds: a minimum of 60 per cent of the total was to be allocated to the Indivisible Fund, 10 per cent to the Cultural Fund, 10 per cent to reserves and 5 per cent to bonuses. This Statute stipulated that membership fees should be 5–100 rubles, and that at least 10 per cent of socialised means of production should be allocated to the Indivisible Fund (*Ustav tovarishchestva po obshchestvennoi obrabotke zemli* (16th edn, 1930), clauses 23–4, 29, 48–9). These Statutes both applied only in the RSFSR.
[22] SKhG, January 7, 1930.
[23] The relevant decrees are summarised in FP, 7–8, 1930, 67.

kulaks from the agricultural credit system.[24] This was followed on February 4, 1930, by a stringently worded decree of Sovnarkom which insisted that all loans to individual peasants which were due for repayment must be paid back to the bank when the peasant joined the kolkhoz, using compulsory procedures if necessary; loans due for repayment after the date of joining would be the responsibility of the kolkhoz itself.[25] During February a vigorous campaign for the immediate elimination of these debts was conducted in the press,[26] and the issue of new loans was made subject to the settlement of past debts in full.[27] Later in February, the collegium of Narkomfin, after a report from the workers' brigade of the electrical engineering works Elektrozavod, resolved to undertake a one-month campaign jointly with Elektrozavod to recover overdue debts in RSKs.[28] Fees to the consumer and agricultural credit cooperatives, and the number of contributors, were also planned to increase substantially. Finally, the kolkhozy were expected to persuade their members to subscribe to the Third Industrialisation Loan, to increase their deposits in the savings banks and to buy 'obligations' for the future purchase of tractors.[29]

No precise figures are available on the results of the campaign. Tractor obligations proved the most popular, and a sum of about 60 million rubles was subscribed (see p. 23 above). Subscriptions amounting to 205 million rubles were taken out for the Industrialisation Loan; only a small part of this sum was actually paid in, however, and payments were particularly sluggish in areas with a higher level of collectivisation. Some 25 million rubles were paid into the agricultural credit system in the form of compulsory deposits. But overdue debts to the agricultural credit system did not fall at all, fees to the cooperatives failed to reach the plan, and deposits in savings banks failed to increase. In most respects, therefore, the campaign was a failure.[30] In consequence, the authorities apparently carried out their threat to refuse loans to recalcitrant kolkhozy.[31]

---

24 FP, 7–8, 1930, 67.
25 SZ, 1930, art. 114.
26 See, for example, SZe, February 14, 1930 (editorial).
27 SZe, March 30, 1930.
28 EZh, February 25, 1930.
29 FP, 7–8, 1930, 66–7.
30 For details see FP, 7–8, 1930, 65–71.
31 Agricultural loans amounting to 235 million rubles were issued to kolkhozy

The financial campaign, reinforcing the natural reluctance of the peasants to hand over their cash to the kolkhozy, undoubtedly inhibited the accumulation of resources in the hands of the kolkhozy themselves. Only a small proportion of the new members actually paid the initial amounts due to the kolkhozy.[32] No precise figures about kolkhoz cash resources in February or March 1930 appear to be available. But there is no doubt that while the collective farmers personally continued to hold cash in large amounts, kolkhoz Funds remained very small, and the level of kolkhoz working capital in the spring of 1930 was described in the agricultural journal as 'almost catastrophic'.[33]

During the retreat from collectivisation the attempt of the state to exact large sums in cash from the peasants and the kolkhozy was called off. As early as February 27, 1930, Syrtsov, who had been extremely active in encouraging financial pressure on the peasantry in previous months, instructed the regional authorities to cease to collect deposits compulsorily, referring to 'difficulties connected with the present organisational period of kolkhoz construction'. He indicated, however, that other payments should be continued.[34] It was not until April 2, 1930, that a decree of TsIK and Sovnarkom withdrew the measures of December 1929 and January 1930: it postponed until November 1 repayment by the kolkhozy of loans to kolkhozy and their members which were overdue, freed them from debts due on property confiscated from the kulaks, cancelled the collection of fees and deposits due to cooperatives and postponed further payment of tractor obligations until the end of the economic year. Kolkhoz payments amounting to over 200 million rubles were cancelled for the economic year 1929/30 alone. At the same time the decree of April 2 emphasised that loans to kolkhozy should, in spite of this loss of state income, reach the figure of 500 million rubles in

---

and MTS in October 1929 – March 1930, which is in excess of what was required in terms of the original plan of 275 million rubles for the year 1929/30, and almost 50 per cent of the revised plan of 500 million rubles (for these plans see p. 122 above), but in January and February 1930 only 33 per cent of the loans planned for the January–March quarter were issued (SO, 3–4, 1930, 19; SO, 6, 1930, 22). This seems to indicate that substantial loans were issued in excess of the plan in October–December 1929 and March 1930, and much smaller amounts during the financial campaign.

[32] SZe, March 9, 1930; in the North Caucasus region, for example, only 7·9 per cent of planned payments had in fact been made by March 1.

[33] NAF, 5, 1930, 42.

[34] FP, 7–8, 1930, 68.

1929/30 which had been approved by the party central committee on January 5, 1930. The kolkhozy were also granted substantial exemptions from agricultural tax.[35] A further decree of April 23 abolished self-taxation of kolkhoz members in the year 1930/31, offered kolkhozy further exemptions from agricultural tax, and made available an additional loan for the spring sowing of 60 million rubles.[36]

All these measures improved the previously impossible financial position of kolkhozy. But they went only a small way towards providing them with adequate working capital. Moreover, the attempt to retain peasants in the kolkhozy on a voluntary basis led the authorities to relinquish in practice the high level of payments into the Indivisible Fund recommended by the model Statute of February 6. The revised model Statute of March 1, 1930, retained the relevant clauses without change. But this could not last. While kolkhozy continued to be urged to collect membership fees from their members in full in money or in easily saleable goods,[37] the 'explanatory note' of April 13, 1930, restricted them to a maximum fee, varying between 5 and 25 rubles according to the wealth of the household.[38] This was much lower than the fees proposed in the model Statute, lower even than the recommendations of the Politburo commission in December 1929 (see p. 120 above).

The proposed size of the Indivisible Fund for the moment remained intact, and this gave rise to much controversy. At a conference of kolkhoz officials in the middle of April, speakers urged that the maximum deduction to Funds of 45 per cent of income, plus a further deduction for those incapable of work, was 'very high', and 'frightened off the poor peasants as well as the middle peasants', because they feared that not enough would remain to feed their families.[39] Appropriate legislation followed during the next few months. On May 31, a circular from Narkomzem and Kolkhoztsentr admitted that most kolkhozy were not strong enough

---

[35] SZ, 1930, art. 230; for the decrees of December 1929 and January 1930, see pp. 122–3 above. According to calculations by the Kolkhoz Bank, kolkhozy were freed from the following payments: share capital and fees due to other organisations, 96 million rubles; debts on land consolidation, 46 million rubles; debts on kulak property transferred to kolkhozy, 10 million rubles; exemption of socialised livestock from agricultural tax, 25 million rubles (IZ, lxxvi (1965), 33–4).

[36] SZ, 1930, art. 261.

[37] SKhIB, 1, April 10, 1930, 22.

[38] SZ, 1930, art. 256.

[39] SZe, April 15, 1930.

economically to carry out deductions even at the minimum level envisaged, and ruled that the deduction should be made not from gross income in money and kind but from income excluding the seed fund, fodder for socialised animals, and sums needed for agricultural tax and for insurance of kolkhoz property:[40] this was roughly equivalent to 'conditional net income' in the accepted terminology. At the XVI party congress in July, Yakovlev stated that only the 'necessary minimum deductions' should be made to kolkhoz Funds (i.e. 10 per cent to the Indivisible Fund and 5 per cent to other Funds) and that 'all the remainder should be distributed to the collective farmers'.[41] A further decree published on July 27, 1930, formally fixed deductions to Funds from income at this level and ruled that any additional deductions must be specifically authorised by a general meeting.[42]

The socialisation of arable farming, including the vast majority of the horses and ploughs of the collective farmers, necessarily involved a substantial increase in Indivisible Funds. The kolkhoz census of May 1930, carried out after the main exodus had already taken place, revealed that 79·0 per cent of kolkhozy had now formed Indivisible Funds, as compared with 48.2 per cent on June 1, 1929. According to the census figures, however, the average Indivisible Fund per household declined from 176 rubles in 1929 to 110 rubles in 1930.[43] Moreover, 34·4 per cent of all Indivisible Funds were acquired from expropriated kulaks, and the proportion was much higher in some kolkhozy, as only 50·1 per cent of kolkhozy possessed Indivisible Funds from this source. Outstanding debts were still large in relation to Indivisible Funds: 455 as compared with 510 million rubles (see Table 7). But the kolkhoz returns for Indivisible Funds were reported to be incomplete, so the size of debts as compared with Funds was exaggerated.[44]

All these figures for Indivisible Funds are certainly unreliable, and provide no more than a general indication of the size of that part of socialised property deemed to be permanently at the disposal of the kolkhozy. The state of kolkhoz accounts, where they existed at

[40] SKhIB, 18, 1930, 7.
[41] *XVI s"ezd* (1931), 642–3; see also Kindeev in PKh, 7–8, 1930, 110–11.
[42] SZe, July 27, 1930.
[43] Calculated from data in Table 7, on the assumption that kolkhozy with Indivisible Funds included the average number of kolkhoz households (18 in 1929 and 70 in 1930).
[44] *Ibid.* p. lv.

all, was chaotic. According to a leading Narkomtorg official, owing to the acute shortage of paper in the countryside, new figures were generally inserted on old tables, and 'in end everything is so confused that it makes the lower officials' heads spin'.[45] At best, accounts were kept on separate sheets of paper, as there were no account books in the kolkhòzy.[46] There was an acute shortage of book-keepers. But there is no reason to doubt the general conclusions of an authoritative report based on returns from the kolkhozy, which showed that monetary working capital was very scarce, and complained that the state made no loans available to tide over the kolkhozy until their income flowed in from the new harvest, the result being that only 'miserly expenditure' was possible during the spring sowing.[47]

In the autumn of 1930, the economic and financial position of the kolkhozy improved considerably. They were more dependent on the harvest for their income than the individual peasants, as both their socialised livestock economy and their non-farming activities were very small: 91·3 per cent of their gross agricultural production came from crops.[48] The socialised sector of the kolkhozy was responsible for 18·2 per cent of all agricultural production, and as much as 25·6 per cent of crop production, and 29·0 per cent of grain.[49] If the production of collective farmers on their household plots is included, kolkhoz production amounted to as much as 23.9 per cent of all kolkhoz and peasant gross output.[50] In the second half of 1930 kolkhozy included some 22–24 per cent of all peasant households and 19–21 per cent of the peasant population.[51] The gross agricultural production per household of kolkhozy, including the household plots, was therefore somewhat higher than that of the

[45] VT, 5, 1930, 13 (Chernov).
[46] EZh, May 27, 1930.
[47] Minaev, ed. (1930), 275–6; see also pp. 137–8 below.
[48] *Materialy po balansu* (1932), 142 (measured in 1928 prices).
[49] *Ibid.* 142; these figures exclude sovkhozy.
[50] See Table 8; these figures are calculated on a slightly different basis from the series cited on p. 169, n. 146, below.
[51] According to *Kolkhozy v 1930 g.* (1931), 8, in May 1930 23.6 per cent of peasant households and 21·0 per cent of the peasant population (or 26·86 million persons) were in kolkhozy; the figures for the number of kolkhoz households in the last few months of 1930 were on average about the same as in May (see vol. 1, Table 16). *Materialy po balansu* (1932), 112–14, 170, 212–13, however, assumes that the kolkhoz population in 1930 was only 23·35 millions, 19·8 per cent of the peasant population and 18·8 per cent of the total agricultural population.

individual peasants, and, as the number of persons per household was lower in kolkhozy, production per head was substantially higher. Kolkhoz income per head from production in 1930 was valued at 160 rubles as compared with 118 rubles for the individual peasant, but these figures may exaggerate the difference.[52] The *money* income of the kolkhozy in 1930 is not known. It is certain to have been low as compared with that of the individual peasants, as almost all the income of the kolkhozy from their collective production was obtained from sales to the official çollection agencies at fixed prices; their opportunities to sell products on the free market were far fewer than those of the individual peasants, or of the collective farmer in his personal capacity.

Considerable efforts were made by the authorities after the 1930 harvest to ensure that the stipulated minimum percentage of net kolkhoz income was allocated to the Indivisible Fund (10 per cent) and to the Social and Cultural Fund (5 per cent). Allocations from kolkhoz income to the Indivisible Fund were henceforth to be made in money and not in kind: a decree of Kolkhoztsentr ruled that products which had been allocated to the Fund must be sold to the official collection agencies at fixed prices, with the obvious intention of putting up the collections and further squeezing the kolkhozy.[53]

Only scattered information is available about the size of the Indivisible and other Funds actually formed by kolkhozy from their income after the harvest of 1930. In four groups of kolkhozy in the North Caucasus and the Central Black-Earth region where a survey was undertaken, the proportion of net income allocated to the Indivisible Fund varied from 6·7 to 17·3 per cent and allocations to Social and Cultural Funds varied from 4·3 to 5·4 per cent; the stipulated minima were 10 and 5 per cent respectively (see p. 126 above).[54]

After the 1930 harvest, the state also brought the financial relaxation of the spring and summer to an end. On September 2,

---

[52] Based on data in *Materialy po balansu* (1932), 212–13, for income from cooperative production and independent production, and for entrepreneurial income, of collective farmers, individual peasants and kulaks; these calculations assume that the kolkhoz population was only 23.35 millions (see n. 51 above); if the kolkhoz population was 26·9 millions, income per head becomes 140 rubles for collective farmers and 122 rubles for individual peasants.

[53] SZe, October 3, 9, 1930.

[54] SRSKh, 6, 1931, 226, 229; seed and fodder Funds, administrative expenditure and depreciation have been deducted from gross income.

1930, a decree of Narkomzem and Kolkhoztsentr sternly ruled that up to 50 per cent of the Indivisible Fund of each kolkhoz must be set aside to cover the outstanding debts; if this amount was insufficient, the percentage of kolkhoz income deducted to the Indivisible Fund must be increased. The remaining half of the Indivisible Fund was to be set aside to be used for capital investment during 1931. Those debts of members of kolkhozy which were not covered by the property they had transferred to the kolkhozy were to be paid from the share of the kolkhoz harvest due to the member concerned, or from his personal earnings.[55] A month later a further decree of Kolkhoztsentr, published on October 3, ordered all overdue debts to be paid at once in the case of the kolkhoz, and within five days in the case of the personal debt of a collective farmer, and announced firm dates for payment of agricultural tax and insurance. The same decree ruled that kolkhozy should transfer money to the village soviet to cover expenditure on economic and cultural needs.[56] The village budget in areas where a high proportion of households was collectivised lost a substantial part of its revenue through the reduction of taxes on the kolkhozy and the cancellation of self-taxation on collective farmers, and Narkomfin had already ruled in May that the kolkhoz must make up the loss.[57]

How far these various provisions were carried out by the kolkhozy in practice is not known. The stringent financial measures of the autumn of 1930 did not, however, completely cancel out the benefits resulting from the legislation of the spring of 1930. Although total income per head (in kind and in money) was higher for kolkhozy than for individual peasants, the taxes paid per collective farmer were much smaller. Direct taxes and compulsory state insurance paid from kolkhoz income amounted to only 1.9 per cent of gross income and 11.3 per cent of taxable income, as compared with 4.0 and 17.8 per cent in the case of individual peasants. Even if personal taxes and insurance paid by collective farmers are included, kolkhozy and individual collective farmers paid only 141 out of the 1,000 million rubles paid by the peasantry in 1930.[58] Moreover, in the economic year 1929/30, kolkhozy received the full sum in agricultural loans proposed in the revised

[55] SZe, September 2, 1930.
[56] SZe, October 3, 1930.
[57] EZh, May 11, 17, 1930.
[58] FP, 1-2, 1931, 29.

plan of January 1930, while loans to individual peasants were drastically reduced.[59] The financial policy of the state in the summer and autumn of 1930, like its grain collection policy (see vol. 1, pp. 355–9), was thus directed towards placing the collective farmer in a position where his remuneration was visibly higher than that of the individual peasant.

But the authorities were equally determined to insist that an increasing proportion of kolkhoz investment should be met by the resources of the kolkhozy themselves. The income side of the agricultural credit plan for the forthcoming economic year 1930/31 included no allocations from the state budget;[60] and the financial plan for the special quarter October–December 1930 allocated only 66 million rubles in agricultural loans to the kolkhozy as compared with 525 million rubles in the twelve months of 1929/30, while an expenditure of 177 million rubles was planned for this quarter from the Indivisible Funds and other resources of the kolkhozy.[61] Simultaneously, the financial viability of the kolkhozy was undermined by the firm ruling that all their 'marketable' products should be sold to the state at low fixed prices. At the end of 1930 the finances available to the kolkhozy were utterly inadequate to provide both for adequate investment and for adequate remuneration of their members. This fundamental defect remained throughout the period of rapid industrialisation.

---

[59] Gross agricultural loans to kolkhozy in 1929/30 amounted to 525 million rubles and net loans (new loans less past loans returned) to 424 million rubles, while individual peasants received gross agricultural loans amounting to only 50 million rubles, while paying back loans amounting to 125 million rubles (FP, 10–11, 1930, 72).

[60] FP, 10–11, 1930, 73.

[61] FP, 10–11, 1930, 74; PKh, 10–11, 1930, 353.

CHAPTER SEVEN

THE PERSONAL INCOME OF THE COLLECTIVE FARMER

(A) THE DISTRIBUTION OF COLLECTIVE INCOME

(i) The background

If the arrangements for distributing a share of the collective income of the kolkhoz to its members were to promote the kolkhoz economy, they would need to provide powerful incentives to collective work; but if they were to be palatable to the collective farmers, they could not depart too far from peasant traditions and experience. The Soviet authorities believed that proper incentives would be provided for kolkhoz labour if, like factory labour, it were remunerated according to its length, skill and intensity. Peasant traditions, on the other hand, suggested two further criteria, which were at variance both with each other and with the needs of an incentive system. On the one hand, the egalitarian tendencies of the mir, which provided land allotments related to the number of 'eaters' in the household, pointed to the need to relate remuneration to the size of the peasant family. On the other hand, if kolkhozy were to be attractive to middle peasants as well as to poor peasants and batraks, it seemed desirable that the past economic success of peasant households should be acknowledged by relating their earnings to the land, implements, animals and money which they brought into the kolkhoz as their share payment.

A major practical obstacle to the introduction of a wage system was that income from agricultural activities, unlike the income of most industrial enterprises, does not flow in evenly throughout the year. It reaches its peak in the months after the annual harvest, and the size of the harvest and of the income from it cannot be accurately assessed in the previous autumn and spring when much of the field work is undertaken. The peasants took this condition of life for granted, but it was obviously difficult to reconcile it with a wage system on factory lines. In the sovkhozy, short-term bank loans before the harvest, and government subsidies in the event of harvest failure, made a wage system possible. But with mass collectivisation, this kind of assistance was beyond the means and contrary to the intentions of a government determined to maximise capital investment in industry and to squeeze resources out of the peasant.

No national system of remuneration had ever been prescribed for the kolkhozy, and on the eve of mass collectivisation all three principles of payment were in use: labour; number of eaters; and land and capital contributed. A national survey of kolkhoz payment systems, and a more detailed study of kolkhozy in Kuban' okrug in the North Caucasus, both undertaken in 1928 (see Table 9), revealed that remuneration related to the collective capital contributed by the peasant was the least important: it affected only 11 per cent of kolkhozy, and even in these the capital was often contributed on a per family or per eater basis, or in proportion to the amount of labour on the kolkhoz undertaken by the household. In a larger number of kolkhozy, and particularly in TOZy, members worked on the collective land with their own horses and implements, and were paid accordingly. In others, the household was remunerated according to the land it held. This system was of major importance in TOZy in the Kuban'; however, here again the land held by each household to a considerable extent corresponded to the number of eaters in the family.[1] In the TOZy attached to the Shevchenko MTS the harvest was distributed according to the area of land held by each household when joining the TOZ, and each household was expected to contribute work in proportion: Markevich argued that this system, 'adapted from peasant thought', had the merit of simplicity, and that the distribution of the harvest in proportion to work would merely result in each household demanding more work.[2] But as a rule payment per eater and payment according to work were more prevalent in all types of kolkhozy, including the TOZy, than payment by capital or land contributed to the kolkhoz.[3] Payment per eater may have been even more

---

[1] Minaev, ed. (1930), 181.
[2] Markevich (1929), 44–8.
[3] According to one report, however, in the Ukraine one-third of income was distributed according to means of production contributed, one-third according to

important than Table 9 indicates: households with more dependants were frequently allocated more work per able-bodied
person than those with fewer dependants.

The kolkhoz congress of June 1928 endeavoured to combine the
advantages of payment per eater and payment according to work: it
approved payment according to work as the best system, but also
proposed that the amount of work made available to kolkhoz
households should be related to the number of eaters. The congress
also approved piece work and payment according to skill, providing
that the differential between skills did not exceed 2:1.[4] Many
different methods of payment according to work were used in
practice.[5] In some kolkhozy the payment scale varied according to
both skill and age;[6] others used a scale depending entirely on age.[7]
Women were frequently paid less than men for a day's work.[8] Some
attempts were made to devise piece-work payments, especially in
Siberia. The more usual system, however, was time payment:
kolkhozy simply recorded the number of days worked.[9] As early as
1926, these units were sometimes known as 'labour days (trudodni)'. At first no adjustment was made for skill, but early in 1929
the tractor column in Chapaev district worked out a system in
which 0·75, 1, 1·25 or 1·5 'labour days' were credited for work in four
grades from 'light simple' to 'responsible skilled'.[10] A publication of
the All-Union Kolkhoz Council also recommended at this time that
the labour days recorded for one day's work should vary from 0·5–1,
according to the age of the worker.[11]

Little information is available about the methods by which the
kolkhozy reconciled such schemes with their seasonal and uncertain

---

work, and one-third according to the number of eaters (B, 22, November 30, 1929,
22).

[4] *Kolkhozy . . . pervyi . . . s"ezd* (1929), 404–5.

[5] For examples see Kindeev (1929), 29–51.

[6] According to KG, 93, November 24, 1929, a commune in Zaporozh'e employed
an eight-grade scale ranging from nine rubles per month (for children engaged in
summer work) to 30 rubles a month for the kolkhoz chairman; the range of the
adult scale was 2:1.

[7] 12–14-year-olds received one unit for a given period of work, 15–18: 1·5, 18–50:
2·0, 50 and over: 1·33 (Kindeev (1929), 81; *Trudy . . . agrarnikov-marksistov* (1930),
i, 91).

[8] For examples see Kindeev (1929), 36–8.

[9] ZKK (1929), 148–9; SZe, June 20, 1930.

[10] Kindeev (1929), 109–10; SZe, June 20, 1930.

[11] Kindeev (1929), 80–1.

income. Many kolkhozy used a provisional payment scale, making advance payments when the work was carried out, and a final adjustment after the harvest; these arrangements were partly financed by advances from various state agencies to the kolkhozy on contracts for sale of their products. In the Central Volga region, a system of work units was used, and a value assigned to the unit after the harvest was sold; an advance payment was made of 50 per cent of the estimated income per unit.[12] The assignment of a firm value to a work unit *after* the harvest, coupled with the use as a unit of 'labour days' varying according to skill, eventually became the main system of remuneration in the kolkhozy (see pp. 142–3 below). Its main features thus dated back to practices already used in some kolkhozy before the mass collectivisation drive.

(ii) The drive for a wage system, summer 1929 – March 1930

At the conference of large kolkhozy in July 1929, the organisation section rejected payment per eater on the grounds that it did not provide incentives to work, and also expressed its disapproval of payment scales which were related to age or sex; instead it called for scales related to skill, and the introduction of work norms and piece work wherever possible. It also resolved that no more than 50 per cent of payments due to members for their work should be made before the end of the economic year.[13]

Propaganda in favour of payment according to work and of piece work continued intermittently during the next six months. At the plenum of the party central committee in November, Kaminsky criticised the 'equalising' and 'consumptionist' tendencies of most kolkhozy,[14] Molotov urged kolkhozy to model themselves on sovkhozy (see p. 3 above), and the plenum resolution stressed in general terms the need to create 'personal interest by every collective farmer in improved productivity of labour (piece work, norms of output, a bonus system, etc.)'.[15] A fortnight after the plenum, an article in the party journal dismissed the system of remuneration prevalent in the Ukraine (see p. 132, n. 3 above) as 'bourgeois', and hinted that it was part of the 'economic programme of the kulak'.[16] In the following month Kaminsky, echoing

[12] ZKK (1929), 153–5.
[13] ZKK (1929), 162.
[14] Cited in VIK, 4, 1962, 59–60.
[15] *KPSS v rez.*, ii (1954), 647.   [16] B, 22, November 30, 1929, 58.

Molotov, told a meeting of members of TsIK that the kolkhoz must base itself in matters of labour organisation on the large sovkhoz and the industrial enterprise.[17] In the same month the peasants' newspaper published a long report, the title of which speaks for itself: 'For Piece Work, For the Correct Organisation of Labour: Against Equalisation, Against the Parasitic Per-Eater System'.[18] But counsels were still to a certain extent divided. The tendency of the middle peasants to sell up their property before joining the kolkhoz called into question the viability of a system based entirely on remuneration for work. On December 15 Yakovlev proposed to the Politburo commission on collectivisation, or to one of its sub-commissions, that part of the remuneration of the collective farmer should be related to the size of his initial share capital and to his contribution to socialised property.[19] But this proposal was implicitly rejected. Early in January 1930, an order of Kolkhoztsentr of the RSFSR stated that payment should be based solely on the quantity and quality of work, with the exception of benefits for sickness or inability to work.[20] At the conference of RSKs a few days later, an official from the Ukrainian Kolkhoztsentr also firmly declared that '*the only measure in distribution must be the number of labour days worked by each collective farmer*', and the newspaper account of the conference reported that the 'overwhelming majority' of delegates opposed distribution per eater, and also rejected payment related to the amount of land contributed by the household to the kolkhoz.[21]

In the enthusiastic atmosphere of the next few weeks many proposals were made to introduce the continuous working week and the seven- or eight-hour day into the kolkhozy.[22] A number of RSKs began to introduce payment scales, the most favoured being a six-grade system with a 2:1 ratio between the top and bottom grades.[23] After the appointment of Yurkin, a former metal worker and sovkhoz director, as chairman of Kolkhoztsentr in the middle of

[17] EZh, December 6, 1929.
[18] KG, 102, December 24, 1929.
[19] Cited from the archives in IISO, [i] (1964), 275.
[20] SKhG, January 4, 1930.
[21] EZh, January 14, 1930.
[22] See for example P, December 24, 1929 (speech at women collective farmers' conference).
[23] For example, Samoilov district, Lower Volga region, and Samara okrug, Central Volga region; the Shevchenko okrug, however, was reported to be going over to a system of 'labour days', recording the hours and days worked, but without a firm payment scale (P, January 16, 1930).

January 1930, a vigorous effort was made to apply the industrial wage system in the kolkhozy; the treatment of the collective farmer as an industrial worker was later described as 'a general tendency which predominated in the *apparat* of the kolkhoz and cooperative system in the first stage of mass collectivisation'.[24] In February kolkhozy were instructed to organise 'labour bureaux' during the first 15 days of March; they should then prepare work norms in order to go over piece work, preference being given where possible to individual rather than group norms. At first no detailed instructions were issued about how the norms should be prepared, and kolkhozy bombarded the central authorities with telegrams demanding specific instructions.[25] On February 25, Kolkhoztsentr eventually issued instructions which were modelled closely on sovkhoz and industrial practices.[26] Details were also published of two proposed payment scales, in which work was graded according to skill and responsibility: mechanised kolkhozy were recommended to adopt a seven-grade scale with a spread of 3:1, and non-mechanised a five-grade scale with a spread of 2:1.[27] These instructions, though published a few days later than Stalin's article of March 2, marked the climax of the unsuccessful attempt by the authorities to introduce a wage system in the kolkhozy.

This system, in which all remuneration depended on the quantity and quality of work, was a complete break with peasant tradition. Payment per eater and payment related to the amount of land and capital contributed to the kolkhoz by the household were completely excluded in favour of a wage system in which earnings depended on payment scales related to work norms prepared by the kolkhozy along industrial lines. Quite apart from the break in

---

[24] VTr, 7–8, 1930, 33.

[25] SZe, February 27, 1930.

[26] SZe, March 5, 6, 1930. An example of a model norm (actual quantities to be inserted by the kolkhoz on the basis of local conditions): one day's sowing with an 11-row sower (ten-hour day) was normed at four hectares; the norm for the rate of pay for one day's sowing was one ruble; so the rate for sowing one hectare was 25 kopeks. Separate norms were suggested for animal and mechanical drawing power, based on a ten-hour and an eight-hour day respectively.

[27] SZe, March 5, 6, 1930; this scheme earlier appeared as a proposal in an article by a deputy chairman of Kolkhoztsentr, Ya. Terletskii, in SZe, February 8, 1930. Although the Kolkhoztsentr instructions were supposed to apply to the whole kolkhoz system, Khlebotsentr at this time recommended a nine-grade scale (SZe, February 27, 1930). A conference of Lower Volga kolkhozy recommended a six-grade and a four-grade scale, each with a spread of 2:1 (P, February 25, 1930).

peasant tradition which it represented, the attempt to prescribe an advance payment in rubles and kopeks for particular farm tasks was wishful thinking of an extreme kind. It assumed that the central authorities, and the board of each kolkhoz, were able to predict accurately the size and value of the forthcoming harvest. It also assumed that the kolkhoz held or could acquire enough working capital to pay its members in advance of the harvest. Many official documents and statements at the time assumed that a substantial part of his 'wage' would be handed over to the collective farmer immediately. The model Statute of February 6, 1930, repeating the proposal of the conference of large kolkhozy in the previous July (see p. 134 above), declared:

> Payment for the work of members of the artel shall be carried out by the following procedure: during the economic year, for food and other needs, members of the artel shall be paid in advance (in kind or in money) not more than 50 per cent of the amount accruing to them for the work. At the end of the economic year a final settlement of payment for work shall be carried out.[28]

Nothing was said in the Kolkhoztsentr instructions of February 25 about advance payments, but the discussions during the course of February at times went further than the 50 per cent maximum advance payment proposed in the Statute, and assumed that a collective farmer, like an industrial or sovkhoz worker, would be paid a full wage immediately.

In view of the acute shortage of financial resources in the kolkhozy (see p. 127 above), immediate payment of substantial sums for the spring field work was obviously impossible. In some areas, advances on contracts, which were made available to the kolkhozy in cash, were used to pay part of the wages due to the collective farmers.[29] But as a general rule payments to collective farmers were small, and even more frequently were not made at all. Vareikis' claim that the provision about advance payments 'is not applied anywhere in practice' was something of an exaggeration.[30]

---

[28] P, February 7, 1930 (clause 15).

[29] For example, in the Urals (FP, 5, 1930, 67); the extent of this practice has not been established. An untypical report from Rossoshanskii okrug, Central Black-Earth region, stated that 30 per cent advance payments were 'universally' made (I, April 19, 1930).

[30] NAF, 3, 1930, 32: this statement was made sometime in February.

But even kolkhozy which were particularly the object of official care and attention, such as the Ural Gigant, incurred large debts to their members.[31] Former batraks and poor peasants tended to rely on wages and casual earnings for a large part of their income, and were supposed to be given priority in wage payments by the kolkhoz. But many of them received nothing, and in consequence were among the first to leave the kolkhozy.[32]

The instructions from Kolkhoztsentr about methods of payments were almost completely disregarded. The regional authorities often failed to pass on the instructions from the centre, and issued numerous circulars and formulas of their own.[33] The labour departments of the kolkhoz system were often weak, even at the republican level: the labour department of the Ukrainian Kolkhoztsentr had only two members of staff, and regional kolkhozsoyuz labour departments were also inadequately staffed.[34] At the lower levels, according to one report, 'no work has been done on payment scales and norms'.[35] Narkomtrud was supposed to send 15,000 book-keepers and accountants to the kolkhozy by April 1, but even after a 'government mobilisation' in the Moscow region only 6,371 were sent.[36] In the kolkhozy, even simple work records were often lacking, though 'all literate people were mobilised' to act as clerks. Work norms were rarely prepared; and, even where records were kept, time payment predominated in the overwhelming majority of cases.[37]

In an endeavour to cope with their acute shortage of cash without antagonising their members, kolkhozy frequently resorted to the issue of what were variously known as 'bonds', 'receipts' or

[31] In Gigant unpaid wages amounted to 400,000 rubles, even though half the 'wages' were paid in kind (FP, 5, 1930, 67).

[32] NAF, 5, 1930, 42–3 (Tsil'ko). In the Lower Volga region a kolkhoz conference proposed that 50–60 per cent advance payments should eventually be made, but that new kolkhozy should make advance payments mainly to batraks and poor peasants, up to a maximum of 20 per cent of the estimated total remuneration (P, February 25, 1930); an investigation of the region undertaken in March revealed, however, that 'even batraks and poor peasants do not normally receive advance payments' (I, April 19, 1930).

[33] P, May 10, 1930 (referring to the okrugs in the Ukraine); SZe, April 2, 1930 (survey of kolkhozy in Urals, Siberia and North Caucasus).

[34] VTr, 7–8, 1930, 34.

[35] I, March 27, 1930.

[36] SZe, April 3, 1930; 'large numbers' of these failed to arrive.

[37] SZe, April 2, 1930 (survey of kolkhozy in Urals, Siberia and North Caucasus).

'coupons' (bony, raschetnye kvitantsii, raschetnye talony); these were a mixture between an internal currency, available for use within the kolkhoz for the purchase of goods, and a promissory note. At first the kolkhoz authorities argued that these devices were essential, and Narkomfin agreed to experiment with them in communes, but at the beginning of March Narkomfin condemned them as 'money surrogates'.[38]

Even after the publication of Stalin's famous article on March 2, the authorities showed little inclination or aptitude to cope with the practical problems of remuneration. The revised model Statute of March 1, 1930, merely repeated the provision of the previous Statute which permitted advance payments up to a maximum of 50 per cent of earnings.[39] Evidence of discontent among collective farmers about the failure to pay them appeared frequently in the press in March and April. The survey of kolkhozy carried out during March (see p. 138, n. 33, above) reported that collective farmers, believing that they were expected to work for nothing, exhibited a 'formal (kazennoe) indifferent attitude' to their work: no-one anywhere explained to them that *'payment cannot be a firm magnitude, guaranteed irrespectively of the financial and economic position of the kolkhoz'*.[40] In Khoper okrug, everyone tried to avoid agricultural work, and instead to do such things as cartage for which the kolkhoz received immediate payment and the collective farmer was accordingly paid in cash. In an *ekonomiya* (major sub-division) of one very large kolkhoz only 120 persons turned up for work out of 600 households; in the same kolkhoz some collective farmers had already been credited with wages amounting to 150–200 rubles, but no-one had thought about whether this debt could be honoured.[41] At the end of March, with the spring sowing under way in many regions, a senior agricultural official reported that questions of payment and distribution of the harvest *'are now disturbing every collective farmer'*, and urged that a conference should be called within a month to sort matters out.[42] On April 2, perhaps in a moment of despair, Yurkin, in a letter written jointly with the deputy chairman of the agricultural cooperatives, announced an All-Union Competition to find out the best experience of labour organisation in

[38] EZh, March 1, 1930; FP, 5, 1930, 14–15.
[39] P, March 2, 1930.
[40] SZe, April 2, 1930.
[41] I, March 2, 1930.
[42] SZe, March 30, 1930 (Tsil'ko).

kolkhozy, with 100,000 rubles in prize money; Kalinin was appointed chairman of the jury.[43] But this was too late for the spring sowing. Perhaps the most remarkable feature of the spring of 1930 is that sowing took place quite successfully in the kolkhozy even though collective farmers were working on credit for an unknown amount of payment, often not knowing even the system by which they would be paid.

(iii) The emergence of the labour-day system, April–July 1930

In the middle of April 1930, a Conference of Officials of the Kolkhoz System met under the auspices of Narkomzem and Kolkhoztsentr specifically to discuss questions of labour organisation; and at the end of July 1930 a USSR Conference of Officials of the Kolkhoz System devoted much of its time to the same subject.[44] During this period, substantial progress was made towards designing a viable system for the remuneration of the collective farmer. Three main sets of decisions were adopted. First, the financial position of the kolkhozy was improved. Secondly, wage payments were replaced by payment according to 'labour days (trudodni)'. Thirdly, payment by capital contributed and payment per eater were again permitted in addition to payment according to work.

The financial position of the kolkhozy was improved both by reducing their obligations to the state (see pp. 124–5 above) and by a firm ruling that advance payments to members should not be permitted. The 'explanatory note' of April 13 insisted that payments for labour should be made only from the harvest or from other income.[45] The provision for advance payments in the model Statute was thus effectively rescinded; henceforth it was recognised that the collective farmer could not be treated like a factory worker, but must remain a peasant in the sense that his main income depended

---

[43] SZe, April 2, 1930.

[44] These conferences were reported in SZe, April 15, 17, and July 25, 27, 30, 1930; references to them in the following pages are taken from these newspaper accounts.

[45] SZ, 1930, art. 256. In practice the new harsher regulation was also applied to smiths, saddlers and other artisans, who were accustomed to be paid immediately, and to bargain over the price charged for a job rather than be paid on a fixed scale, and now had to await the harvest before receiving payment. According to I. Mezhlauk, their 'great dissatisfaction with the extremely sharp break with the traditional forms of payment' led them 'almost everywhere' to leave the kolkhozy (SZe, May 8, 1930).

upon and must await the results of the harvest, and must be received in kind, as well as in money. With the kolkhozy now free of their main financial obligations until after the harvest, Narkomfin again firmly banned their attempts to create 'money surrogates'.[46]

The second set of decisions in April–July 1930 replaced money wages by the 'labour-day' system, the main features of which continued until the 1960s. Under the labour-day system, a development of arrangements already in use in some kolkhozy before 1930 (see pp. 133–4 above), the number of units of work performed by a collective farmer are recorded, and after the harvest the available kolkhoz income, in money and in kind, is distributed among the collective farmers in proportion to the number of units recorded for each farmer. The 'labour day' is a unit of account; skilled work is allocated more 'labour days' for one actual day's labour than unskilled work, and piece work can be accommodated to the system by recording a 'labour day' for the achievement of a definite work norm rather than for working a certain number of hours. The system solved two central problems of remuneration in the kolkhoz: the income of the collective farmer was made to depend on the 'quantity and quality' of his or her labour, while at the same time the amount paid out depended on the income actually received by the kolkhoz as a whole during the year.

At the kolkhoz conference in April 1930, delegates from local kolkhozsoyuzy argued that firm money wages were impossible, and that all calculation should be made in terms of labour days. In his summing-up of the discussion, Gei, a member of the Kolkhoztsentr board, unwilling to forget the alluring dreams of previous weeks, still advocated the retention of a wage system in the largest fully-mechanised kolkhozy, but freely admitted that kolkhozy which did not come into this category (in fact virtually all kolkhozy at this time) must go over to labour days. Immediately after the conference a *Pravda* editorial sternly condemned the 'mechanical transfer of the

---

[46] EZh, May 17, June 12, 1930. At a conference on kolkhoz finance held on May 8, 1930, a speaker from the Urals reported that an 'investigating group' had found that while *bony* were 'not dangerous', they could cause great complications to currency issue in the long term, but several speakers cautiously defended the practice on the grounds that there was no other way of increasing the working capital of kolkhozy; it was attacked by Goldenberg and Vaisberg (EZh, May 11, 1930). The repetition of the ban in strong terms by Narkomfin on November 10, 1930 (*Finansy i sotsialisticheskoe khozyaistvo*, 5, February 20, 1931, 19) indicates that such substitutes continued to be issued.

system and methods of the large-scale industrial enterprise directly to the kolkhoz', and declared that all talk of a wages system must cease; instead, a system should be introduced which was simple and comprehensive, and took into account the number of days or hours worked by each collective farmer, as well as their level of skill, work norms and quality of work.[47] Neither the conference resolution nor the *Pravda* editorial specifically endorsed the labour-day system, however, and the editorial even declared that the introduction of a single system of remuneration in all kolkhozy was unnecessary.

On June 6, 1930, an instruction of Kolkhoztsentr officially endorsed the labour-day system, proclaiming that it would inculcate firmly in every collective farmer the knowledge that his income was determined by the total earnings of the kolkhoz and by his own work as a share in this total. The instruction announced that a model labour-day scheme would be sent out 'in the very near future',[48] but no such scheme appears to have been made available in the course of the summer of 1930. A long article in the agricultural newspaper described a possible scheme in some detail: collective farmers meeting work norms approved by the kolkhoz would be credited with 'normal labour units' or labour days according to a five-grade scale, the number of labour days credited increasing according to skill from one in grade 1 to two in grade 5. At the end of the year, the distributable income of the kolkhoz in kind and money would be divided by the total number of labour days earned by all kolkhoz members in order to establish what the collective farmer should receive per labour day.[49] But this proposal did not receive official endorsement, and on July 1, 1930, a lengthy decree of Kolkhoztsentr, while again supporting distribution according to the number of labour days, still made no detailed provisions.[50] A resolution of the presidium of the central control

[47] P, April 18, 1930.

[48] SKhIB, 15, 1930, 8; as far as is known, this is the first occasion on which remuneration by 'labour days' was approved in an official order. The 'explanatory note' of April 13, 1930, by insisting that payment should be in kind as well as in money (see pp. 140–1 above) in effect rejected the money-wage system, but it did not specifically mention labour days.

[49] SZe, June 20, 1930 (A. Deikin); the author also proposed that bonuses and fines for good and bad work should be imposed on a five-point scale.

[50] SKhIB, 19–20, 1930, 31. On June 29, 1930, a circular/instruction of Kolkhoztsentr ruled that administrative expenditure should not exceed 2–3 per cent of kolkhoz income, or 1–1½ per cent in the case of kolkhozy with total incomes in excess of 15,000 rubles a year; all administrative posts in kolkhozy should be paid

commission and the collegium of Rabkrin of July 9, 1930, called upon Kolkhoztsentr to issue directives on methods for distributing income in kolkhozy by July 15, and to study existing experience within a month,[51] but the resolution apparently remained without practical effect. In August, Narkomfin and Kolkhoztsentr further strengthened the status of the new system by ruling that all accounts with collective farmers were to be kept in labour days, and not switched to a monetary form until the end of the economic year.[52] But all detailed elaboration was left to the local kolkhozsoyuzy.

The third set of decisions in April–July 1930 made important concessions to the principles of payment by capital contributed and per eater. The 'explanatory note' of April 13, 1930, ruled that 5 per cent of the gross harvest, and of the income from socialised dairy cattle, should be set aside for distribution on the basis of the property transferred by the collective farmer or the household to the socialised funds.[53] This decision was surprising in view of the hostility of the central authorities to such arrangements in the past; like the decision to permit collective farmers to retain their own livestock, it was a bid to attract middle peasants to the kolkhozy, and was presented as such in the press.

The central authorities were less willing to reintroduce payment per eater. In this case they did not make a deliberate concession to the wishes of the majority of the peasants, but conducted a piecemeal retreat in the face of overwhelming pressures and difficulties. The explanatory note of April 13 ruled that payment was to be based on the quality and quantity of the work of the collective farmer or of the household, in accordance with the

---

not by a fixed salary or guaranteed wage but out of the results of the harvest, in money and in kind, on the same basis as collective farmers as a whole; the income received could not exceed the highest income received by a collective farmer, except that a mark-up of up to 40 per cent of basic pay could be awarded by decision of the general meeting; the instruction did not specifically mention labour days (SKhIB, 18, 1930, 12).

[51] I, July 15, 1930; the same resolution stated that 'the kolkhoz and cooperative system pays no attention to the norming of administrative expenditure, as a result of which cases occur of its excessive growth', and called upon Kolkhoztsentr to work out within a month a scale of general expenditure and standard schemes for administrative staff related to the size of the kolkhoz. A later decree of Narkomzem and Kolkhoztsentr merely reiterated the provision that administrative expenditure should not exceed a fixed proportion of total income (SZe, September 2, 1930).

[52] P, August 2, 1930.

[53] SZ, 1930, art. 256.

decisions of the general meeting of the kolkhoz; this seemed to exclude per-eater payments.[54] This was a very sensitive issue. In the mir, families with a small number of able-bodied adults traditionally received a separate land allotment for each eater, and those leaving the kolkhoz continued to do so; harder work by the adult members of the family could therefore partly compensate for the larger number of dependants. In the kolkhozy, many collective farmers strongly supported the allocation of part or all of the harvest per eater as more equitable than allocation solely in terms of work done. According to I. Mezhlauk, 'a fairly wide stratum of middle and poor peasants' found distribution solely by labour days so unacceptable that they would leave, or refuse to join, the kolkhoz,[55] while Kindeev argued that distribution per eater of part of the harvest in kind was 'more flexible and satisfactory in the eyes of the collective farmers'.[56] Reports from the provinces confirmed the strength of these feelings. In an RSK in the Urals a tendency was noted in favour of an 'egalitarian system';[57] at a conference of kolkhozy in the Lower Volga region 'strivings to equalisation' were expressed, especially in relation to payments to the kolkhoz management.[58] And while Yakovlev claimed that women were generally favourable to piece work because it was likely to achieve equality between the sexes more rapidly,[59] women in a German kolkhoz in the Crimea, supported by some of the men, argued that 'piece work puts us in the position of workers and puts the leading comrades we elect in the position of masters', and were not convinced by experience until the end of 1930.[60]

At the conference of kolkhoz officials in the middle of April 1930, Markevich, more attuned than most leading officials to peasant reactions, accordingly suggested that part of the harvest should be distributed per eater; the Kolkhoztsentr representative countered by the usual proposal that more work should be given to adult collective farmers in households with a large number of dependants.[61] The conference accepted the latter solution, and on this

[54] SZ, 1930, art. 256.
[55] SZe, May 8, 1930.
[56] PKh, 7–8, 1930, 111.
[57] P, January 16, 1930.
[58] P, February 25, 1930.
[59] *6 s"ezd sovetov* (1931), No. 16, p. 17.
[60] SZe, January 15, 1931.
[61] A discussion article in P, June 7, 1930, argued that only unskilled work should

basis resolved that the quantity and quality of labour should be the sole criterion for distribution. The argument continued during the next three months. In a discussion on the model kolkhoz Statute in the agricultural newspaper, I. Mezhlauk proposed that one-third to one-half of kolkhoz income should be distributed according to the number of eaters, and one-half to one-third according to labour days.[62] Most other contributors to the discussion were on the whole hostile to this suggestion, on the grounds that it would reduce work incentives: 'workers who earn identical wages', one writer argued, 'also live unequally because of the difference in their families'.[63] The instruction of June 6, 1930 (see p. 142 above) firmly stated that income must be distributed among collective farmers according to the quality and quantity of work, and the decree of July 1, 1930, reiterated this principle and suggested ways of allocating more work to larger families. Nevertheless, prominent officials in Kolkhoztsentr were careful to stress that each kolkhoz had the right to determine its own methods of remuneration: the right approach, according to a member of the board of Kolkhoztsentr, was to encourage kolkhozy to keep distribution per eater to a minimum, but not to prevent the introduction of a scheme such as I. Mezhlauk's if a kolkhoz were in favour of it.[64]

At the XVI party congress in July, several speakers advocated partial remuneration on a per-eater basis. Lominadze, now secretary of the Transcaucasian party committee, argued that some distribution per eater would in any case be required in 1930 as in some cases 'during the period of hesitations' 25–30 per cent of collective farmers refused to work.[65] A collective farm chairman, describing remuneration per eater as 'a matter very near to the hearts of the collective farmers', declared that without it 'family people would be unable to live in the kolkhoz'.[66] In face of such arguments, Yakovlev wavered in his reply to the discussion, and retreated to the principle that arrangements should not be re-

---

be allocated so as to even out income between families of different size: skilled collective farmers should be permanently and fully employed.

[62] SZe, May 8, 1930.

[63] SZe, June 10, 1930; some contributors argued that households with a large number of eaters should be allowed to retain two cows instead of one for their personal use.

[64] SZe, June 24, 1930 (Gei).

[65] *XVI s"ezd* (1931), 196.

[66] *Ibid.* 619.

gulated in detail from the centre; he conceded that no objections would be raised if the kolkhoz 'set aside a certain part of its food products for members with large families', and that no special regulations were needed to enable them to do so.[67]

After the congress, the line that each kolkhoz should be allowed to take its own decision about the system of remuneration was treated as authoritative. An unsigned article in the agricultural newspaper, while claiming optimistically that the overwhelming majority of collective farmers preferred distribution by quality and quantity of work, insisted that 'we do not have the right to abstract outselves from the habits and customs of the peasant'; the system adopted in each case must be accepted by the peasant as 'the most suitable system from the point of view of *his conceptions* about the measures necessary to strengthen the kolkhoz and secure its further growth'.[68] A *Pravda* editorial a week later also argued that, while remuneration according to work was preferable, '*the collective farmer must decide himself*' about remuneration per eater and by capital contributed.[69] In the agricultural newspaper the Uzbek Narkomzem and Kolkhoztsentr were criticised for decreeing that only remuneration according to work was permissible, while the Central Volga region was equally criticised for its ruling that 50 per cent of the harvest should be distributed on a per-eater basis; the newspaper suggested that remuneration per eater should be introduced only 'on the initiative of the masses', and only up to a maximum of one-third of distributed income.[70] In the next few months, the authorities stuck more or less firmly to the position that they preferred a system of remuneration solely according to work, but would not prevent kolkhoz members from following the principle of partial distribution per eater if they chose to do so. A decree of Kolkhoztsentr stated that remuneration should be by quantity and quality of labour but added the significant phrase 'as a rule';[71] a later decree of Narkomzem and Kolkhoztsentr, by condemning distribution *solely* per eater as a '*direct distortion*', implied that *some* distribution per eater was permissible.[72] Meanwhile, further legislation (see p. 126

---

[67] *Ibid*. 644.
[68] SZe, July 16, 1930; Yakovlev's reply to the debate at the party congress was on July 10.
[69] P, July 23, 1930.
[70] SZe, July 18, 30, 1930.
[71] SZe, July 27, 1930.
[72] SZe, September 2, 1930.

above) sought to ensure that collective farmers would receive a substantial share of kolkhoz income.

(iv) The harvest of 1930

The decisions of April–July 1930 failed to eliminate the prevailing muddle; and, coming in the midst of the main agricultural season, the sharp changes in policy even confused matters further.

The previous official policy of encouraging wage systems along industrial lines continued to have repercussions. Wage systems were introduced in some kolkhozy, particularly in larger ones, and the decisions of the April kolkhoz conference were sufficiently ambiguous, or sufficiently lacking in authority, to allow kolkhozy and local authorities to continue their efforts to introduce a wage system, though always on the basis of 'promise to pay' after the harvest. In May a report from a large kolkhoz in the Kuban' described with approval the use of a nine-grade scale based on sovkhoz practice, with a wage rate of 80k – 2r 80k for a ten-hour day.[73] As late as May 30, 1930, a conference of chairmen of kolkhozy and village soviets in Vladimir district, Ivanovo region, resolved that 'piece payments shall be immediately introduced for basic activity, on the basis of work norms and the approved wage scale'.[74] Many local officials believed that a wage system was immediately feasible in the kolkhozy, and looked on the withdrawal of official support as pusillanimous and temporary. The wage system died hard. As late as the autumn of 1930, an article in an agricultural journal, based on experience in the North Caucasus, suggested that payments in money terms should be fixed in advance and adjusted in accordance with the results of the harvest.[75] In September 1930, a decree of Narkomzem and Kolkhoztsentr drew attention to the continuing practice of recording labour in the form of a money wage, and condemned it as 'contradicting the main principles of kolkhoz construction'.[76] In the autumn of 1930, many kolkhozy which persisted in fixing payments in money terms found themselves able to pay a mere 30 kopeks or less per 'ruble' recorded, while others became heavily indebted to their members.[77] At the VI congress of

[73] P, May 9, 1930.
[74] *Kollektivizatsiya* (Ryazan', 1971), 430.
[75] NAF, 9, 1930, 114.
[76] SZe, September 2, 1930.
[77] SRSKh, 8, 1931, 150.

soviets in March 1931, Yurkin still complained that piece work was 'often' valued in money terms, with 'very unfortunate results', and that 'kolkhozy are often confused with sovkhozy in the localities'; he criticised demands that collective farmers should get a guaranteed wage as 'a kulak slogan'.[78] In the discussion of Yurkin's report, a speaker from the Lower Volga region defended calculation in advance of the harvest of the amount of money and products to be distributed per labour day, but in his reply Yurkin repeated his warning that no promises or hints of promises should be made to collective farmers before the harvest.[79] This was evidently a point of tension between the regime and the peasants. According to a later account, 'kulaks' disrupted kolkhoz general meetings when the introduction of a labour-day system was proposed, arguing that 'collective farmers will get nothing if the kolkhozy go over to labour days, but if all work is calculated in money they will get something from the kolkhoz or the state, this year or next'.[80]

But the kolkhozy in which a wage system was introduced were certainly a small minority; and, with the adoption of the new legislation on labour days in June 1930, many of these abandoned the wage system with alacrity. But June was very late in the season; sowing was complete everywhere, and harvesting was soon to begin. At the kolkhoz conference in July, a representative of the board of Kolkhoztsentr reported that as late as the middle of July most kolkhozy had not yet discussed their arrangements for distributing the harvest, and claimed that the instructions issued by local kolkhozsoyuzy were complicated and incomprehensible.[81] The collective farmers lacked even an approximate idea of the grain and money they would personally receive. Vareikis pointed out:

> The absence of a clear perspective for the collective farmer, ignorance and lack of confidence about how the harvest will be divided and how the division of income between the individual members of the kolkhoz will in practice be arranged: all this has been a source of many misunderstandings, hesitations and disillusionments by the collective farmer.[82]

[78] *6 s"ezd sovetov* (1931), No. 17, 9–10.
[79] *Ibid.* No. 18, 11; No. 20, 53.
[80] SRSKh, 8, 1931, 150 (report of a kolkhoz conference held in the summer of 1931).
[81] SZe, July 30, 1930.
[82] B, 10, May 31, 1930, 41.

Records of the work performed by collective farmers were absent or chaotic. Their work during the spring period was very often not recorded at all (see p. 138 above). Though the elaborate proposals for record keeping made earlier in the year gave way to simpler methods from April onwards, it was not until late in the summer, if at all, that record books became generally available.[83] For most brigade leaders, keeping even simple records of the work performed by the collective farmers was a novel and difficult task; many reports bore witness both to their incompetence and to their hostility to the complexity of the system.[84] At the VI congress of soviets in March 1931, Yakovlev, declaring that *'where there are no records there is no large-scale economy'*, cited many examples of inaccurate records.[85] Even when records were accurate, they were usually passed direct to the kolkhoz management, and the collective farmers had no note of the number of labour days they had worked or of the advances they received.[86] The first attempt to remedy this situation was made in a Statute of Narkomfin and Kolkhoztsentr, which ruled that every collective farmer should have an account book (raschetnaya kniga) showing the labour days credited, in addition to the personal account (litsevoi schet) recording the same information which was kept in the kolkhoz office.[87] But by this time much of the harvest work had already been done, and in most kolkhozy no account books (or labour books, as they were later called) were issued until 1931.[88]

[83] The new record forms worked out jointly by Kolkhoztsentr and Rabkrin were not available at the time of the harvest, so kolkhozy had to prepare their own forms (VTr, 7–8, 1930, 39); according to Kindeev, writing in August, 'in the overwhelming majority of the kolkhozy which have been surveyed, records of labour and accounts with members are only now being introduced' (PKh, 7–8, 1930, 111); a typical report from a district in the Lower Volga described the 'chaotic labour records', for which labour record books had not been introduced until August or September (P, October 27, 1930). Even the revised forms for recording work were said to be far too detailed (SZe, August 14, 1930).

[84] See for example P, October 27, 1930 (report from Lower Volga); SZe, January 16, 1931 (report from West Siberia).

[85] *6 s"ezd sovetov* (1931), No. 16, 6–7.

[86] VTr, 7–8, 1930, 39–40; kolkhozy in the Central Volga region issued individual receipts(tabeli) to their members, and elsewhere cheques, stamps or coupons were issued; sometimes different colours were used to indicate different grades of labour—but all these devices were said to be untypical.

[87] P, August 21, 1930.

[88] The decision to issue account books in addition to the personal accounts was made again at a kolkhoz conference in February 1931, and reported in a financial

Some progress was made towards recording the 'quantity and quality' of labour. The grade of work was often indicated: a great variety of systems was in use, with a spread varying between 1:2 and 1:5·75, though 1:3 was usually the maximum.[89] Otherwise records usually simply took the form of a note of the number of hours or days worked. Even this relatively simple operation was beset with difficulties. One 'day's' work might mean anything from 8–14 hours,[90] and there were cases in which one or two hours' work was recorded as one labour day.[91] It was certainly quite beyond the understanding or competence of most brigade leaders, and most members of the kolkhoz boards, to record the amount of work actually performed in a given period by each member, or even by a whole brigade. Just before the harvest, Sheboldaev, writing in the party journal, conceded that 'we shall succeed in going over to piece work only in the case of certain special jobs such as tractor drivers and blacksmiths'.[92] In the majority of kolkhozy, no piece-work system of any kind operated throughout 1930.[93] In most of the remainder, records of work performed were kept solely for groups of collective farmers, or for whole brigades, and not for the individual peasant. Group piece work was defended on the grounds that it was much simpler to record than individual piece work, an important consideration in view of the primitive state of kolkhoz records.[94] Some kolkhoz officials also argued that group piece work encouraged cooperation in small work groups.[95] But this was not the official view. At the VI congress of soviets in March 1931, Yakovlev admitted that brigades and groups were still the basis of piece work 'in most cases', but insisted that individual piece work was 'extremely desirable'.[96]

---

journal as if it were entirely new (*Finansy i sotsialisticheskoe khozyaistvo*, 6, February 28, 1931, 10).

[89] PKh, 7–8, 1930, 108 (Kindeev); according to this account, all the kolkhozy surveyed in the Central Black-Earth region used a grading system, 48 per cent of those in the North Caucasus and 43 per cent in the Lower Volga region.

[90] SZe, June 20, 1930.

[91] *6 s"ezd sovetov* (1931), No. 16, 16.

[92] B, 11–12, June 30, 1930, 59.

[93] According to a report in VTr, 7–8, 1930, 34, although the largest kolkhozy used work norms, in at least 50 per cent of the kolkhozy time work was the only method; a survey, reported by Kindeev in PKh, 7–8, 1930, 107, showed that work norms were used only in a minority of kolkhozy in all the regions surveyed.

[94] PKh, 7–8, 1930, 107.   [95] SZe, January 16, 1931.

[96] *6 s"ezd sovetov* (1931), No. 16, p. 13.

The problem of ensuring that work was performed properly received some attention. In February 1930, a Lower Volga kolkhoz conference recommended that a four-grade scale should be used to measure quality.[97] In March, a Kolkhoztsentr instruction ruled that the quality of all agricultural work must be evaluated, and work should be formally 'accepted' on completion;[98] this was a grandiose suggestion, as this was the term used to describe the act of transfer of completed capital construction projects from state building agencies to state customers. Proposals to introduce bonuses and penalties for good and bad work were made later in the year (see p. 142, n. 49 above). But in practice, with very rare exceptions, no attempt was made to record the quality of work. Rewards and sanctions for good or bad work were therefore not possible, although they were obviously particularly important when piece work was being introduced.

The confusion of the spring sowing period, when vast numbers of peasants were leaving the kolkhozy, the belatedness and inaccuracy of the records of the work of the collective farmer, and the failure of many collective farmers to work in the kolkhoz fields, made it inevitable that the income from the harvest should be distributed by simplified methods. Zealous local authorities frequently claimed that the majority of kolkhozy were distributing the harvest according to the quantity and quality of labour contributed.[99] But many reports to the contrary appeared in the press. In some cases, a monthly grain ration was issued to collective farmers;[100] in others, flour was issued instead of grain;[101] food was often issued on a per-head basis to collective farmers working in the fields.[102] All these arrangements were rejected by the authorities, whose elaborate instructions included a provision that food could be issued during field work only by a resolution of the kolkhoz general meeting, and that such food must be deducted from the amount due to the collective farmer concerned from the harvest.[103] But distribution per eater nevertheless predominated. A survey by Kindeev showed

[97] P, February 25, 1930.
[98] I, March 17, 1930.
[99] See, for example, B, 14, July 31, 1930, 25; P, October 27, 1930; *6 s''ezd sovetov* (1931), No. 16, 6.
[100] *Ibid*. No. 20, 3.
[101] P, October 18, 1930.
[102] SZe, September 2, 1930.
[103] SZe, September 2, 1930.

that many kolkhozy distributed most of the harvest in kind on a per-household or per-eater basis: in these kolkhozy food grains were distributed solely per eater, and straw for fuel etc. were distributed per household; only fodder was distributed according to labour days, and even here the number of animals possessed by each household was taken into account.[104] At the VI congress of soviets, both Yakovlev and Yurkin reported that grain had been distributed per eater in the 'overwhelming majority' of kolkhozy.[105]

By the autumn of 1930, owing to the general shortage, the physical distribution of consumer goods was a crucial element in the real income of the peasants. But here, too, arrangements within the kolkhozy were apparently little influenced by the principle of remuneration according to work. Industrial consumer goods were distributed on a per-head basis in some places,[106] while in others they were simply made available at the discretion of the salesman in the village shop, and those who were not working tended to get there first.[107]

Thus the collective farmers received much of their share of the harvest, and their main supplies of industrial consumer goods, on a per-head basis. Only their collectively earned money income was distributed on the basis of labour days, and (see p. 156 below) this was a minor part of their total money income. In these circumstances, they could hardly have attached much importance to distribution on the basis of labour days.

While the authorities were temporarily compelled by force of circumstances to allow remuneration on a per-eater basis, the decision of April 13, 1930, to conciliate the middle peasant by distributing 5 per cent of the gross harvest in proportion to the property invested by the collective farmer in socialised Funds (see p. 143 above) was considerably modified in the course of 1930. A survey of a large number of kolkhozy by a group of instructors of Kolkhoztsentr concluded that 5 per cent was too high in areas in which MTS or former kulak property provided a substantial part of

---

[104] PKh, 7–8, 1930, 111.
[105] *6 s"ezd sovetov* (1931), No. 16, 6; No. 17, 14. Yakovlev's account was said to be based on direct enquiries to a large number of kolkhozy in face of contrary claims from many regional authorities.
[106] *6 s"ezd sovetov* (1931), No. 20, 3; SZe, October 12, 1930.
[107] SZe, October 12, 1930.

the capital used by the kolkhoz.[108] In June, a member of the board of Kolkhoztsentr accordingly proposed that property invested by collective farmers in socialised Funds should be deemed to include former kulak property, and that the appropriate proportion of 5 per cent of the harvest should be distributed to batraks and poor peasants.[109] Former kulak property constituted a substantial proportion of the Indivisible Funds of the kolkhozy (see p. 126 above), so this proposal, which was apparently widely put into practice, was a major modification of the original decision.[110] It was also proposed that in kolkhozy served by MTS the capital of the MTS should count in the allocation of the 5 per cent, the appropriate proportion being placed in the Indivisible Fund of the kolkhoz and used to purchase shares of Traktorotsentr, but this arrangement was not enforced in practice.[111] But the most important qualification to the original decision was that the 5 per cent deduction should not be paid in kind but in money made available by selling the products concerned to the collection agencies at fixed prices:[112] payment in rubles declining in value in conditions of goods shortage was obviously worth very much less in real terms than payment in kind. In the event, some payment was made: in groups of kolkhozy surveyed in the Central Black-Earth region and the North Caucasus, the percentage of gross income paid out under this head was reported to have varied from 3·5 to as much as 9·0 per cent.[113] But certainly the authorities reinterpreted their original decision in such a way as to diminish the amount paid in real terms to those collective farmers who had originally possessed more property.

At least 4 million of the 5 million peasant households which remained in the kolkhozy throughout 1930 joined after October 1, 1929, and for these 4 million households this was their first agricultural season as collective farmers. The traditional incentives

---

[108] SZe, October 9, 1930; the survey was presumably made in the spring, but its date was not given.

[109] SZe, June 24, 1930.

[110] Some discussion took place on whether the sums allocated should be set against their debts to the kolkhoz in the case of the numerous indebted poor peasants (SZe, August 6, 1930); I have not found out whether this was done.

[111] SZe, October 9, November 28, 1930.

[112] SZe, October 9, 1930.

[113] SRSKh, 6, 1931, 229.

of individual peasant agriculture had vanished for ever, with the important exception of their work on the household plot. The emergence of new incentives depended on the successful design and adoption of a new system of remuneration by the Soviet authorities; and on the accurate keeping of simple records for every collective farmer, and of more complex records for every collective farm, of a kind of which the Russian peasants had no experience. The authorities blundered in the first three months of 1930, introducing a system which was completely inappropriate to the conditions of its time. No new system emerged until the middle of 1930, and even then the barest outline of the new system was provided by the central authorities. Moreover, the new system, though ingenious and, given adequate resources, feasible, was complicated, and no mass training in the most elementary techniques had been provided for the hundreds of thousands of brigade leaders and tens of thousands of kolkhoz clerks or book-keepers who were required to operate it.

It is not surprising that, according to numerous reports published after the 1930 harvest, the confusion and incompleteness of the arrangements for reducing and remunerating the work of the collective farmer had very harmful effects on his performance. Without the exceptionally favourable weather conditions of 1930, disaster could hardly have been averted. At the VI congress of soviets in March 1931, Yakovlev, summing up the results of 1930, described the pernicious consequences of merely recording the number of days worked without any attention to the amount of work performed. Collective farmers got up at 8 a.m. in the busiest period of field work, and then chatted to their neighbours and prepared for work leisurely; when they were ready to go to the field, it was already by old peasant custom time for lunch (obed). Because no attention was paid in the remuneration system to quality, ploughing was rushed, leaving the soil in such a state that it damaged the machines; sowing was also hasty; grain was tied up badly so that some of it fell off the carts, and was left in the straw during threshing.[114] In a West Siberian kolkhoz 'brigade leaders had to go round and wake up members of the brigade in the mornings, and the meals were unduly prolonged'.[115] In a kolkhoz in central European Russia, the chairman had to kill a bull calf

---

[114] *6 s''ezd sovetov* (1931), No. 16, pp. 12, 15–16.
[115] SZe, January 16, 1931.

illegally and divide it up among a group of collective farmers in order to get them to cut hay in a remote part of the kolkhoz; 'the trouble is', a peasant remarked, 'that somehow people don't work on the *kolhoz* as they do for themselves. They are not as interested'.[116]

But even these troubles were relatively minor. Collective farmers were unclear about the remuneration they were to receive. They knew that most of the harvest was to be distributed on a per-eater basis irrespective of work done. They had alternative sources of income in their household plot and their animals. Money income was now of little value in view of the goods shortages. For all these reasons they were often very reluctant to work in the collective fields at all. In the Ukraine and the North Caucasus, for example, only young people turned up for work in the early stages of the harvest.[117] Elsewhere, peasants appeared for work belatedly when they discovered that remuneration was to be based on labour days,[118] or that the kolkhoz had decided to distribute grain per eater only to those households which had done a reasonable amount of work in the collective fields.[119] But on a kolkhoz in the Central Black-Earth region peasants who had not worked were permitted to pick cabbages, and were able to perform nearly as many labour days as those who had worked throughout the summer.[120] Yakovlev claimed that 'in every kolkhoz you can hear them saying "what's the use of working, you will get your share anyway"'.[121]

The situation varied, however, from kolkhoz to kolkhoz and from area to area. Other reports indicated something of a clamour to work for the kolkhoz, presumably in areas where agricultural labour was abundant and in kolkhozy where the peasant believed that the harvest would be distributed on the basis of labour days. In these cases, the adult members of families with large numbers of dependants were frequently allocated more work.[122] Where agricultural labour was abundant, kolkhozy often tended to allocate most of the work to former batraks and poor peasants, leaving the former middle peasants almost idle.[123] From this evidence of

---

[116] Hindus (1934), 328.   [117] VTr, 7–8, 1930, 35.
[118] P, October 27, 1930 (Lower Volga).
[119] P, October 27, 1930 (Lower Volga); *6 s"ezd sovetov* (1931), No. 18, 7.
[120] *Ibid.* No. 18, 7.
[121] *6 s"ezd sovetov* (1931), No. 16, 8.
[122] *Ibid.* No. 16, 15.
[123] VTr, 7–8, 1930, 35. The case for doing this was that the former middle

unwillingness to work in many places and an overabundance of labour in others, no firm conclusions can be drawn. On the basis of an extensive survey Yurkin claimed at the VI congress of soviets that only 40 per cent of collective farmers in all participated in harvest work in 1930;[124] this was misleading, however, as most of those not participating were women, who traditionally played a rather minor part in harvest work as such.

Firm figures about the income distributed to collective farmers by the kolkhozy in 1930 are almost completely lacking. By far the most important product distributed in kind was grain. If our calculations are correct, the kolkhozy retained about 3$\frac{1}{4}$ tons per household (see vol. 1, Table 15), and a substantial part of this was distributed to their members. They also received that part of the money income of the kolkhoz which remained after the payment of taxes and economic expenses, and allocations to the Indivisible and other Funds. But the money income of the kolkhoz was small, as it consisted almost entirely of payments by the collection agencies in fixed prices for grain and other agricultural products; a survey in eight areas of the USSR showed that in the agricultural year 1930/ 31 only approximately 17$\frac{1}{2}$ per cent of the money income of collective farmers came from the kolkhoz.[125]

The distribution of substantial quantities of grain to the collective farmers, at first encouraged by the authorities as a way of demonstrating to individual peasants that they would be better-off in the kolkhozy, had embarrassing consequences. Collective farmers sold some of their grain on the free market; this was not illegal, but was regarded as most improper.[126] Seeking to forestall such behaviour, some local authorities endeavoured to restrict grain distribution to the minimum needs of the collective farmer for personal consumption, and to maximise the distribution of money

---

peasant would tend to have more animals from which he could obtain products and income privately, and early in 1930 a Kolkhoztsentr decree had apparently ruled that priority in the allocation of work should be given to batraks and poor peasants; but at the kolkhoz conference in April 1930 Kolkhoztsentr recognised that this decree had 'forgotten the interests of the middle peasant' (SZe, April 15, 1930).

[124] *6 s''ezd sovetov* (1931), No. 17, p. 15.

[125] Unweighted average of percentages for two peasant social groups in eight areas, calculated from data in IISO, ii (1968), 334.

[126] See SRSKh, 8, 1931, 151.

income. The Central Volga regional authorities stipulated that collective farmers who earned more than the permissible grain consumption norm in terms of labour days should simply be paid the money value of grain earned in excess of the norm, with the value calculated at the low official collection prices, while collective farmers who earned less than the norm should be permitted to buy grain at wholesale prices.[127] This system prevented grain sales on the free market, but at the price of greatly reducing the incentive to work on the collective lands.

(v) The triumph of piece work and the labour day, end of 1930

The Soviet authorities drew the lesson from this experience that the new system should be applied more consistently and more vigorously. After the successful completion of the harvest, and of the first stage of the grain collections, the attitude of the central press to remuneration per eater became far more critical.[128] The previous official view that the collective farmers must make their own decisions about the best system was abruptly modified. In July, distribution of the harvest on a per-eater basis was regarded as a traditional peasant attitude, to be handled with understanding and even sympathy. In October, an editorial in the agricultural newspaper castigated it as a 'kulak principle'.[129] The freedom of choice for the collective farmer was removed at a stroke. At the kolkhoz conference in January 1931, Yurkin, in his opening report, stressed the importance of work norms and piece work, and condemned hostility to them as due to '"eateristic" attitudes'; and he again firmly condemned the equal division of the results of labour as 'wrecking in character' and as advocated by kulaks.[130] In his concluding report to the conference on behalf of Kolkhoztsentr, Tataev declared: 'The eater principle, payment by the day, and so

---

[127] *Kak raspredelyat'* (Samara, 1930), 7–8, 10–11, 15, 17–26.

[128] See for example SZe, October 23, 1930.

[129] SZe, October 26, 1930. The charge was incongruous, because per-eater distribution was simultaneously treated as a 'variant of consumptionist communism' (NAF, 10, 1930, 38). This was in connection with proposals made by Vareikis earlier in the year for a system of remuneration in which payments in kind from the harvest of grain, potatoes and fodder would be made on a per-head basis (NAF, 3, 1930, 32–3); these were now described as liable to 'disorganise the system of labour payment', and as 'depriving the kolkhoz of conditions enabling improved labour productivity' (NAF, 7–8, 1930, 103).

[130] SZe, January 14, 1931.

on, are a joke, although they still exist'.[131] The kolkhoz conference again recommended that income should be distributed solely by labour days, and adopted a scheme for the division of kolkhoz labour into four grades, credited with 0·7–1·5 labour days.[132]

At the VI congress of soviets in March 1931 Yakovlev reported that Stalin, during the preliminary discussion of issues confronting the congress, had stated that distribution according to work, the securing of the interest of the collective farmer in the results of his work, and proper records were 'the cornerstone of our congress of soviets'.[133] Yakovlev's report provided an elaborate defence of distribution according to work, and presented numerous examples purporting to demonstrate that piece work substantially increased productivity. He still admitted, however, that large families had a good case for demanding a minimum allocation of work: 'I do not think the kulaks talked them into it, they are simply defending their own interests'.[134] In its resolution the congress condemned the per-eater principle as the first of two 'very important and most harmful faults in the work of the kolkhozy in 1930' (the other was the bad organisation of labour):

> In all cases it involved the disruption of the material interest of the collective farmer in the results of kolkhoz production, a sharp reduction in labour productivity and as a result the reduction of the income of the kolkhoz. In such kolkhozy some collective farmers, the best and most class-conscious, the most devoted to the common cause, worked honestly, but others shirked work and used the kolkhoz as a means of profiting from the labour of others, of grabbing more from common labour and working less. The distribution of income (both in money and in kind) not by the quantity and quality of labour contributed by the collective farmer but per head is very often advocated by kulaks and other enemies of the kolkhoz, trying to disrupt the kolkhoz system. Such adherents of living on other people's work must be most decisively rebuffed, even expelling them from the kolkhoz.

Instead the rule for all collective farmers and kolkhozy must be: 'he who works more and better, receives more; he who does not work,

[131] SZe, January 19, 1931.
[132] For this scheme see Wronski (Paris, 1957), 22–33.
[133] *6 s"ezd sovetov* (1931), No. 16, pp. 17–18.
[134] *Ibid.* No. 16, pp. 15, 17–18.

receives nothing'; 'piece work evaluated in labour days' must be applied on a mass scale for all the main agricultural activities'.[135] After the experience of the first year of mass collectivisation, piece work and the labour day were firmly enshrined as the instruments by which work for the kolkhozy by its members would be remunerated.

(B) EARNINGS FROM PRIVATE SALES

In the autumn and winter of 1929–30 it seemed obvious in party circles that work for the kolkhoz would soon embrace the whole economic activity of the collective farmer, and that he would no longer grow his own products for sale. During the grain collection campaign in the autumn of 1929, articles in economic journals and in the daily press stressed the virtues of the planned supply of industrial goods to the villages in return for agricultural products, and argued that the market relations of the 1920s were being replaced by planned commodity-exchange.[136] Soon even the somewhat market-oriented term 'commodity-exchange (tovaroobmen)' temporarily dropped out of use. At the plenum of November 1929, the party central committee castigated 'the panic-stricken demands of the Right-wing opportunists for the unleashing of "free turnover" for the capitalist elements' and declared that the party was 'preparing conditions for the development of planned product-exchange (produktoobmen) between town and country'.[137]

In the autumn of 1929, prices on the free market rose drastically,[138] while on the official market industrial goods were often unobtainable. The incentive for peasants and collective farmers to take their products to the free market was overwhelming. For the moment, however, the authorities were hesitant about the extent to which all private trade could be eliminated immediately. In December 1929, Mikoyan argued that 'the role of market spontaneity is gradually being folded up', and that meat and dairy

---

[135] *Resheniya*, ii (1967), 289.

[136] See for example VF, 5, 1929, 3–19 (L. Shanin); *KTs . . . na 1929/30* (1930), 222.

[137] *KPSS v rez.*, ii (1954), 645.

[138] According to the official Gosplan index of retail prices, by January 1930 the prices of agricultural goods were 60·3 per cent and the prices of industrial goods 46·2 per cent above the January 1929 level on the private market; the index stood at 475 and 358 (1913 = 100) as compared with 204 and 207 in socialised trade (SO, 3–4, 1930, 107).

products would be the next to be brought under control in the process of mastering the whole food chain 'systematically, and reconstructing it on a socialist foundation'. He conceded, however, that areas which had completed their grain collection plan should be allowed to 'go over to spontaneous flow (samotek)'.[139] Later in the same month Chernov argued even more strongly that the grain collection campaign had 'to a considerable extent *eliminated market relations between town and village*', though he also assumed that in 1930 'an insignificant part of marketed grain' would go to bazaars, and that 'non-organised intra-peasant turnover' would continue.[140]

In the new year, the abolition of unorganised trade was treated by leading officials as an urgent task. In February, at a conference on 'exchange and distribution', a Narkomtorg spokesman called for '100 per cent inclusion of the worker's budget in the socialised sector of trade'; to this end a 'unified plan of product-exchange between town and village' must replace collection plans for particular agricultural products in 1930.[141] In many areas, local markets and bazaars were closed in an endeavour to force all rural trade into official channels.

This policy was, soon repudiated. In his speech of February 20, 1930, Syrtsov declared that while relations with the kolkhozy would in the future move towards direct product-exchange they would at first remain 'within the formal framework of monetary deals'; two market systems existed, one controlled by the state and the other involving the private sector (the second market, according to Syrtsov, included both direct deals between state organisations and trade in food products by milk-women and on stalls).[142] The resolution of the party central committee on March 14, 1930, instructed party organisations: '*forbid* the closing of markets, *re-open* bazaars and *do not hinder* the sale of their products on the market by peasants, including collective farmers'.[143] At the XVI party congress, Stalin declared 'we are not yet abolishing NEP, for private trade and capitalist elements still remain, commodity turnover and the money economy still remain'.[144] Collective farmers were now

---

[139] P, December 7, 1929.
[140] *Torgovo-promyshlennaya gazeta*, December 29, 1929; he claimed that intra-peasant turnover was 'not marketed grain to the full extent'.
[141] EZh, February 14, 1930 (Vinogradskii).
[142] B, 5, March 15, 1930, 43-4.
[143] *Resheniya*, ii (1967), 196.
[144] *XVI s"ezd* (1931), 37.

entitled to possess their own farm animals and to the permanent use of a household plot (see pp. 105–6 above), and—for the moment—to dispose of the resulting production as they thought fit.[145]

The production from the non-socialised economies of collective farmers was a substantial proportion of the total production of the kolkhoz sector: collective farmers grew large quantities of fruit and vegetables on their household plots, and owned personally most of the livestock in the kolkhozy. According to Gosplan calculations, 30 per cent of the gross income of the kolkhoz sector from farming in money and kind came from the personal economies of the collective farmers (see Table 8).[146] How much of this production was sold on the free market is not known. Total rural incomes from free-market sales in 1930 have been variously estimated at 2,800 and 3,300 million rubles.[147] A survey of peasant money incomes in eight areas in the agricultural year 1930/31 disclosed that in almost every region collective farmers obtained a smaller proportion of their money income from sales on the market than individual peasants; the proportion was nevertheless substantial.[148]

As a result of the strengthening of the personal economy of the collective farmers, and the restoration of the free market, inequality between former poor peasants and former middle peasants persisted, as the supporters of socialisation had feared. In each of the eight areas surveyed former poor peasant households, whose individual economies were relatively weak, earned a substantially smaller proportion of their income from sales on the market than

---

[145] A special issue in 1930 was the land sown individually in the autumn of 1929 and transferred to the kolkhoz by new members when they joined. Land consolidation regulations had already warned against disturbing these sowings in the process of forming the kolkhoz fields from the strips (SZe, February 9, 1930), and the 'explanatory note' of April 13, 1930, ruled that the harvest from them was to belong to the collective farmer concerned (SZe, April 13, 1930).

[146] According to an alternative calculation 28·8 per cent of the 'production income' of kolkhozy in kind and money, valued at 1930 prices, came from 'independent' production (*Materialy po balansu* (1932), 212–13).

[147] Malafeev (1964), 131; FP, 3–4, 1931, 23.

[148] IISO, ii (1968), 334; 25 per cent of the money income of collective farmers and 33 per cent of the income of poor and middle individual peasants came from sales on the market (unweighted average of poor and middle peasant groups of collective farmers and individual peasants in eight areas; this rough calculation probably underestimates the difference, as it gives too much weight to ex-middle peasants in kolkhozy, where they were a minority, and to poor peasants among the individual peasants).

former middle peasants, and this was evidently a major reason why their total money incomes were also much lower.[149]

(c) EARNINGS FROM OTKHODNICHESTVO

The most urgent question for collective farmers before the harvest of 1930 was the immediate income they could earn from work outside the kolkhoz. At the end of the 1920s otkhodnichestvo was very substantial. In the summer of 1929, over 2 million people were employed on seasonal timber cutting and logging, and 1·5 million on seasonal building work, and a high proportion of these came from the countryside. In addition, more than 3 million people were employed in seasonal agricultural work in kolkhozy and sovkhozy, individual farms, and sugar-beet, cotton and tobacco plantations, and several hundred thousand others in seasonal industries, making a total approaching 7 million in all.[150] According to Narkomtrud surveys, 4·3 million of these came from the countryside.[151] In 1930, owing to the vast expansion of capital construction, the demand for building labour was expected to reach 2·16 million at the height of the season against 1·31 million in 1929;[152] labour shortages, and a consequent pressure on wages, were anticipated.

The enormous expansion of the kolkhozy at the end of 1929 and in the first two months of 1930 threatened to disrupt the traditional market arrangements through which seasonal labour had been recruited from the countryside. The number of collective farmers required for seasonal labour of all kinds during 1930 was first estimated at 1·5 million, and later at 2 million persons.[153] But the kolkhozy, anxious to retain as much labour as possible, sometimes endeavoured to prevent their members from leaving for seasonal work. According to one report, otkhodnichestvo ceased in RSKs;[154] according to another, collective farmers going to work in Baku

---

[149] *Ibid.* 332–5; unfortunately this summary by a Soviet historian of archival data is tantalisingly inadequate.

[150] *Industrializatsiya SSSR, 1929–1932 gg.* (1970), 359; for earlier figures, see vol. 1, pp. 12, 48.

[151] VTr, 2, 1930, 54, 58–60.

[152] *Industrializatsiya SSSR, 1929–1932 gg.* (1970), 386–7 (Narkomtrud report reprinted from the archives).

[153] SZe, February 12, March 11, 1930; these estimates were published before the exodus of peasants from the kolkhozy in March and April 1930.

[154] ZI, January 24, 1930.

without permission were treated as deserters.[155] When kolkhozy permitted their members to undertake seasonal work, they often made large deductions from their earnings. In the Lower Volga region, many kolkhozy tried to requisition all the wages their members earned on sovkhozy, and pay them at kolkhoz rates; elsewhere, deductions amounted to 40–50 per cent of earnings; the situation was described as *'complete anarchy'*.[156]

Confronted with these difficulties, Narkomtrud and Kolkhoztsentr proposed rival solutions. Uglanov, the People's Commissar for Labour, complaining of the great labour shortage in the lumber industry, in building, and in loading and unloading in transport, called for a decree instructing kolkhozy to release their seasonal workers.[157] Kolkhoztsentr, however, insisted that collective farmers must obtain permission from the board of their kolkhoz before taking part in seasonal work, and proposed that all recruitment of seasonal labour should be undertaken by contracts between labour agencies and the kolkhozy.[158] The standpoint of Kolkhoztsentr prevailed. A draft decree from Kolkhoztsentr was approved by the Politburo on February 25, 1930,[159] and on March 3 a circular of Narkomzem, Kolkhoztsentr, Vesenkha and Narkomtrud announced an elaborate system for the central planning of seasonal labour from the kolkhozy. 'Control figures for otkhodnichestvo' were to be prepared at the centre, and issued by Kolkhoztsentr of the USSR to the republican Kolkhoztsentry. On this basis, plans showing the number of collective farmers to be released from each kolkhoz should be prepared by the okrug labour departments and kolkhozsoyuzy, and the okrug labour departments of Narkomtrud, or the economic agencies concerned, should, before April 1, sign agreements with the individual kolkhoz boards. Work-orders (naryady) issued on the basis of these agreements were compulsory, both for the kolkhoz and for the collective farmer concerned. Collective farmers were permitted to undertake seasonal work only when issued with a work-order by the kolkhoz board; the work was to be carried out under a group leader who would carry a document informing the employing agency of the percentage of wages which

---

[155] P, February 26, 1930; see also P, February 17, 1930; SZe, February 12, 1930.
[156] P, February 26, 17, 1930; SZe, February 12, 1930, June 28, 1930 (referring to the period before the March legislation).
[157] ZI, January 28, 1930.
[158] SZe, February 12, 1930.
[159] *Industrializatsiya SSSR, 1929–1932 gg.* (1970), 589.

was to be passed to the kolkhoz board.[160] These arrangements, if effective, would enable the central authorities to direct increasingly scarce seasonal labour to priority objectives, while at the same time ensuring that kolkhozy were not deprived of essential labour and did receive a share of the outside earnings of their members. But for the collective farmer they would represent a considerable restriction on his freedom to undertake seasonal work as compared with the position of the individual peasant.

The publication of this strongly-worded circular as late as the beginning of March reflected the confusion which prevailed at this time. Before it was published, the relaxation of the collectivisation drive at the end of February and the beginning of March had already affected otkhodnichestvo. While the model Statute of February 6 made no reference to otkhodnichestvo, the Statute of March 1, 1930, stipulated that deductions to kolkhoz income from outside earnings by collective farmers should be within the limits 3–10 per cent.[161] A fortnight later, on March 16, a Sovnarkom decree accused local soviets and kolkhoz organisations of causing 'great harm to the national economy' through their restrictions on the free departure of peasants to seasonal work, and instructed local authorities to prosecute those responsible.[162] The provisions of the model Statute and the decree did not abrogate the circular of March 3, but they by-passed it, for now a collective farmer was entitled to go freely to seasonal labour on his own initiative, as well as through the new contract system, providing he paid the stipulated proportion of his income to the kolkhoz.

In practice, the circular of March 3 was almost completely ineffective. In the Ukraine, only 5,307 of the 120,754 seasonal workers recruited were obtained through contracts;[163] in the Lower Volga, only a quarter of the kolkhozy followed official procedures; the situation was similar in other areas. Instead, 'spontaneity and lack of planning' prevailed.[164] From March onwards, substantial numbers of peasants went to work in the towns,[165] and frequent

---

[160] *Sbornik . . . prikazov po promyshlennosti, 1929/30,* No. 22, circular 41; ZI, March 4, 1930; see also SZe, March 11, 1930.

[161] I, February 7, March 2, 1930; the limits were repeated in categorical terms in later circulars of Kolkhoztsentr (SZe, April 4, 1930; SKhIB, 1, 1930, 18).

[162] SZ, 1930, art. 206.

[163] P, October 4, 1930.

[164] PKh, 7–8, 1930, 102 (Kindeev).

[165] P, June 29, 1930, disk. listok 24 (A. Golovanov).

reports appeared of disruption in the kolkhozy caused by the flow of labour to outside work. Kolkhozy were described in which families with many dependants were abandoned, and almost all the people remaining to work on the farm were schoolchildren.[166] Other reports, however, described continued restrictions by the kolkhozy: according to Vareikis, in the Central Black-Earth region the collective farmer was frequently subject to 'a considerable limitation of his personal freedom compared with his position before joining';[167] in the Central Volga region, only 5·5 per cent of all able-bodied collective farmers were released for seasonal work.[168]

Evidence about the extent to which the kolkhozy adhered to the stipulated limits on deductions from the incomes of their members from outside work also reveals great variations in kolkhoz practices. After the publication of the model Statute on March 2, some kolkhozy still deducted up to 50 per cent of these incomes, and even retained all the earnings of collective farmers who undertook casual outside work for a day or two.[169] A survey of 30 kolkhozy later in the summer showed that 21 made no deductions at all, while the other nine deducted amounts varying from 5 to 50 per cent.[170]

The extent of these personal and financial restrictions imposed by the kolkhozy on otkhodnichestvo in the summer of 1930 cannot now be established. The pressure on kolkhoz managements to retain labour was considerable: in many areas they were extremely short of labour at the peak of the agricultural season, both because their members were reluctant to work on the collective land (see pp. 154–5 above), and because their labour requirements were higher than in the individual peasant sector, owing to the larger cultivated area per household which the kolkhozy retained in the spring of 1930 (see vol. 1, pp. 308–9). All accounts agree that non-farming activities, and particularly otkhodnichestvo, were less important in the kolkhoz sector than in the individual sector. In 1930, the kolkhoz sector (including both the individual and the collective activities of collective farmers) earned only 18·6 per cent of non-farming gross rural income, as compared with 25.9 per cent of farming income (see Table 8). In all the eight areas covered by

---

[166] SZe, June 10, 1930; PKh, 7–8, 1930, 102, also reported that outside work 'often produced a critical situation for the whole economy of the kolkhoz'.

[167] B, 10, May 31, 1930, 40–1.

[168] NAF, 7–8, 1930, 111.

[169] SZe, March 30, April 2, 1930.

[170] PKh, 7–8, 1930, 102 (Kindeev).

the survey of rural money incomes in 1930/31, the percentage of money income received from non-farming earnings was higher for individual peasants than for collective farmers.[171] Another report showed that collective farmers, who constituted about 20 per cent of the peasant population, earned only 16.8 per cent of all peasant wage incomes.[172]

In a startling reversal of past trends, the total supply of seasonal labour to the towns fell considerably during the harvest period. The total number of building workers declined by 187,000 in August 1930, as compared with the previous month, while it increased in August 1929. The shortage of labour was partly due to the large increase in demand: the number of building workers in August 1930, estimated at 1·78 million, was as much as 56·6 per cent higher than in August 1929.[173] But in many reports the shortage was also attributed to the desire of kolkhoz managements to retain labour.[174]

With the acute labour shortage which resulted from the growing pressures of industrialisation, the authorities saw the flexible arrangements of 1930 as purely temporary. The availability of surplus labour in the kolkhoz, and the need to make use of it, was a persistent theme in the last few months of 1930. An article in the agricultural journal, envisaging an expansion of the seasonal labour force from 7 to 15 million in the course of two or three years, argued that it would become a second branch of collective production; it should be planned by the kolkhoz, and the kolkhoz should have the power to oblige its members to participate in it.[175] In August, Kolkhozsentr conducted a successful drive to recruit 20,000 collective farmers to work in the Donbass, where labour was extremely scarce; the collective farmers retained all the rights of members of kolkhozy, were awarded various privileges in relation to the harvest, and their wages were made subject only to the minimum deduction into kolkhoz income, but the kolkhoz was required to refuse to accept them back if they left the mines.[176] Reviewing this experience, a Narkomtrud official called for individual kolkhozy and particular areas to be attached to particular

---

[171] IISO, ii (1968), 335.

[172] *Materialy po balansu* (1932), 212–13; for the kolkhoz population see p. 127, n. 51, above.

[173] *Industrializatsiya SSSR, 1929–1932 gg.* (1970), 387.

[174] See for example *ibid.* 389, 392; this is a Narkomtrud report from the archives.

[175] NAF, 9, 1930, 67, 70–1.

[176] P, August 22, 1930; SZe, December 16, 1930.

economic agencies, so as to avoid all possibility of competition, and for the system of contracts with the kolkhozy to become the general rule.[177] At the conference on kolkhoz labour in January 1931, Barchuk, after reviewing the experience of 1930, announced that 9·6 million seasonal workers would be required in 1931, and called for the establishment of a system of control figures for otkhodnichestvo, based on labour balances, and broken down to districts and to obligatory plans for every kolkhoz; for the time being, unplanned otkhodnichestvo by individual collective farmers would also be permitted. To encourage the collective farmers to participate, the deduction to kolkhoz income from their earnings should be cut to from 3–10 to 2–3 per cent, they should be entitled to receive part of kolkhoz production in kind throughout their period of work, and their family should get a full share of products in kind even if they had not fulfilled their quota of labour days. At the same time, kolkhozy should develop artisan production in order to use up surplus female labour.[178] On these proposals, otkhodnichestvo, and non-agricultural production generally, would be an expanding element in the income of the collective farmers, and they would be subject to a comprehensive national plan for the training and allocation of seasonal labour.

(D) REMUNERATION AS A WHOLE

The main features of the arrangements for the remuneration of the collective farmer which were established by the autumn of 1930 persisted throughout the Stalin period and beyond. This was not a unified or even a coherent system, but a mixture of different systems and devices, traditional and new, introduced piecemeal in the course of the struggle to adapt the individual peasant to the new collective way of life.

Even after the retreat from collectivisation in the spring of 1930, the Soviet leaders took it for granted that the socialised sector of the kolkhoz would soon come to predominate overwhelmingly in the economic activity of the collective farmers, and provide the major source of their income. Over 90 per cent of the sown area of the

[177] SZe, December 16, 1930; VTr, No. 12, 1930, 75–6 (both articles by I. Fominykh).
[178] SZe, January 17, 1931.

kolkhoz was socialised, and the state allocated its machinery, money, manpower and advice almost exclusively to the socialised sector. While the household plot and privately-owned animals were officially permitted from the spring of 1930, the authorities confidently expected that these activities, and the income from them, would rapidly diminish with the strengthening of the socialised sector.

The products of the kolkhoz, like those of the individual peasant farm, were intended both for personal consumption by members and for sale, and collective farmers received their share of socialised income both in kind and in money. Income in kind was received mainly in grain, the principal product of the socialised sector of the kolkhoz. On average the collective farm household retained far more grain than the individual household, and this was a major factor impelling individual peasants to join, or rejoin, the kolkhozy in 1931.

But the arrangements for remunerating collective work did not offer adequate incentives to replace the stimulus provided to the individual peasants by the market, and by the need to produce food for their own consumption. The ingenious system of labour days successfully adjusted the level of payment of the peasants for their work before and during the harvest to the size of the income available for distribution after the harvest. But it proved very difficult to design work norms suitable for the immense variety of jobs and territory in the USSR, and still more difficult to penalise shoddy, and reward conscientious, work. In the autumn of 1930, the novel labour-day system was not yet much used in practice, and all these weaknesses seemed to be temporary administrative difficulties which would be overcome with experience; the authorities were confident that the system would work smoothly once it had fully replaced payment per eater. But in the ensuing decades these temporary administrative difficulties permanently haunted the kolkhoz.

The good harvest, and the high level of grain distribution in 1930, partly obscured an even more fundamental problem. The aim of the state was to remove as much production as possible from the kolkhoz through the official collections. In future years, with lower harvests, and with many more peasants in the kolkhozy, the grain collectors were more strict towards the kolkhozy, and they retained much less grain per household than in 1930; the unwillingness of the collective farmer to work on the collective lands became a permanent difficulty of the kolkhoz economy. Even in 1930, while grain distributions were high, the collective money income available for distribution was small; the kolkhozy received nearly all their money income from sales to the official collection agencies at fixed prices, now only a fraction of free-market prices. Because their money income from collective work was low, the collective farmers looked to their personal economies not only for food, apart from grain, but also for most of their money income, much of the rest of it being earned from otkhodnichestvo and other personal non-agricultural activities. Collective farmers received on the free market four or five times as many rubles for a product from their household plot than for the same product grown collectively and sold to the state. So even in 1930, the Indian summer of the kolkhoz system, their efforts and enthusiasm were directed to their personal economy; their work on the collective lands was less conscientious, and undertaken only for the minimum number of days required to obtain essential supplies of grain. A substantial increase in payment for collective work could change these priorities; but in the next quarter of a century this did not take place.

In 1930, the authorities were concerned to demonstrate un-ambiguously that it was more profitable to be a collective farmer than an individual peasant. It is not possible to assess accurately the income in 1930 of collective farm households in kind and in money in comparison with individual peasant households. Taking their total income in kind from the collective sector and their household plot together, their income in grain exceeded that of the individual peasant, but they undoubtedly consumed less meat and dairy products per head, as the total number of animals per household in the kolkhozy was lower than in the individual peasant sector (see vol. 1, p. 339). The average money income of a kolkhoz household in 1930/31 was estimated in a sample survey at only 591 rubles as compared with 605 rubles for an individual peasant household. Some monetary expenses which were paid by the individual peasant out of his income were, however, borne from the collective money income of the kolkhoz (for example, the purchase of fodder and harness for horses); when these expenses are taken into account, money income in 1930/31 could have been as high in the collective farm household as in the household of the individual peasant.[179] On the other hand, the cash held by the average collective farm

---

[179] IISO, ii (1968), 333.

household in the agricultural year 1930/31 was estimated at only 60 rubles as compared with 79 rubles held by the individual peasant.[180] Certainly the collective farmers did not have obviously larger money incomes than the individual peasants; and, in their total income in kind, the higher availability of grain must be set against the lower availability of meat and dairy products. In spite of the advantages of the kolkhozy in land allocation and state support, the average total income of the collective farm household did not substantially exceed that of the individual peasant. This was partly because most collective farmers were former batraks and middle peasants, who came into the kolkhozy with relatively little capital. For the peasants outside the kolkhoz, the advantages of membership were not overwhelmingly demonstrated by the outcome of the harvest of 1930.

[180] *Ibid.* 337.

CHAPTER EIGHT

CONCLUSIONS

Before the collectivisation drive of the winter of 1929–30, only a small minority of peasants belonged to kolkhozy, and most kolkhozy included only a minority of the households in the settlement of which they formed a part—on June 1, 1929, the average number of households per kolkhoz was only 17·7. Three-fifths of the 55,000 kolkhozy were TOZy, and the typical kolkhoz did not go beyond the partial socialisation of arable farming. Collective farmers were remunerated by a variety of payment systems, most prominent among which were payment for time devoted to collective work, and payment 'per eater', i.e. according to the number of members of the household. These small kolkhozy were simple in their structure and organisation. But in two important respects they were techni-cally more advanced than the individual peasant economies which surrounded them. First, on most kolkhoz land, the fields of the crop rotation were not divided into strips, and this made for more efficient farming. Secondly, over one-third of all kolkhozy used or had access to a tractor. In consequence, yields were somewhat higher on kolkhoz lands than on comparable lands cultivated by individual peasants. But the economic advantages of the kolkhozy were not sufficient to persuade most individual peasants to relinquish voluntarily their traditional way of life.

For the party leaders, however, the kolkhozy had very obvious attractions. The proportion of grain production sold to the state was much higher for kolkhozy than for individual peasants. And the leaders were convinced that mechanisation and scientific farming on industrial lines would lead to a rapid expansion of agricultural production, and, together with the development of collective forms of agriculture, would resist and eventually eliminate petty capi-talism in the countryside.

At the height of the collectivisation drive, comprehensive collectivisation came to imply that more advanced forms of kolkhoz organisation should prevail immediately. In December 1929–

February 1930, central and local kolkhoz authorities and local party organisations encouraged the immediate establishment of giant kolkhozy in which there was a high level of socialisation: the socialisation of all livestock was often advocated, and a large question mark appeared against the future of the personal household plots of collective farmers. Kolkhoztsentr approved a system for remunerating collective farmers which closely followed the industrial wage system. Trotsky commented acidly on these developments: 'An obvious contradiction: the wider the scale of forced collectivization, and consequently the lower its technical base, the higher is the type of social relations that the utopian-bureaucratic leadership wants to impose'.[1]

This precipitate shift towards higher forms of kolkhozy was not, however, a deliberate strategy planned in advance by Stalin and the Politburo. Stalin was silent or ambiguous about all these questions in his published pronouncements. In his speech of December 27, 1929, he even appeared to be unresponsive to the pressure for a high degree of socialisation, in marked contrast to his firm pronouncement in favour of the elimination of the kulaks and his insistence on the viability of collectivisation without mechanisation (see p. 87 above, and vol. 1, pp. 197–8, 391–2). No firm recommendations about kolkhoz organisation were made by the central committee. These matters were deliberately left to 'local initiative'. This was a time when, in all spheres of the economy, and of political, intellectual and cultural life, far-reaching plans and alternative sets of proposals were prepared and feverishly debated, with little detailed interference from the central party authorities.

But this 'system-building' was carried out within a definite political framework, in which the radical restructuring of society was regarded with approval, and traditional approaches were treated as manifestations of Right deviation. In these tumultuous months, it seemed to many party leaders and activists at every level that enthusiasm and improved organisation could solve all problems. Stalin and his associates evidently decided that this was a time of revolutionary break-through, in which manifestations of revolutionary élan, however extreme, should not for the moment be discouraged; and they were themselves captivated by this mood, and encouraged it, when only their own positive intervention could

---

[1] *Writings of Leon Trotsky (1930)* (New York, 1975), 112 (article of February 13, 1930).

have restrained the lower party organisations. Some statements by party leaders even supported more radical forms of kolkhoz organisation, though in rather general terms. Thus at the plenum of the central committee in November 1929 Molotov urged the kolkhozy to 'model yourselves on the sovkhozy', and shortly afterwards Kaganovich enthusiastically praised the Gigant kolkhoz in the Urals in a well-publicised report. There is also some evidence to suggest that behind the scenes Stalin encouraged the extravagant proposals about socialisation within the kolkhozy made by Ryskulov and others.

In the optimistic atmosphere of December 1929 – February 1930, the proposed forms of organisation seemed logical and coherent to enthusiastic adherents of rapid collectivisation. They argued that if the kolkhoz were to manage its own tractors, it must be a giant, approaching the size of an administrative district; otherwise its tractor economy would be small and inefficient. The district-kolkhoz would also enable the development of food-processing enterprises and industries using agricultural raw materials, which would be quite uneconomical on the scale of a single village. And, given that the experience of Khoper okrug had shown that large-scale farming could be conducted efficiently with horses and ploughs, it also seemed advantageous to establish giant kolkhozy in advance of mechanisation, and to replace the inefficient crop rotations of rural settlements, formed more or less accidentally in the course of history, by planned rotations on an inter-village basis. Such arguments in favour of the district-kolkhoz in 1930 rehearsed those in favour of the establishment of agricultural communes containing thousands of households in China in 1958.

The case for socialisation of livestock rested on similar premisses. Large-scale livestock farms within the kolkhozy would yield great economies of scale. And socialisation of livestock was made urgent by the widespread slaughter which began in the summer of 1929. Leading party officials insisted that livestock must be incorporated in the collective sector of the kolkhozy before it was destroyed. They also argued that, with middle peasants and even well-to-do middle peasants joining the kolkhozy in large numbers, the socialisation of livestock was essential to prevent social inequality; without socialis-ation, a kulak class might emerge within the kolkhozy on the basis of private livestock (this was a fear shared by Trotsky).

The decision to introduce a wage system within the kolkhoz based on payment for skill and quantity of work made it clear that the giant fully-socialised kolkhoz was not intended, at any rate by the central kolkhoz authorities, as a move towards communism, with payment according to need, but was instead modelled on the contemporary Soviet state factories, with their socialist system of payment according to work. But the notions of kolkhoz organisation which prevailed in the early weeks of 1930 were nevertheless wholly unrealistic. The farming skills and organisational experience required for the successful establishment of giant fully-socialised kolkhozy were completely lacking in the Soviet Union, and the state was quite unable, and unwilling, to make available even the minimum of resources required for such an immense reorganisation. When collectivisation was at its peak in March 1930, much of this ambitious programme remained without practical consequences. Giant kolkhozy were established only in a minority of cases. The payment of wages to collective farmers was usually impossible owing to the shortage of cash in the kolkhozy. Much livestock was socialised—with disastrous results—but even here the authorities paid most attention to the socialisation of seeds, horses and ploughs, essential to the success of the spring sowing.

The retreat from radical forms of kolkhoz organisation was an integral part of the retreat from collectivisation. It was shown in vol. 1 that the Politburo, fearing a catastrophic failure of the spring sowing, decided to call for a retreat when faced by widespread unrest among the peasants in many areas in February 1930. One of the major elements in this unrest was hostility to the attempts to introduce new forms of kolkhoz organisation. The giant kolkhozy lacked good communications and experienced organisers, and were remote from and alien to the collective farmers. The confusion of the arrangements for remuneration, and the universal absence of adequate payments, were further causes of resentment. The socialisation of livestock was the feature of kolkhoz organisation which aroused the greatest hostility, particularly among women collective farmers, who were responsible for tending the animals.

In the spring and summer of 1930 these schemes were all abandoned. The giant kolkhozy were dissolved, and the principle was restored that the boundaries of the kolkhozy should correspond to those of existing villages or settlements. The artel form of kolkhoz was henceforth strongly favoured in preference to the commune. The main fields, and the horses and ploughs of the collective farmers, were socialised, but most livestock remained in the ownership of the collective farm household, which was also guaranteed the right to its household plot for growing fruit and vegetables. The attempt to introduce a wage system was also abandoned, and replaced—in principle, though not yet in practice—by the ingenious 'labour-day' system: the collective farmer was rewarded according to work, but at the same time his or her earnings were treated as a residual or dividend, paid from what was left over from kolkhoz income in kind and in money after deliveries to the state had been completed and taxes paid, and after allocations had been made to the Indivisible and other Funds of the kolkhoz.

The resentment among the peasants aroused by the general process of collectivisation resulted in a purely temporary retreat by the authorities, *reculer pour mieux sauter*, and forcible collectivisation was resumed within less than a year (see vol. 1, ch. 9). But the 'kolkhoz compromise', the dual economy of socialised farming on collective lands (the former *nadel*), and private or personal farming on the household plot (the former *usad'ba*), has continued as a permanent feature of the kolkhoz economy; the kolkhoz has continued to be based on the traditional settlement or village; and the labour-day system began to give way to a wage system only in the 1960s.

In 1930, this was certainly not the intention. The authorities believed that the rapid growth of the socialised sector would soon make personal livestock and the household plot unprofitable and superflous, or at any rate quantitatively insignificant, and that the growing prosperity of the kolkhozy would soon make it possible to go over to a wage system.

These hopes rested on two false assumptions. First, it was supposed that within a few years Soviet agriculture would be the most technologically advanced in the world, with a higher level of production per head of population and per hectare than in the United States; this would rapidly reduce the household plots to insignificance. This was a false assumption about industry rather than agriculture; it accepted as feasible the over-optimistic revised five-year plans for the production of tractors and agricultural machinery, which were officially approved in the spring and summer of 1930 (these plans will be discussed in vol. 3). The second false assumption was that, with growing prosperity, the pressure of the state to acquire kolkhoz production at low prices would diminish, and collective farmers would receive an increasing flow of industrial consumer goods in return for the state collections; this would, it was supposed, make collective work far more attractive economically than work on the household plot. In fact after 1930 agricultural production declined, and the growing requirements of the capital goods' industries also led to a decline in the availability of industrial consumer goods. But state demands to acquire the production of kolkhozy at low prices did not diminish, and work on the collective lands was poorly remunerated. The household plot and private livestock therefore continued, as in 1930, to be far more rewarding than work on the collective lands, and remained a major source of urban and rural food supplies which the state did not try to eliminate by compulsion, and was unable to eliminate by competition. And the continuing poverty of the kolkhozy made the introduction of a wage system impossible.

The incorporation of private livestock in the kolkhoz system was primarily a victory for the former middle peasant households, and particularly for the female members of those households, as former middle peasant households possessed far more animals than former poor peasants and batraks. These inequalities were limited by the restrictions imposed on the number of animals which a kolkhoz household could own, but they remained a feature of the kolkhoz economy. They were soon overshadowed, however, by the emergence in the course of the early 1930s of new types of social and economic division within the kolkhoz, between the chairman and the other kolkhoz administrators, the brigade leaders and the rank-and-file collective farmers.

A further change completed the establishment of what continued to be the main features of kolkhoz organisation for over a quarter of a century. The decision in the spring of 1930 that each kolkhoz should be based on an existing settlement or village carried with it the consequence that tractors and other major items of agricultural machinery should not be owned by individual kolkhozy, which could not in the near future own enough machinery to be able to maintain and repair it efficiently. Whether the Machine-Tractor Stations should be managed by the state-owned Traktorotsentr, by the kolkhozsoyuzy or by the agricultural cooperatives still remained a matter of controversy. In September 1930, however, a central committee resolution gave clear priority to Traktorotsentr. Little is known about the circumstances of this decision. While it was obviously influenced by the decline of the cooperatives during the collectivisation drive, and by the weakness of the kolkhozsoyuzy, it proved to be a first major step towards the formal concentration of the management of the kolkhoz system in the hands of the state.

The kolkhoz, as it emerged in 1930, was thus in an ambiguous position. Formally it was owned and managed by its members as a cooperative organisation. In practice, while the influence of the members over its economic behaviour was not negligible, a large part of its production was appropriated by the state at nominal prices, and its economic activities were controlled by state officials and party activists acting under instructions from the state, and (where they existed) by the state or cooperative Machine-Tractor Stations. On the other hand, a substantial part of the production of collective farmers came from their household plots and could be sold by them at market prices; this was a wedge of personal or private economy built into the kolkhoz itself.

At the end of 1929, the social nature of the kolkhoz was the subject of intense debate. Larin argued that for an economic unit to be socialist it must be the property of the state and not of a particular group of individuals, and its members must work for the whole society; the kolkhoz was therefore not a socialist but a transitional type of economy, in which the collective interests of its members could result in a clash of interests with the state. Stalin, however, insisted that the kolkhoz was a form of socialist economy, in which the main instruments of production were socialised and land belonged to the state; the kolkhoz did not contain exploiting and exploited classes, and, although 'elements of class struggle' existed within the kolkhozy, these would soon die away. Nothing specific was said about the household plot or privately owned livestock, which were assumed to be of minor and diminishing significance, and they were not designated as 'socialist' (on the grounds that they formed part of the kolkhoz economy) until some years later. But ever since Stalin's pronouncement at the end of 1929 the kolkhoz has invariably been treated in Soviet publications as part of the socialist economy; even earlier, kolkhozy which resisted the demands of the state were castigated as 'bogus', as having, as it were, cast themselves out of the socialist economy.

With almost the whole of industry state- or cooperatively-owned, and with private trade (except bazaar trade by individuals) virtually eliminated, it followed, on the official Soviet definition, that after the completion of comprehensive collectivisation and the elimination of the individual peasant economies the whole Soviet economy would be socialist. In December 1930, the plenum of the party central committee accordingly announced that the successful completion of the plan to collectivise 50 per cent of all peasant households by the end of 1931 would result in 'an absolute predominance of socialist elements over the individual sector in the countryside', and would 'complete the construction of the foundation (fundament) of the socialist economy of the USSR', a 'victory of world-historical significance'.[2] Stalin's unambiguous definition of the kolkhoz as a 'form of socialist economy' had provided the basis for a speedy announcement of the triumph of socialism in one country.

[2] *KPSS v rez.*, iii (1954), 81.

TABLES

Table 1. Stock of tractors by social sector, October 1, 1928–January 1, 1931

(a) Number

	A. In sovkhozy	B. In MTS, including cooperative columns	C. In agricultural cooperatives	D. In kolkhozy and their group associations	In MTS, kolkhozy and cooperatives (B+C+D)	E. In individual households	Total
Stock on October 1, 1928	6719	—	6673	10854	17257	2487	26733
Net increase in 1928/29	2959	2387	-2904	8255	8008	-2487	8210
Stock on October 1, 1929	9678	2387	3769	19109	25265	—	34943
Net increase in 1929/30	15275	18414	-3769	1469	16114	—	31389
Stock on October 1, 1930	24953	20801	—	20578	41379	—	66332
Net increase in October–December 1930	2732	10313	—	-7299	3014	—	5746
Stock on January 1, 1931	27685	31114	—	13279	44393	—	72078

(b) Horse-power (thousands)

Stock on October 1, 1928	77·6	—	66·7	108·9	175·6	24·9	278·1
Net increase in 1928/29	45·8	23·9	−8·7	77·2	92·4	−24·9	113·3
Stock on October 1, 1929	123·4	23·9	58·0	186·1	268·0	—	391·4
Planned allocation for 1929/30	220	85·	—	57·	142·	—	362·
Net actual increase in 1929/30	322·1	233·2	−58·0	37·3	212·5	—	534·6
Stock on October 1, 1930	445·5	257·1	—	223·4	430·5	—	926·0
Net increase in October–December 1930	37·6	115·4	—	−75·5	399	—	77·5
Stock on January 1, 1931	483·1	372·5	—	147·9	—	—	1003·5

Sources: Calculated from *Nar. kh.* (1932), 145, except plan for 1929/30, which is calculated from *K'Ts . . . na 1929/30* (1930), 123, 131.

Table 2. Machine-Tractor Stations and tractor columns, 1929–1930

(a) Plans for 1929 and 1930

Date of plan	Planned period	System of Traktorotsentr				Cooperative system (Khlebotsentr)		
		Number of MTS	Number of tractors	Tractor h.p. (thousands)	Sown area (thousand ha)	Number of MTS and columns	Number of tractors	Sown area (thousand ha)
June 5, 1929[1]	1929/30 By spring		5000+	100	1000[a]			
December 16, 1929[2]	1930	104[b]	5200		520–624[c]			
February 1, 1930[3]	{ By spring 1930	159	5555[4]		1490[4d]			
	1929/30	214			1970[4e]			
February 13, 1930	1930					490[5f]	18000[5f]	

(b) Fulfilment in 1929 and 1930

Date	Number of MTS	Number of tractors	Tractor h.p.	Sown area	Number of MTS and columns	Number of tractors	Sown area
Spring 1929	1[6]			24[6]	45[5fg]	1182[5fg]	70[7g]
September 1929					61[5f]	2045[5f]	
February 1930					185[5f]	5000+[5f]	
May–June 1930	158[8h]	7102[8h]	87[8h]	2000[4i]	465[9i]	12500[9ji]	2200[9k]
December 31, 1930	360[10l]	31114[11l]	372.5[11l]				

Sources: [1] SZ, 1929, art. 353.
[2] BU NKZ RSFSR, No. 52, 1930, p. 15.
[3] SZ, 1930, art. 130.
[4] NAF, 6, 1930, 121–3.
[5] P, February 13, 1930 (Belenky).
[6] Markevich (1929), 35.
[7] P, July 13, 1929.
[8] *Sols. str.* (1935), 310, 312.
[9] NFK, May 15, 1930, 13 (Belenky).
[10] PS, 3–4, 1931, 77–9 (decree of January 21, 1931).
[11] *Nar. kh.* (1932), 145.

Notes: [a] Arable area.
[b] P, September 12, 1929, announced a Traktorotsentr plan to establish 100 new MTS in 1929/30 (see p. 20 above).
[c] 5,000–6,000 hectares per MTS.
[d] 1·31 million hectares grain plus 0·18 million hectares cotton.
[e] 1·75 grain arable plus 0·20 cotton, 0·01 sugar beet and 0·01 soya.
[f] This figure refers to the RSFSR; there were 36 columns and MTS in the Ukraine in the autumn of 1929 (Danilov (1957), 364).
[g] The number of cooperative MTS and columns is given as 58 and the number of their tractors as over 1,500 in P, July 13, 1929.
[h] June 1, 1930.
[i] By June 15, 1930; includes grain and cotton; this figure seems improbably high.
[j] Immediately before spring sowing.
[k] By May 1, 1930.
[l] Includes MTS and columns transferred from the cooperatives.

Table 3. Average number of households per kolkhoz, June 1,
1928–September 1, 1930

	June 1, 1928	June 1, 1929	October 1, 1929	January 1, 1930	March 1, 1930	September 1, 1930
USSR	12·5	17·7	28·5	63·5	132·7	58·0
RSFSR	12·5	16·9	28·0	71·4	136·5	56·3
Including:						
Western	10·0	11·3	14·9	26·4	47·3	30·1
Moscow	14·5	15·6	21·3	58·0	77·4	28·8
Ivanovo-						
Industrial	11·2	12·7	15·6	51·6	57·3	26·8
Central						
Black-Earth	14·5	20·6	32·7	141·8	253·4	54·4
Ural	11·0	20·3	33·1	101·1	226·6	45·7
Central Volga	15·5	17·9	31·5	45·7	196·4	68·5
Lower Volga	11·0	17·7	46·9	288·3[a]	480·6	108·4
North Caucasus	12·1	16·1	35·6	341·5	262·0	186·0
Siberia	12·9	20·4	27·9	26·5[a]	56·4	44·1
Ukraine	12·6	19·9	33·1	47·6	123·1	55·2
Uzbekistan	14·3	15·0	20·8	26·5[a]	96·6	68·2

Source: Calculated from data in *Ezhegodnik po sel. kh. 1931* (1933), 440–3.

Note: [a] Based on very low figures given in source for number of households collectivised (see vol. 1, Table 17, notes b, c and d).

Table 4. Kolkhozy by type of Statute,[a] 1927–1930

	Number				Percentage			
	Communes	Artels	TOZy	Total	Communes	Artels	TOZy	Total
June 1, 1921	n.a.	n.a.	n.a.	n.a.	20[1]	65[1]	15[1]	100[1]
June 1, 1927[b]	1335[4]	7134[4]	6363[4]	14832[2]	9·0[3]	48·1[3]	42·9[3]	100
June 1, 1928[c]	1847	11390	19694	32931	5·6	34·6	59·8	100
June 1, 1929[c,d]	3416	18440	33043	54899	6·2	33·6	60·2	100
October 1, 1929[b]	4654[9]	20773[9]	42019[9]	67446[9]	6·9[8]	30·8[8]	62·3[8]	100
May 1930	7342[10]	62006[10]	14522[10]	84050[10e]	8·8[3]	73·7[3]	17·3[3]	99·83[f]

Sources: [1] See Lewin (1968), 109–10.
[2] *Kolkhozy v 1930 g.* (1931), 6.
[3] *Ibid.* 12.
[4] Derived from sources 2 and 3 above.
[5] *Kolkhozy v 1928 g.* (1932), 2.
[6] *Kolkhozy v 1929 godu* (1931), 2.
[7] *Sdvigi* (1931), 22.
[8] *Ibid.* 30.
[9] Derived from sources 7 and 8 above.
[10] *Kolkhozy v 1930 g.* (1931), 78.

Notes: [a] All these figures refer to the Statute as which the kolkhoz was registered, not the 'economic type'.
[b] Excludes Yakut ASSR (17 kolkhozy on June 1, 1928).
[c] The number of kolkhozy 'by economic type' were:

	June 1, 1928	June 1, 1929
Communes	3335	3327
Artels	3796	17062
TOZy	16862	26661
Total	[23993]	[47050]

(*Kolkhozy v 1928 g.* (1932), pp. iv, 66; *Kolkhozy v 1929 godu* (1931), pp. xliv, 4). Kolkhozy by economic type exclude kolkhozy without collective sown area in 1928 and kolkhozy without a socialised branch of the economy in 1929 (in the 1929 figures, the Ural region is included by registered Statute and not by economic type).

[d] Excludes Yakut ASSR, Mari autonomous region and an okrug of Kirgiz ASSR. Total number of kolkhozy in the USSR on this date was 57045 (*Sdvigi* (1931), 22); oddly, the percentages of different types for the whole USSR given in *Sdvigi* (1931), 32, and elsewhere are identical with those given above for 54,899 kolkhozy; the above figures are more likely to be reliable.

[e] Total number of kolkhozy for this date is given as 85,950 in *Sdvigi* (1931), 22, and figures close to this are given in other sources; again, the percentages of different types of Statute given in this source (*ibid.* 30) are the same as those given for the lower number of kolkhozy in our source 10.

[f] Kolkhozy without a productive branch of agriculture are excluded from these percentages.

Table 5. Socialisation of draught animals in kolkhozy, 1929–1930 (thousands)

	Total number of draught animals in kolkhozy	Number of socialised draught animals in kolkhozy	Socialised draught animals in kolkhozy as percentage of total
June 1, 1929[1a]	703	312	44·4
January 1, 1930[2b]	2110	370	17·4
February 1, 1930[2]	5160	2760	51·8
February 10, 1930[2]	8430	5670	67·2
February 20, 1930[2]	10530	8550	81·2
March 1, 1930[2]	11930	9350[c]	78·3
May 1930[1d]	5020	4774	95·1

Sources: [1] *Kolkhozy v 1930 g.* (1931), 10–11.
  [2] I, March 9, 1930; figures published during the campaign (e.g. in SZe, February 11, 21, 1930 referring to February 1 and 10) differ only slightly from these.
Notes: [a] Excluding Yakut ASSR.
  [b] Given as January 20, 1930, in source.
  [c] Number on March 10 was 10·3 million (SO, 3–4, 1930, 109).
  [d] Excluding Tadzhik SSR, and Kirgiz and Yakut ASSRs.

Table 6. Socialised livestock, 1929–1930 (thousands)

(a) Socialised livestock in sovkhozy and kolkhozy

	May–June 1929			May–June 1930		
	Sovkhozy	*Kolkhozy*	*Total*	*Sovkhozy*	*Kolkhozy*	*Total*
Cattle	204	386	590	757	3620	4377
Sheep and goats	1203	695	1897	2754	5650	8605
Pigs	54	126	180	181	769	950

Source: *Nar. kh.* (1932), 188–9, 655–6; sovkhoz and kolkhoz figures for 1929 are from a complete census; method of collecting sovkhoz figures for 1930 is not stated; kolkhoz figures for 1930 are from tax returns sent via village soviets to Narkomfin.

(b) Socialisation of cows in kolkhozy

	Total number of cows in kolkhozy	Number of socialised cows in kolkhozy	Socialised cows in kolkhozy as percentage of total
June 1, 1929[a]	[704]	169	24·0
May 1930[b]	[4779]	1620	33·9

Source: *Kolkhozy v 1930 g.* (1931), 10–11; these figures are from the kolkhoz census of 1929 and 1930 and therefore differ slightly from those in Table 6(a); thus in the source for Table 6(a) the number of socialised cows in kolkhozy is given as 174,000 in 1929 and 1,413,000 in 1930.

Notes: [a] Excluding Yakut ASSR.
[b] Excluding Tadzhik SSR, and Kirgiz and Yakut ASSRs.

Table 7. Debts and Indivisible Funds (IFs) of kolkhozy, 1929–1930

	June 1, 1929					
	% of kolkhozy with outstanding debts	Total of outstanding debts (mr)	Outstanding debt per kolkhoz with debts (r)	% of kolkhozy with IFs	Total value of IFs (mr)	IF per kolkhoz with IF (r)
TOZy	92·0	55·4	2257	39·2	10·0	956
Artels	92·9	59·7	3769	55·5	31·3	3301
Communes	97·7	37·8	11623	83·5	30·8	11071
All kolkhozy	92·7	152·9	3504	48·2	72·0	3173

Source: [1] *Kolkhozy v 1929 godu* (1931), 126–7.
  [2] *Kolkhozy v 1930 g.* (1931), 200–1.

Note: Indivisible Funds include the money value of permanently socialised buildings, animals, implements, etc.
For a further explanation of this table see pp. 118–19 and 126–7 above.

			May *1930*		
% of kolkhozy with outstanding debts	*Total of outstanding debts (mr)*	*Outstanding debt per kolkhoz (r)*	*% of kolkhozy with IFs*	*Total value of IFs (mr)*	*IF per kolkhoz with IF (r)*
79·0	29·6	2600	69·0	32·5	3200
85·4	306·7	5800	79·8	358·0	7200
92·1	118·1	17500	92·5	119·3	17600
84·8	454·6	6400	79·0	509·9	7700

Table 8. Peasant income in money and kind by social sector, 1930[a]
(million rubles)

(a) Gross income (gross production)

| | Farming | | Non-farming | | Total | |
	Amount	%	Amount	%	Amount	%
Kolkhozy	3691	18·1	536	7·0	4227	15·1
Collective farmers: individual sector	1587	7·8	886	11·6	2473	8·8
Individual peasants	15100	74·1	6197	81·3	21297	76·1
Total	20377	100·0	7619	100·0	27996	100·0

(b) Standard net income[b]

| | Farming | | Non-farming | | Total | |
	Amount	%	Amount	%	Amount	%
Kolkhozy	2673	18·9	536	7·0	3209	14·7
Collective farmers: individual sector	1195	8·4	886	11·6	2081	9·6
Individual peasants	10293	72·7	6197	81·3	16490	75·7
Total	14160	100·0	7619	100·0	21780	100·0

Source: FP, 1–2, 1931, 26.
Notes: [a] Preliminary estimates by Gosplan; for details see original source, pp. 24–31. Includes most income in kind (money income was estimated at 11,779 million rubles (see vol. 1, Table 7)).
[b] Gross income less raw material inputs produced within the sector.

Table 9. Methods of remuneration in kolkhozy, 1928

(a) Kolkhozy by method of remuneration (percentage of all kolkhozy in group)

	TOZy	Artels	Communes	All kolkhozy
According to need	2·1	6·8	18·6	5·4
According to contribution to collective capital	9·8	13·6	11·2	11·0
According to labour force[a]	71·6	80·6	78·2	73·2
According to number of eaters	40·4	43·1	48·8	41·2
According to land	20·7	11·2	2·0	16·3
According to animals	7·2	5·6	1·3	5·7
According to work by means of production of members in kolkhozy	26·0	14·1	5·6	20·4

Source: *Kolkhozy v 1928 g.* (1932), 56–7, 136–7.
Notes: General note: the columns add up to more than 100 per cent, as kolkhozy reporting more than one method of remuneration are counted more than once.
  [a] '*Po rabochei sile*'—according to labour force, or labour power; presumably this heading covers both payment by work done, and payment according to number of members of household working for the kolkhoz.

(b) Kolkhozy in Kuban' okrug by main method of remuneration (as % of total number of kolkhozy in okrug)

Payment for non-socialised means of production	6·7[a]
Per eater[b]	18·9[a]
Per family[b]	7·8[a]
For work done	14·4[c]
For work done (with a minimum payment per eater)	25·6[d]
For work done (with socially organised consumption)	13·3[e]
Other	13·3
Total	100·0

Source: Minaev, ed. (1930), 183–6.
Notes: [a] TOZy only.
  [b] Eater or family provides a definite amount of labour, including non-socialised implements and animals.
  [c] Artels and communes.
  [d] TOZy with more than 50 per cent of sown land socialised, artels and communes.
  [e] Communes only.

Table 9 *(contd.)*

(c) Collective production distributed in kolkhozy of Kuban' okrug by method of remuneration (as percentage of total distributed production)

Method of distribution	In TOZy with 50 per cent or less of sown land collectivised	In TOZy with more than 50 per cent of sown land collectivised	In artels	In communes	In all kolkhozy
For work done	22·4	14·6	50·6	45·5	35·7
Per person working	—	—	0·8	2·3	1·1
Per eater	3·4	17·8	22·5	17·6	17·3
Per family	5·6	2·4	5·2	0·4	2·2
Per kolkhoz member	9·1	9·4	0·2	—	3·5
For amount of land held	43·0	44·5	7·5	—	18·2
For amount of capital paid in	4·3	3·7	1·9	—	1·8
For means of production made available	8·6	4·0	—	—	1·9
For 'non-normed' needs (social services etc.)	3·6	3·6	11·3	34·2	18·3
Total	100.0	100.0	100.0	100.0	100.0

Source: Minaev, ed. (1930), 174.

(d) Kolkhozy in Kuban' okrug in which remuneration was based on capital paid in, 1928 (as percentage of total kolkhozy in the okrug)

	Kolkhozy with remuneration based on capital paid in	Including: Kolkhozy in which capital paid in on per-eater basis	Kolkhozy in which capital paid in on per-family basis	Kolkhozy in which labour required is proportionate to capital paid in	Other kolkhozy with remuneration based on capital paid in
TOZy	9·1	2·2	2·2	2·1	2·6
Artels	4·8	0·0	0·0	4·8	0·0

Source: Trudy . . . agrarnikov-marksistov, ii (1930), i, 31.

GLOSSARY OF RUSSIAN TERMS AND ABBREVIATIONS USED IN TEXT

AIK	agro-industrial'nyi kombinat (agro-industrial combine)
aktiv	activists (politically-active members of a community)
art.	article
ASSR	Avtonomnaya Sovetskaya Sotsialisticheskaya Respublika (Autonomous Soviet Socialist Republic)
bai	rich peasants (in Kazakhstan)
batrak	rural labourer
CC	Central Committee [of Communist Party] (Tsentral'nyi komitet)
CP(b)T	Communist Party (Bolsheviks) of Turkmenia
CPSU(b)	Communist Party of the Soviet Union (Bolsheviks)
disk. listok	diskussionyi listok (discussion sheet)
Ekoso	Ekonomicheskii Sovet (Economic Council [of the RSFSR; equivalent to STO for the USSR])
Gosbank	Gosudarstvennyi Bank (State Bank)
Gosplan	Gosudarstvennaya Planovaya Komissiya (State Planning Commission)
GPU	*see* OGPU
Khlebotsentr	Vserossiskii Soyuz Sel'skokhozyaistvennykh Kooperativov po Proizvodstvu, Pererabotke i Sbytu Zernovykh i Maslichnykh Kultur (All-Russian Union of Agricultural Cooperatives for the Production, Processing and Sale of Grains and Oil Seeds)
khutor	peasant farm with fields and cottage enclosed

KNS	komitet nezamozhnykh selyan (committee of poor pesants [in Ukraine])
kolkhoz	kollektivnoe khozyaistvo (collective farm)
kolkhozsoyuz	soyuz sel'skokhozyaistvennykh kollektivov (union of agricultural collectives)
Kolkhoztsentr	Vserossiskii (*from November 1929* Vsesoyuznyi) Soyuz Sel'skokhozyaistvennykh Kollektivov (All-Russian *from November 1929* All-Union) Union of Agricultural Collectives)
komsod	komissiya po sodeistviyu khlebozagotovkam (commission to assist the grain collections)
koopsoyuz	soyuz kooperativnykh obshchestv (union of [agricultural] cooperative societies)
kopek	1/100 ruble
mir	peasant commune (= zemel'noe obshchestvo (land society), obshchina)
MTS	Mashinno-traktornaya stantsiya (Machine-Tractor Station)
Narkomtorg	Narodnyi Komissariat Vneshnei i Vnutrennoi Torgovli (People's Commissariat of External and Internal Trade)
Narkomzem	Narodnyi Komissariat Zemledeliya (People's Commissariat of Agriculture [of RSFSR up to December 1929, then of USSR])
NEP	Novaya ekonomicheskaya politika (New Economic Policy)
obshchina	peasant commune (= zemel'noe obshchestvo (land society), mir)
OGPU (GPU)	Ob''edinennoe Gosudarstvennoe Politicheskoe Upravlenie (Unified State Political Administration [Political Police])
okrug	administrative unit between region and district (see Technical Note in Volume 1)
orgraspred	organizatsionno-raspredelitel'nyi otdel (Organisation and Distribution Department [personnel department of party central committee])
otkhodnichestvo	'going away' to seasonal work outside one's own village or volost'
otkhodnik	peasant who goes away from village or volost' for seasonal work

otrub	peasant farm with fields only enclosed
pud	0.01638 tons[1]
pyatikratka	fine up to five times value of grain not delivered
Rabkrin	Narodnyi Komissariat Raboche-Krest'-yanskoi Inspektsii (People's Commissariat of Workers' and Peasants' Inspection)
RSFSR	Rossiiskaya Sovetskaya Federativnaya Sotsialisticheskaya Respublika (Russian Soviet Federative Socialist Republic)
RSK	raion sploshnoi kollektivizatsii (district of comprehensive collectivisation)
ruble (rubl')	unit of currency, at par = £0·106 or $0·515
skhod	gathering or general assembly of mir
sovkhoz	sovetskoe khozyaistvo (Soviet [i.e. state] farm)
Sovnarkom	Sovet Narodnykh Komissarov (Council of People's Commissars)
Soyuzkhleb	'Union Grain' (All-Union association (ob''edinenie) of Narkomtorg)
Soyuzmyaso	'Union Meat' (All-Union association (ob''edinenie) of Narkomtorg)
stanitsa	large village in North Caucasus
STO	Sovet Truda i Oborony (Council of Labour and Defence [Economic sub-committee of Sovnarkom])
TOZ	tovarishchestvo po sovmestnoi (*or* obshchestvennoi) obrabotke zemli (association for the joint cultivation of land [simplest form of kolkhoz])
Traktorotsentr	Vsesoyuznyi tsentr mashinno-traktornykh stantsii (All-Union Centre of Machine-Tractor Stations)
tsentner	0·1 tons
TsIK	Tsentral'nyi Ispolnitel'nyi Komitet (Central Executive Committee [of Soviets of USSR])
Vesenkha	Vysshii Sovet Narodnogo Khozyaistva (Supreme Council of National Economy [in charge of industry])

---

[1] Metric tons are used throughout this volume.

volost'   rural district (before 1930, intermediate between village and uezd)
Zernotrest Vsesoyuznyi trest zernovykh sovkhozov (All-
           Union Trust of [New] Grain Sovkhozy)

ABBREVIATIONS OF TITLES OF BOOKS AND PERIODICAL PUBLICATIONS USED IN FOOTNOTES

(For full titles, see appropriate section of Bibliography; items listed below are periodical publications unless otherwise stated.)

B	*Bol'shevik*
BO	*Byulleten' Oppozitsii*
BP	*Byulleten' ekonomicheskogo kabineta prof. S. N. Prokopovicha*
BU NKZ RSFSR	*Byulleten' uzakonenii . . . NKZ RSFSR*
EO	*Ekonomicheskoe obozrenie*
EZh	*Ekonomicheskaya zhizn'*
FP	*Finansovye problemy planovogo khozyaistva*
I	*Izvestiya*
IISO	*Istochnikovedenie istorii sovetskogo obshchestva*
IS	*Istoriya SSSR*
IZ	*Istoricheskie zapiski*
KG	*Krest'yanskaya gazeta*
KGN	*Krest'yanskaya gazeta: izdanie dlya nizhne-vol'zhskogo kraya*
KTs . . . na . . .	*Kontrol'nye tsifry narodnogo khozyaistva SSSR na . . .* (books)
NAF	*Na agrarnom fronte*
NFK	*Na fronte kollektivizatsii*
P	*Pravda*
PKh	*Planovoe khozyaistvo*
PS	*Partiinoe stroitel'stvo*
SKhG	*Sel'skokhozyaistvennaya gazeta*
SKhIB	*Sel'skokhozyaistvennyi informatsionnyi byulleten'*
SO	*Statisticheskoe obozrenie*

SRSKh	*Sotsialisticheskaya rekonstruktsiya sel'-skogo khozyaistva*
SU	*Sobranie uzakonenii*
SZ	*Sobranie zakonov*
SZe	*Sotsialisticheskoe zemledelie*
SZo	*Sotsialisticheskoe zemleustroistvo*
TsIK 2/V	*2 [Vtoraya] sessiya Tsentral'nogo Ispolnitel'nogo Komiteta* (book)
VI	*Voprosy istorii*
VIK	*Voprosy istorii KPSS*
VT	*Voprosy torgovli*
VTr	*Voprosy truda*
ZI	*Za industrializatsiyu*
ZKK	*Za krupnye kolkhozy* (book)

BIBLIOGRAPHY

Letters used as abbreviations for items in the bibliography are listed on pp. 197–8. All other books are referred to in the text footnotes either by their author or editor, or by an abbreviated title (always including the first word or syllable) when there is no author or editor, and by date of publication.

Place of publication is Moscow or Moscow–Leningrad, unless otherwise stated.

Only items referred to in the text are included in the bibliography.

SECTION I NEWSPAPERS, JOURNALS AND
OTHER PERIODICAL PUBLICATIONS

Bol'shevik
Byulleten' ekonomicheskogo kabineta prof. S. N. Prokopovicha (Prague)
Byulleten' Oppozitsii (bol'shevikov-lenintsev) (Paris)
Byulleten' uzakonenii i rasporyazhenii po sel'skomu i lesnomu khozyaistvu: ezhenedel'nyi offitsial'nyi organ NKZ RSFSR
Ekonomicheskaya zhizn'
Ekonomicheskoe obozrenie
Finansovye problemy planovogo khozyaistva (*Vestnik finansov* until no. 2, 1930)
Finansy i sotsialisticheskoe khozyaistvo
Istoricheskie zapiski
Istochnikovedenie istorii sovetskogo obshchestva
Istoriya SSSR
Izvestiya
Kollektivist
Krasnyi Khoper (Uryupinsk)
Krest'yanskaya gazeta
Krest'yanskaya gazeta: izdanie dlya nizhne-vol'zhskogo kraya
Materialy po istorii SSSR
Na agrarnom fronte

Na fronte kollektivizatsii
Nizhnee Povol'zhe (Saratov)
Partiinoe stroitel'stvo
Planovoe khozyaistvo
Povol'zhskaya pravda (Stalingrad)
Pravda
Sbornik postanovlenii i prikazov po promyshlennosti
Sel'skokhozyaistvennaya gazeta (*Sotsialisticheskoe zemledelie* from January 29, 1930)
Sel'skokhozyaistvennyi informatsionnyi byulleten'
Sobranie uzakonenii i rasporyazhenii RSFSR
Sobranie zakonov i rasporyazhenii SSSR
Sotsialisticheskaya rekonstruktsiya sel'skogo khozyaistva
Sotsialisticheskoe zemledelie (*Sel'skokhozyaistvennaya gazeta* until January 28, 1929)
Sotsialisticheskoe zemleustroistvo
Statisticheskoe obozrenie
Statistika i narodnoe khozyaistvo
Torgovo-promyshlennaya gazeta (*Za industrializatsiyu* from beginning of 1930)
Voprosy istorii
Voprosy istorii KPSS
Voprosy torgovli
Voprosy truda
Za industrializatsiyu (*Torgovo-promyshlennaya gazeta* until end of 1929)

SECTION II   BOOKS IN RUSSIAN

Administrativno-territorial'noe selenie Soyuza SSR i spisok vazhneishikh naselennykh punktov, 8th edn (1929)
Andreev, A. A., *Uspekhi i nedostatki kolkhoznogo stroitel'stva, rech' na Rostovskom partaktive 18 marta 1930 goda* (Rostov, 1930)
Andreev, A. A., *Uspekhi kollektivizatsii na Severnom Kavkaze: doklad v politbyuro TsK VKP (b) v kontse noyabrya 1930 g. i postanovlenie TsK VKP(b) ot 10–1–1931 g.* (Rostov, 1931)
Anisimov, N., ed. *Brigadnaya sistema organizatsii truda v kolkhozakh* (1931)
Bauer, A. A., Iogansen, A. A., Khizhnyakov, V. V., and Khmelev, N. N., *Kollektivnoe zemledelie: spravochnaya kniga dlya zemledel'-cheskikh artelei, kommun i tovarishchestv* (1925)

Bogdenko, M. L., *Stroitel'stvo zernovykh sovkhozov v 1928–1932 gg.* (1958)

Chigrinov, G. A., *Bor'ba KPSS za organizatsionno-khozyaistvennoe ukreplenie kolkhozov v dovoennye gody* (1970)

Danilov, V. P., *Sozdanie material'no-tekhnicheskikh predposylok kollektivizatsii sel'skogo khozyaistva v SSSR* (1957)

Danilov, V. P., ed. *Ocherki istorii sel'skogo khozyaistva v soyuznykh respublikakh* (1963)

Direktivy KPSS i sovetskogo pravitel'stva po khozyaistvennym voprosam: sbornik dokumentov, vol. I, *1917–1928 gody* (1957)

Drozdov, A., *Organizatsiya truda i raspredelenie dokhodov v kolkhoze* (1930)

Ezhegodnik po sel'skomu khozyaistvu Sovetskogo Soyuza za 1931 god (1933)

Gaister, A. I., ed., *Zhivotnovodstvo SSSR: dinamika skotovodstva, kormovaya baza, myasnoi balans* (1930)

Industrializatsiya SSSR, 1929–1932 gg.: dokumenty i materialy (1970)

Ivnitskii, N. A., *Klassovaya bor'ba v derevne i likvidatsiya kulachestva kak klassa (1929–1932 gg.)* (1972)

Kak raspredelyat' urozhai i dokhody v kolkhozakh (ukazaniya kraikolkhozsoyuza i kraizemupravleniya, utverzhdennye kraiispolkomom) (Samara, 1930)

Kalinin, M. I., *Izbrannye proizvedeniya,* vol. II, *1926–1932 gg.* (1960)

Kindeev, K. Ya., *Organizatsiya truda v kolkhozakh* (1929)

Kolkhozy: pervyi vsesoyuznyi s"ezd kolkhozov (1–6 iyunya 1928 g.) (1929)

Kolkhozy v 1928 g.: itogi obsledovaniya kolkhozov (1932)

Kolkhozy v 1929 godu: itogi sploshnogo obsledovaniya kolkhozov (1931)

Kolkhozy v 1930 g.: itogi raportov kolkhozov XVI s"ezdu VKP (b) (1931)

Kollektivizatsiya sel'skogo khozyaistva na Severnom Kavkaze (1927–1937 gg.) (Krasnodar, 1972)

Kollektivizatsiya sel'skogo khozyaistva Tsentral'nogo promyshlennogo raiona (1927–1937 gg) (Ryazan', 1971)

Kollektivizatsiya sel'skogo khozyaistva: vazhneishie postanovleniya Kommunisticheskoi partii i Sovetskogo pravitel'stva, 1927–1935 (1957)

Kollektivizatsiya sel'skogo khozyaistva v Srednem povol'zhe (1927–1937 gg.) (Kuibyshev, 1970)

Kommunisticheskaya partiya Sovetskogo Soyuza v rezolyutsiyakh i resheniyakh s"ezdov, konferentsii i plenumov TsK, 2nd edn, vol. II, *1924–1930,* vol. III, *1930–1954* (1954)

Kontrol'nye tsifry narodnogo khozyaistva SSSR na 1929/30 god, odobrennye Sovetom Narodnykh Komissarov SSSR (1930)

Krot-Krival', S. M., *Skotovodstvo i molochnoe khozyaistvo v sel. khoz. kollektivakh i ikh organizatsiya i vedenie* (1926)

Malafeev, A. N, *Istoriya tsenoobrazovaniya v SSSR (1917–1963 gg.)* (1964)

Markevich, A. M., *Mezhselennye mashinno-traktornye stantsii*, 2nd edn (1929)

Materialy po balansu narodnogo khozyaistva SSSR za 1928, 1929 i 1930 gg. (1932)

Minaev, S. V., ed., *Sotsialisticheskoe pereustroistvo sel'skogo khozyaistva SSSR mezhdu XV i XVI s"ezdami VKP(b)* (1930)

Narodnoe khozyaistvo SSSR v 1958 godu: statisticheskii ezhegodnik (1959)

Narodnoe khozyaistvo SSSR: statisticheskii spravochnik 1932 (1932)

Nemakov, N I., *Kommunisticheskaya partiya – organizator massovogo kolkhoznogo dvizheniya (1929–1932 gg.): po materialam nekotorykh oblastei i kraev RSFSR* (1966)

Nifontov, V. P., *Zhivotnovodstvo SSSR v tsifrakh* (1932)

Plan kollektivizatsii v vesennyuyu sel'kokhozyaistvennuyu kampaniyu 1930 g. (1930)

Pravila vnutrennego rasporyadka sel'skokhozyaistvennoi arteli, 8th edn (1929)

Pyatiletnii plan narodno-khozyaistvennogo stroitel'stva SSSR, 3rd edn, vols. I, II(i), II(ii), III (1930)

Resheniya partii i pravitel'stva po khozyaistvennym voprosam, vol. II, *1929–1940 gody* (1967)

Sdvigi v sel'skom khozyaistve SSSR mezhdu XV i XVI partiinymi s"ezdami: statisticheskie svedeniya po sel'skomu khozyaistvu za 1927–1930 gg., 1st edn (1930), 2nd edn (1931)

Selunskaya, V. M., *Rabochie-dvadtsatipyatitysyachniki* (1964)

Shestnadtsataya konferentsiya VKP(b): aprel' 1929 goda: stenograficheskii otchet (1962)

XVI [Shestnadtsatyi] s"ezd Vsesoyuznoi Kommunisticheskoi partii (b): stenograficheskii otchet, 2nd edn (1931)

6 [Shestoi] s"ezd sovetov Soyuza SSR: stenograficheskii otchet (1931)

Slin'ko, I. I. *Sotsialistichna perebudova i tekhnichna rekonstruktsiya sil'skogo gospodarstva Ukraini (1927–1932 rr.)* (Kiev, 1961). (In Ukrainian)

Sotsialisticheskoe stroitel'stvo SSSR: statisticheskii ezhegodnik (1935)

Stalin, I. V., *Sochineniya*, vols. XI, XII (1949)

Trudy pervoi Vsesoyuznoi konferentsii agrarnikov-marksistov, 20.xii–27.xii.1930 [sic 1929], vols. I, II(i) and II(ii) (1930)

Ustav tovarishchestva po obshchestvennoi obrabotke zemli, 16th edn (1930)

Vlasov, N. S., and Nazimov, I. N., *Nedelimye fondy i struktura sredstv v kolkhozakh* (1930)

2 [*Vtoraya*] *sessiya Tsentral'nogo Ispolnitel'nogo Komiteta Soyuza SSR 5 Sozyva: stenograficheskii otchet* [November 29 – December 8, 1929] (1929)

Vyltsan, M. A., *Ukreplenie material'no-tekhnicheskoi bazy kolkhoznogo stroya vo 2-i pyatiletke, 1933–1937 gg.* (1959)

Za krupnye kolkhozy: materialy 1-go Vserossiiskogo soveshchaniya krupnykh kolkhozov (1929)

SECTION III   BOOKS, THESES, ETC. IN OTHER LANGUAGES

Abramsky, C., ed., *Essays in Honour of E. H. Carr* (London, 1974)

Avtorkhanov, A., *Stalin and the Soviet Communist Party: a Study in the Technology of Power* (Munich, 1959)

Carr, E. H., *Socialism in One Country, 1924–1926*, vol. I (London, 1958), vol. II (London, 1959)

Carr, E. H., and Davies, R. W., *Foundations of a Planned Economy, 1926–1929*, vol. 1 (London, 1969)

Jasny, N., *The Socialized Agriculture of the USSR: Plans and Performance* (Stanford, 1949)

Lewin, M., *Russian Peasants and Soviet Power: a Study of Collectivization* (London, 1968)

Male, D. J., *Russian Peasant Organisation before Collectivisation: a Study of Commune and Gathering, 1925–1930* (Cambridge, 1971)

Miller, R., *One Hundred Thousand Tractors: the MTS and the Development of Controls in Soviet Agriculture* (Cambridge, Mass., 1970)

Wesson, R. G., *Soviet Communes* (New Brunswick N. J., 1963)

Wheatcroft, S. G., 'Soviet Grain Production Statistics for the 1920s and the 1930s', unpublished Discussion Papers SIPS 13 (Centre for Russian and East European Studies (CREES), University of Birmingham, 1977)

Wheatcroft, S. G., 'Views on Grain Output, Agricultural Reality and Planning in the Soviet Union in the 1920s', unpublished M.Soc.Sc. thesis (Centre for Russian and East European Studies (CREES), University of Birmingham, 1974)

Wronski, H., *Rémunération et niveau de vie dans les kolkhoz: le troudoden* (Paris, 1957)

NAME INDEX

SUBJECT INDEX